ONE IN A HUNDRED

ONE IN A HUNDRED

John W. Leeger

Copyright ©1999 by John W. Leeger.

Library of Congress Number: 99-91435
ISBN #: Hardcover 0-7388-0772-9
         Softcover 0-7388-0773-7

All rights reserved. No part of this book may be reproduced or transmitted in any form or by any means, electronic or mechanical, including photocopying, recording, or by any information storage and retrieval system, without permission in writing from the copyright owner.

This book was printed in the United States of America.

To order additional copies of this book, contact:
Xlibris Corporation
1-888-7-XLIBRIS
www.Xlibris.com
Orders@Xlibris.com

CONTENTS

COLUMBIA 11
MONTEREY 45
AYER 129
ASMARA 171
ALEXANDRIA 347

FOR MY PARENTS.

Many of the characters in this book are
based upon people who may still be living.
Names have been changed to protect their privacy.

COLUMBIA

YOU'RE IN THE ARMY NOW....

Greetings:

In the summer of 1966, like thousands of other guys, I received my official letter from Uncle Sam. Mine, however, arrived the day after I took delivery of a brand new 1966 Pontiac GTO convertible. It was just what I needed. I looked for some way to get into Navy music. Or Army music. Or **any** music. But it was not to be. So the Army Security Agency seemed like the next best bet: my friendly recruiter volunteered that only the top 10% were allowed into the ASA. I figured that in such company, the extra two years would be little enough in trade for the assurance that I would probably get out alive. Well....Maybe....

Realizing that a monthly car payment of $104.00 would be difficult on a starting salary of $90.60, I asked around to determine what to do. Everyone gave me the same advice: call the dealer, and see if he would take the car back (keeping my $750.00 down payment, of course) and preserve my good credit rating. The dealer was very understanding; said it happens all the time. So on my way to Basic Training, I drove to the dealer and gave the car to them. Goodbye to civilian life: "You're in the Army, now."

Fort Jackson, South Carolina, was everything I had expected of an Army Basic Training camp—and then some! I reported in on August 26, so it was hot, and of course, there was no air conditioning. They lined us up and introduced us to the man who would be our god for the next eight or ten weeks. His name was Sergeant Williams, but we were to call him nothing other than *Drill Ser-*

geant—and that at the top of our lungs. He was not a tall man, about five feet six inches, but he was quick to assure us that he was the meanest SOB any of us had ever encountered. He looked ageless—as though he had been 35 years old for a century. His uniform was so heavily starched that it squeaked. Even in the field during the weeks to come, he always looked like he had just put on a fresh uniform.

They marched us over to the barber shop for the ritual shearing. I wore my hair short at that time, so it wasn't too much of a shock for me, but some of the guys had conniptions! I couldn't believe the amount of hair that was piled around the chairs. One of the objectives of Basic Training, of course, is to remove all traces of individuality. And that haircut was the first big leveler! Everyone looked a whole lot sillier than they had when they arrived—and a whole lot more like everyone else.

Next we were marched to our barracks. The building must have been built before the First World War, but it was immaculate. There were two floors. Each had one large open room. The downstairs room held two rows of six bunk beds. At one end was a bathroom (which we now had to learn to call the *latrine* or the *head*) that was equipped with a trough urinal, four toilets, and six sinks, as well as a shower room with six faucets. We found that modesty was not to be encouraged—everyone watched everyone else do everything. At the other end of the lower level were two small rooms for the Drill Sergeants. Upstairs there were rooms for the squad leaders over the latrine. That left space in the big room up there for two rows of eight bunk beds. Sixty of us were to share this one little building! It turned out not to be too much of an inconvenience, however, as the only things we did in there were sleep, use the bathroom (Oops! Sorry—I meant the latrine, of course.), and clean up. We found that everything was to be highly organized, and *clean*, oh so clean! If there were such a thing, we would have earned a Ph.D. in cleaning by the time we got out of Basic Training.

We were told that our Basic Training course wouldn't start for two weeks, but the Army had things for us to do. There was plenty of KP (Kitchen Police) duty to go around. We peeled potatoes, washed dishes, loaded the milk dispensers, and generally did everything but cook. Some of us were even lucky enough to get to clean out the grease pit. This was a concrete cube about three feet on a side that was set in the ground behind the mess hall. Drain water went through a series of traps there to filter the grease out of the drain water. Cleaning out the grease pit was a nastier job than I could ever have imagined. We were told we wouldn't be allowed off the base until after we had finished six of the eight weeks of Basic Training. We weren't even to leave the barracks area. I wrote more letters in those eight weeks than in the rest of my life. We found the slave wages we were paid were another non-hardship—Uncle Sam took care of everything.

During our second week of KP, a bunch of us were peeling potatoes and telling stories about our civilian lives. I chimed in with the heartbreaking story of giving up my new GTO for the privilege of serving in the Army. One of my new friends said,

"You poor sap. Haven't you heard of the Soldiers and Sailors Relief Act?"

"Ohhhhhh, I don't think I **want** to hear this."

"The Soldiers and Sailors Relief Act says that if you are drafted or enlist under pressure of the draft, all your bills can be reduced to whatever level you can afford. As soon as I knew my number was going to come up, I went out and bought a new Corvette. It's in a garage in Columbia, now. And get this—I pay $5.00 a month for it. Isn't that great?"

Well, I didn't think it was so great! That night I dreamed about my beautiful, fire-engine red GTO convertible. My neighbor in the upper bunk told me in the morning that he thought I had been having a nightmare. Yeah. That just about summed up the way I felt.

BASIC TRAINING

When Basic Training finally started, we were all excited, and ready for the change. After all, we had endured two solid weeks of mess hall duty, and nothing could be worse than continuous KP....Could it?

Well, of course it could!

Monday morning at 5:30 a.m. (0530 hours, in military jargon) Sergeant Williams and three of his cronies exploded into the barracks. The lights went on, and they started banging on lockers and shouting encouraging things such as:

> "Drop your cocks and grab your socks! Turn out of those racks! Your Uncle Sam isn't paying you to lie around all day! I want all you men dressed out and in formation in the Company Street in ten minutes."

Ten minutes?! Well, you never saw such a rush for the bathroom! We managed to form what we thought was a pretty good formation by the appointed time. In the predawn dark we were told exactly who we were. The drill sergeants seemed to only talk at only one level—loud.

> "Stand at attention! Straighten up there, you! You are the sorriest-looking bunch of maggots I've ever seen! But we're going to change that! Aren't we?"

"...."

"I asked you a question! Aren't we going to change that?"

"Yeah!" we replied.

"What the hell was that? When you address me I only want to hear, *Yes, Drill Sergeant,* or *No Drill Sergeant!* Is that clear?"

"Yes, Drill Sergeant."

"I can't heeear you!"

"Yes, Drill Sergeant."

"What the hell kind of maggots are you? I STILL can't hear you!"

"YES, DRILL SERGEANT!"

"That's better! Now, we are going to run IN FORMATION down to the exercise ground at that end of the company street where we will have our first Physical Training! PLATOON, ATTENTION! RIGHT FACE! ON THE DOUBLE! FORWARD...MARCH! Pick it up! I want no stragglers!"

The exercise ground turned out to be a stretch of asphalt about 150 feet by 300 feet. We would get to know it well. For the next 30 or 40 minutes, we did calisthenics. Most of us weren't up to the pace he demanded. It was brutal! When, at last, he told us to get back into formation, we thought it was over. But, of course, it wasn't. After telling us what a worthless bunch of maggots we were several more times, he started us running around the exercise ground. We ran for 15 or 20 minutes. By now, nearly everyone thought that death was imminent. Sergeant Williams ran with us, however, and shouted *encouragement* to us all—particularly the ones at the back of the pack.

"Get the lead out of your ass, Private! Lift those legs! Pump your arms! What's the matter with you? Think you can't go any farther? Move your ass, troop, I'm not done with you yet!"

By the time we got back to the barracks, it was 6:45 a.m. Everyone was drenched with sweat. We were given 15 minutes to get cleaned up, and then we were marched to the mess hall. We were famished. One thing you could say for Basic Training, though; if the food in the mess hall wasn't the greatest, there was plenty of it, and you could eat as much as you wanted.

Initially, we were taught all the important minutiae that make a good soldier:

> How to march in formation,
> How to turn properly,
> How to fold our Army issue uniforms and lay them out in our lockers and foot lockers,
> How to spit shine our shoes and boots,
> How to polish brass,
> How to wax the barracks floor so we could see ourselves in it,
> The proper way to clean toilets and urinals,
> What the various rank insignia meant,
> Who to salute, and how,
> How to address officers,
> How to keep our gig lines straight.

Now this last was a typical bit of Army arcanery. You were expected to keep the opening of your fatigue shirt, the opening of the zipper flap on your pants, and the right side of your shiny brass belt buckle in a straight line. If one of the drill sergeants detected the tiniest deviation, you were immediately gigged (punished) for your transgression. The usual punishment was 20 pushups, but sometimes the drill sergeants had other prescriptions to aid our memories. You can imagine how difficult it was to remember your gig line when you had just finished crawling under barbed-wire fences, or slithering over, under, or around numerous other obstacles. We did a lot of pushups.

Those of us who smoked learned how to field strip their butts. That sounds pretty obscene, but refers to the practice of taking your cigarette butt apart, scattering the remaining tobacco, and putting the remaining paper (and the filter, if your cigarette was so equipped) in your pocket for proper disposal later. If a drill sergeant found a cigarette butt, the whole company was made to sweep the area. The drill sergeants would line us up in the duck walk position (squatting with your butt low) and walk us from one end of the company area to the other, picking up all trash as we went. After the first time we did that, even those of us who didn't smoke were constantly on the look out for cigarette butts, and we disposed of them when we found them.

We marched everywhere. Some of the guys had to learn their left feet from their right. But eventually everyone could stay in step. All the training areas seemed to have been located as far as possible from the barracks area. We marched and we marched. For the first couple of weeks most of what we learned was marching.

Occasionally there were movies. These movies hadn't been made in Hollywood, and they didn't tell the sort of stories we were accustomed to seeing on the silver screen. Instead, we learned about the horrors of venereal diseases, the effects of various types of chemical weapons, elementary first aid, and things not to do with a rifle.

Ah, the rifle....In 1966 the M16 was reserved for the lucky folks serving in Vietnam. In basic training we learned on its older brother, the M14. Essentially the same, the M14 had a heavier, wood stock, as opposed to the high-tech plastic stock of the M16, and the ones we were issued wouldn't fire in the fully automatic mode. We learned how to take it apart, clean it, put it together, and march with it, and what to call it. You never called your rifle anything but a rifle. If you made the terrible mistake of calling it a gun, you were required to hold it overhead with one hand, with your elbow straight. Then, with the other hand you pointed first at the rifle and then at your crotch, and at the top of your lungs you shouted,

>"This is my rifle! This is my gun! This is for killing!
>This is for fun!"

The drill sergeants delighted in this game, and would keep the unfortunate example performing this drill for long periods of time.

Yes, we learned a lot about our rifles, but we didn't learn how to shoot them for a long while. Most of the time, the rifles were left in the barracks when we went on our little marches. None of us minded leaving them behind: it meant that much less weight to carry. Full packs weighed about 40 or 50 pounds. After a few miles, they felt more like 400 pounds, so the extra burden of a rifle was a good thing not to have.

Finally, we were going to put the training to practice and learn to shoot. We marched much farther than we had before and found ourselves at the firing range. Picture acres of empty South Carolina scrub grass. About 50 firing positions had been set up. These consisted of a fox hole, and a few sand bags. Off in the distance were the targets. We got an hour-long lecture concerning exactly what we would be doing, and how to do it. Then we were separated into groups of 50. The first group was issued ammunition, loaded up, and walked to the firing positions. When everyone was in place, the sergeant in charge shouted,

"All right, men, get into the firing pits!"

Down the firing line, everyone jumped into his fox hole. One fellow seemed to have a trampoline in the bottom of his: he came up like he had springs on his soles. The sergeant hollered,

"What the hell do you think you are doing, maggot? You in position 16...get into that fox hole!"
"I can't get in there, Sergeant...there's a snake in that hole!"
"Is that so...?"

The sergeant walked down and stood next to the shaking soldier. He looked down in the fox hole, then said:

"Well, I'll be damned. Give me that rifle, troop."

With that, the sergeant took aim and fired into the pit. Then he had the soldier jump into the pit and remove the snake. What he brought out was a six-foot rattlesnake! From that moment, when we were told to get into fox holes, everyone knocked on the side, or threw something in first. The sight of that soldier bouncing out of the fox hole kept us all amused—and careful. After that, the actual shooting was anticlimactic.

HAND-TO-HAND

One day we were marched to a new location, and seated on bleachers for the typical indoctrination lecture. We were told that we would be taught how to protect ourselves using only our hands. After witnessing the firepower that an M14 provided, we were well aware that if all we had were hands and our enemy was armed, we would be history. The lecture droned on and on—it seemed that we were going to learn how to talk our enemies to death. Then the lecturer asked if anyone would like to participate in a demonstration. Now the lecturer was my platoon sergeant, Sergeant Williams. He was only about five feet six inches tall, and probably weighed about 150 pounds, so he didn't appear to be very menacing. But the members of his platoon remembered that during one of his lectures, he had let slip that he was the only person in the Army who held an Expert Badge in hand-to-hand combat. That made 60 people I knew who would not want to volunteer for this little demonstration.

One fellow, however, shot up his hand immediately. He was called down to the open space in front of the bleachers. Then from behind the bleachers, out stepped Sergeant Lewis. Now, Sergeant Lewis **looked** the part of a master of combat. He was about six feet four inches tall and weighed about 240 pounds—and there didn't appear to be any fat on him. He had a mean-looking scowl to complete the intimidating portrait.

We were told that the poor Private who had volunteered would first show how he would defend himself from Sergeant Lewis's attack with a (wooden) bayonet. Then Sergeant Lewis would demonstrate one of the correct ways. Our attention was riveted to the spectacle that was about to take place. I wondered how the unfortunate Private would get through the rest of Basic Training in a body cast. Then, the exhibition began. Light on his feet as a cat, Sergeant Lewis approached the Private and lunged at him with the wooden bayonet. The Private responded by breaking Sergeant Lewis's arm. As the poor Sergeant lay there moaning in pain, we looked at one another in awe. It turned out, of course, that the Private had a black belt in karate. He maintained that he hadn't meant to hurt Sergeant Lewis, but that the Sergeant had fallen poorly when he was flipped.

The Sergeant and the Private were led off in different directions—one to the hospital, and the other to parts unknown. I never saw him again. Later I wondered if he had been a plant, and the whole exhibition a sham. But if that were the case, the Sergeant had taken some acting classes somewhere, because he looked like he was in a great deal of pain. What's more, his platoon was assigned to another Sergeant....

Hand-to-hand combat instruction was fairly enjoyable. We didn't do any real fighting (at least, the exercises were not intended to be serious), but it was nice to be out in the open and doing something other than mindlessly running around in circles or doing calisthenics. The actual exercises were held in what were called pits. There were about 10 of these, and they consisted of nothing more than 25-foot diameter circles ringed by sandbags and filled with sand. Generally the Drill Sergeants stood in the middle of the pits and directed operations.

On one occasion, Sergeant Williams was in our pit. Way over by the bleachers, one of the other sergeants was using a megaphone to tell us about the next exercise. I was not being as attentive as I should have been, since I was kidding around with the guy standing next to me. All of a sudden, Sergeant Williams said,

> "Leeger! How much would you bet that I could take one step from where I'm standing and plant both of my heels between your eyes?"
>
> "Uh....I wouldn't want to bet on that, Drill Sergeant,"

I stammered back. Then, all my platoon mates chimed in with,

> "C'mon, Sergeant Williams, show us!"
> "Yeah! I'd bet five dollars you can't do it."
> "Go on. Show us, Sergeant Williams!"

And other encouraging words. What a bunch of friends! Fortunately, Sergeant Williams declined to remake my face, and instead insisted that I pay closer attention to what the other Sergeant was saying. You can bet that I was all ears!

SKINNY

One of the black guys in our platoon was named Skinny. Now, I'm sure he had a complete name, but all any of us ever knew him as was Skinny. He was from Philadelphia, and proud of it! He was very young, immature (none of us, in fact, were epitomes of maturity), not very bright, and not well educated. Whenever someone said something that he approved of (or disapproved of, for that matter), he would say,

"GOTTalMIGHTy DAWG!"

He was very lighthearted—he treated the whole Basic Training experience as a wonderful opportunity organized just so that he could have fun. He was fun to be around, except for one thing: he didn't smell very good. And the odor got progressively worse as the weeks went by. No one could remember seeing Skinny take a shower. Now, remember that Basic Training had started in September when it was still plenty hot in South Carolina, and we had been working up a good sweat every day for four or five weeks. As you can imagine, he would have been a natural for a "before" advertisement for Mennen Speed Stick.

Several of us talked to him, and tried to get him to understand that there was nothing personal involved, but he just wasn't pleasant to be down wind of. All of our tact was for naught: the smell kept getting stronger and stronger. We went to Sergeant Williams, and explained the problem. His advice was succinct:

"He's your platoon mate. You take care of it."

That night after lights out some of the guys held a meeting. It was decided that drastic action was required. Not wanting to put up with the smell for another day, the guys (there must have been 10 or 12 of them) snuck over to Skinny's bunk. They yanked him out of bed, and pulled his blanket over his head and upper body. Then they dragged him, kicking and screaming, into the shower where the water had been left running. They held him under the shower for a long time. His blanket was soaked and so, more importantly, was Skinny. The message finally got through—from that day on, Skinny showered every day. From then on, not only was he fun to be around, but he wasn't even bad to be down wind from.

BREAKUP

The previous July, while in Summer Theater, I had gotten engaged to a lovely girl named Janet Boyd. She was one of the dancers/singers in the chorus. She was aware of the fact that I had been drafted, but our plan was for me to get through Basic Training and then get married. Because I had enlisted for the Army Security Agency, I was pretty confident that I wouldn't be sent to Vietnam, and that Janet would be allowed to accompany me to duty assignments after Basic. I called her twice a week, and wrote at least once a week. She wrote back from East Carolina University, where she was enrolled.

During the fifth week of Basic Training we were told that we would have a pass that weekend. I was ecstatic! I called around and found that I could afford a train ticket to Raleigh, North Carolina. From there, it was about an hour and a half drive to Greenville and my fiancee. I figured I could hitchhike that distance in a couple of hours.

The weekend pass didn't start until 8:00 a.m. Saturday, and we had to be back by 8:00 p.m. Sunday. Saturday morning we fell out for reveille at 7:00. Everyone was excited about getting off the base for a day and a half. Someone must have been so excited that his brain went out of gear, because lo and behold, when Sergeant Williams stepped up to give us the morning lecture he found a cigarette butt on the ground in front of him.

"Well, well, well....What do we have here? You men think you're going to get out of here and leave me with a filthy, dirty company area?"

"No, Drill Sergeant!"

"You're goddamn right you're not. Form up in a line across the street! Assume the position! Now clean this place up!"

Everyone was afraid that this was some kind of tactic to deny us all or part of our leave. I was really worried that I would miss the train to Raleigh. We duck-walked as quickly as possible, making certain not to miss anything. Finally Sergeant Williams decided that the area was clean enough for us to be allowed to go. We formed up again, got a short lecture, and were released.

I made the train for Raleigh. By the time we arrived in Raleigh it was dark out—and raining. I took a cab to the highway where I intended to hitch hike, and got out in the rain. I wasn't there for very long when a big Buick pulled up. The passenger window rolled down.

"Kinda wet to be out, ain't it. Where are you headed?"
"I'm going to Greenville, sir."
"Well, get in. I can give you a ride to I-95. From there you're on your own."

I was grateful to get into the warm, dry car. I strapped on my seat belt while he got underway, leaned back, and relaxed a little bit. It didn't last for long. He picked up the whiskey bottle between his legs, took a big swig, and said,

"Here, kid. Have a drink."
"Uh....No thanks sir."

It appeared as though he had been drinking quite a bit, because our progress down the road was not too smooth or steady. After about five minutes, I decided I would sooner catch a cold than a tree. I asked him to pull over, and got out. My luck had to get better from this point, I decided. I was, however, out in the country with no cover, getting wetter by the minute. I hiked down the road about a mile until I came to an overpass. At least I was dry. Finally, after about half an hour, someone picked me up. He drove me to I-95 and let me off. I only waited there about 15 minutes before someone gave me a ride all the way to Greenville. Well, now I knew my luck had turned.

Unfortunately, my luck was just beginning to self-destruct. When I finally got to Janet's dorm, my spirits were soaring. Not having any place to stay, we walked over to the theater which, as usual, was unlocked. We went inside and sat down. Then she said those magic words,

"I can't marry you, John."

Well, they certainly weren't the words I was expecting, but they magically took my soaring spirits and dashed them to the ground. She said she had decided she couldn't do anything until she finished her degree. Worse than that, she had decided to call off the engagement, because of the time involved. Oh, sure, she said she still loved me—she just didn't love me enough to commit or to wait.

I was devastated. We talked all night, but I couldn't change her mind. In the morning, she and a friend of ours gave me a ride to I-95. We kissed goodbye.

I stood there on the side of the road crying like a baby. Eventually, I got myself somewhat under control, and put out my thumb. Soon enough, a fellow stopped and picked me up. He was driving to Miami, and needed someone to keep him awake. He had left the day before from Montreal, and was driving nonstop. I managed to keep him awake all the way to where I needed to get off in South Carolina. It was a matter of minutes before someone stopped and gave me a ride all the way to Fort Jackson.

I made it back before the deadline, went into the barracks, and sat down, desolate. After a while, John McKenzie came over,

"What's the matter, man? You haven't moved a muscle since you sat down. What happened?"

I told him. But as I talked I came to a conclusion: I would go AWOL (Absent WithOut Leave). This was usually a court-martial offense, and could result in any number of unpleasant punishments. But I didn't care. She was more important to me. I would leave right away. John suggested we take a walk and talk a little more, before I set out. He walked me all over the base, and finally talked me out of it. Eventually, I was grateful to him. He had put himself in jeopardy, because we were supposed to be in the barracks at 8:00, and we didn't get back until 9:30.

In the months to come, I wrote to Janet often, and called when I could. But it was to no avail: her mind was made up. And I never saw her again.

Eventually, I got over it. I even consoled myself with the fact that at least she hadn't sent me a "Dear John" letter.

* * * * *

Among the many things that John told me while trying to get me to not go AWOL was a funny story which he assured me had actually happened to him. He had been working on a Master's Degree in Forestry at the University of Pennsylvania before he was drafted. His thesis project was to be an in-depth study of all the flora and fauna of a certain tract of state forest that the University had available for them. He was to spend a weekend there gathering data.

He left early on Friday, and made his way to the little cabin on the tract. There was still a lot of daylight, so he went out and started collecting samples. When it started to get dark, he went back to the cabin, and prepared to put the samples in little vials of water, to keep them fresh. That's when he discovered he had left the box full of sample vials at the University. He wracked his brain, trying to think of something to use temporarily, so he wouldn't have to drive back to school. Finally, he hit upon a possible solution. He drove back to the tiny town he had come through just before he reached the forest, and found the general store was still open. He went in, and waited until he was alone with the little old man who appeared to be the proprietor.

> "What'll it be, son?"
> "Uh....Well....I...uh...need a gross of prophylactics."
> "Huh?"
> "Uh, you know....rubbers. I need a box of rubbers."
> "Did you say a gross?"
> "Yes, sir."

The fellow looked at him for a minute, then went back into the storeroom. He came out after a minute or two blowing dust off a box,

> "You're in luck, son. I just happen to have a whole box."
> "Great. I'll take it."

He went back to the cabin with his prize, and spent the little remaining daylight filling rubbers with water, putting his samples in them, tying them off, and labeling them. He hadn't counted well, though, and found that he didn't have enough. So he made his way back to the general store at 10:00 a.m. the next morning. The same little man was working there,

> "What'll it be today, son?"
> "Uh, I need 27 more prophylactics. And, by the way, three of the ones you sold me last night had holes in them."

The proprietor looked at him as seriously as he could, then replied,

> "Hope it didn't spoil your weekend."

John hadn't bothered to explain what he needed so many condoms for the night before. Now he hastened to set the old man's mind at ease. They laughed about it, eventually. And I laugh about it to this days.

GAMES SOLDIERS PLAY

In addition to allowing us to shoot some really keen guns (rifles), we got to practice other fun things. First, there was gas mask training. We stood around in the company area for hours practicing putting the things on when Sergeant Williams shouted the magic word,

"GAS!"

The masks smelled bad, weren't comfortable, and had to be strapped on tightly to keep the offensive chemicals out—at least that's what the good sergeant said. He would walk up to each of us, and tug all our straps to make certain they were as tight as they could be. I sincerely hoped I'd never have to wear one of the things in action: after about 15 minutes, I would develop the kind of headache you read about in medical journals.

We had several lectures about the various types of gas that might be used on the battlefield, and those that had been used in the past. We were told that we would be exposed to CS, the milder form of tear gas. CN, the nastier stuff, contains a nausea agent—the theory was that it's hard to aim a gun when you're throwing up. Then, of course, there were things like Mustard Gas, and the various nerve gases. For obvious reasons, we wouldn't be exposed to these things. But then, as we were to find, CS was nasty enough.

Then it was time for the actual gas training day. We marched out to a remote site. We were told to relax for a few minutes while the drill sergeants finished their preparations. Those who smoked, did. The rest of us sat down on the logs that were scattered around. We were just getting comfortable when one of the drill sergeants came running into the midst of us with his gas mask on and dropped a CS gas bomb. A couple of the guys managed to choke out the word gas while everyone scrambled to get their masks on. We found very quickly that you **do** have to have all the straps tight, and that the things do work. A couple of the guys didn't get their masks on before the irritation became too great for them to remain in control of themselves. They went running into the woods, bouncing off trees.

Eventually, the gas dissipated enough for the drill sergeants to tell us we could take off our masks. My eyes and nose stung a bit, even though I thought I had put my mask on pretty quickly. We retired to the bleachers for another lecture. The other guys found their way out of the forest and received some additional training in putting on their masks.

After lunch we had another lecture, and then it was time for Uncle Sam's sadism of the day. One at a time, we put our gas masks on, and were taken into a large tent that was full of CS gas. Inside sat two drill sergeants in gas masks. You had to take off your mask and shout your name, rank, and serial number. I wasn't too worried. Even after I saw other guys come out of that tent with their noses and eyes streaming, I thought that it wouldn't get to me like that. After all, I had studied vocal performance for years, and had enormous lung capacity.

When I was finally in the tent, I could feel little places stinging on my neck where the sweat reacted with the gas. The drill sergeant told me to begin. I took a huge breath, closed my eyes, took off my gas mask, and shouted,

"John W. Leeger. Private. RA14965654!"

The sergeant waited a bit and said,

"I didn't hear you, private."

As quickly as I could, without taking a breath, I shouted again,

"John W. Leeger. Private. RA14965654!"

But it wasn't going to be. Once again, the sergeant said,

"I didn't hear you, private."

It was becoming increasingly obvious that he would keep this up until I took a breath, so I took a breath and coughed out,

"John W. Leeger. Private. RA14965654!"

They finally let me out. Like everyone else, my nose and eyes were streaming, and everything from my neck up itched like crazy. After everyone had gone through the ordeal, we were given another lecture. During the next break, they dropped another gas grenade, but no one got caught napping that time. We were grateful to fall in and march back to the barracks that night.

* * * * *

After so many weeks of PT (Physical Training) we were in pretty good shape. Before we took the PT test at the end of Basic, however, we had to go through the obstacle course. This was probably the most enjoyable activity of the whole eight weeks. The obstacle course covered several acres, and included all kinds of things to run through, crawl over, climb, or jump off. Most were made of logs, but there were rope ladders, swings, and ropes to climb or shinny down. It was like a playground for grown ups. Nearly everyone enjoyed it. I thought that there might be a market for playgrounds like that.

* * * * *

Then it was time for grenade training. Now this was some serious stuff. We were shown several familiar items that had been exposed to hand grenades—it was a sobering experience. One of the drill sergeants held up a barely-recognizable steel helmet. It had been shredded—blown out from the inside. We were told that a recruit had dropped his grenade, and instead of letting the drill sergeant kick it down the emergency hole, had thrown his helmet on it and fallen on it. If that was actually what happened, the recruit must have been allowed to go home in a box.

To get to the throwing area you went down a ramp between dirt walls until you were in a trench about three feet deep. A wall made of heavy logs with a thick earthen berm on the other side extended another four feet or so above you and protected you from shrapnel from the grenades. At the bottom, the passageway turned to the right. A roof extended over the top, forming a sort of tunnel. A wooden bench provided a waiting area. As you slid closer and closer to your date with explosives you could hear the grenades the other guys had thrown. It may have been imagination, but I swear I could feel the shrapnel hitting the berm behind me.

As you slid down the bench, eventually you came to a wall where the passageway made a 90° angle to the right. There an NCO waited for you. When your time came, you were taken down a short hall and around a 180° angle, this time to the left. Then there was still another 90° angle to the right and you found yourself in the pit.

It was open in the front, save for a low wood and sandbag wall. The ground sloped gently down on the other side of the wall. The two side walls were heavy logs. The range safety officers stood in an elevated area behind you. The front of the range safety officers' area was a thick plexiglass shield—the plexiglass was scratched and pitted. I'm sure the men standing there felt safe, but the plexiglass looked awfully worn to me.

Being right-handed, I stood to the left of the emergency hole with my left side facing the throwing range. The instructor stood directly in front of me. We yelled at each other,

"ASSUME THE POSITION!"
"YES, DRILL SERGEANT!"

I stood with my feet about three feet apart and my hands extended out to my sides. The instructor slapped a grenade in my right hand,

"PREPARE TO PULL THE PIN!"
"YES, DRILL SERGEANT!"

Just as I had been taught, I brought my hands together in front of my chest and stuck my left index finger in the pin ring,

"PULL THE PIN!"
"YES, DRILL SERGEANT!"
"THROW THE GRENADE!"
"YES, DRILL SERGEANT!"

We had been taught to throw the grenade like a football at an angle between 30° and 45°. You were supposed to watch it until it started coming down. I'm not a great athlete, so I must have been loaded with adrenaline, because that grenade looked like it was going to go forever.

"HIT THE DIRT!"

I didn't bother to answer—I hit the dirt. The grenade went off with a terrible roar, and then I **did** hear the shrapnel hit the earth berm and the plexiglass front of the range safety officers' area.

"You threw that thing a country mile, boy."
"Yes, drill sergeant."

I was happy to be through with that exercise. In fact, everyone was happy to be done with that day. No one got killed, or even wounded. The march back to the barracks was very enjoyable.

* * * * *

To assure that troops would not be panicked when exposed to enemy fire, the Army required that recruits crawl on their bellies about 100 yards while drill sergeants fired machine guns over their heads. Just to remind you that there were real bullets in those machine guns, they included tracer rounds, so you could see something flying over you. The guns were fired about four feet over your head, but that was more than close enough for me. To make things even more fun, there were two places where you had to crawl under barbed wire. You did this by rolling over on your back, sliding your rifle under the barbed wire, and then holding the wire up with the rifle and inching under. Then you rolled back over onto your belly and crawled some more. One more little fillip was added for our enjoyment. There were some sand bag bunkers next to the lanes we crawled down, and every once in a while they set off concussion bombs inside them—it felt like artillery shells going off. Instinct made you want to jump away from the noise, but the keening whine overhead kept your face in the dirt.

Soon after we arrived at the range, my squad was marched back to the barracks area to paint lockers. I thought that we were going to get to skip the live fire crawl, but they managed to get us back in time for the evening's festivities. We were the last group in line. As we moved down the side of the field, we could see the tracers going over the field, and we could hear the concussion bombs going off. Finally we filed into the trench at the far end of the field. The instructor yelled,

"OVER THE TOP!"

and away we went. After the first barbed wire obstacle I caught up with the guy ahead of me. He was moving pretty slowly, and I wanted out of there,

"GET OUT OF MY WAY, OR I'LL CRAWL RIGHT OVER YOUR ASS!"

I yelled. He sped up, and we got to the end. Just as I got past the machine gun stand and stood up, the drill sergeant who had been firing over our heads stood up and said,

> "Well, I'll be damned: I'm out of bullets."

Then the fellow in front of me turned around. It was the company commander. He said,

> "I admire your spirit, troop!"
> "Uhhhh...thank you, sir."

We marched back in the dark. I, for one, was happy to be in one piece.

* * * * *

Joseph Lichtenstein was a quiet fellow from Philadelphia. He was the type that the drill sergeants always called *soft*. He was considerably out of shape when he arrived at Basic, and he hadn't improved nearly enough to suit the NCOs. He didn't have much common sense: procedures that seemed logical, if silly in an Army sort of way, to the rest of us, were simply incomprehensible to Joe. He bumbled along from one episode to another, constantly taking guff from the drill sergeants.

The last major excursion we had was a simulated live fire platoon sweep. At the exercise area we lined up 50 across and on command started through the live fire area. As we walked down our individual paths, we came to signs that said things like,

> SHOOT TARGET IN BUNKER AHEAD

or,

JUMP INTO FOXHOLE.

SHOOT TARGET ON RISE AHEAD.

We actually were walking around with rounds in our rifles! The object of the exercise was to hit as many targets as possible, and to keep in rank, so that no one was out in front, or dragging behind. If you were in front or behind, the likelihood of someone accidentally getting shot went up dramatically. You can imagine the length of the safety lecture we got before this one.

Those of us who hadn't gone through the exercise yet could see most of the exercise terrain. When Joe's group started through the exercise area, he was pretty much in the middle, so most of us saw what ensued. Joe started through the exercise on his own clock. When he saw a target, he shot at it—from the hip! He must have thought this was the John Wayne exercise. Sometimes he lagged behind, sometimes he was out front. After the third firing position, the company commander decided that Joe was definitely a menace. He walked down the path, and came up behind him. He shouted,

> "Just what in the hell do you think you are doing, Private!"

With that, Joe turned around to see who was addressing him. He still had the rifle in position to fire from the hip, his finger was on the trigger, and the rifle was pointing more or less at the Lieutenant's belly button.

Many of us who saw what was going on dropped to the ground and tried to make ourselves into moles. The Lieutenant gasped. Then, very calmly, he said,

> "Put the weapon down, soldier."

Joe looked at him, and then looked down at the rifle. His face turned ashen, and he carefully took his finger off the trigger, and moved the rifle so that it was pointing up in the air. The Lieutenant took the weapon from him, removed the magazine, ejected the bullet in the firing chamber, and gave it back to him.

"Come with me, Private. You don't need to go through the rest of this."

He led Joe away. We gave up trying to get underground, and got shakily to our feet. No one said a word for a long time. But we all prayed that, after today, the Army would never consider putting Joe in a combat role.

GRADUATION

Speculation about our next assignments was always accompanied by a lot of tense laughter. We knew that most of us would be sent to that great meat grinder, Vietnam. Some of us had enlisted to lessen the possibility of assignment to Vietnam. Of course, that required a three- or four-year hitch, as opposed to the two- year stint for draftees. But we thought the extra time was worth the additional security.

I had enlisted specifically for the Army Security Agency and language school. According to my recruiter, language school was worth as much as 30 semester hours of college credit through the University of California system. Since I had been studying vocal music, I listed my three preferences as French, German, and Italian. When I was asked to choose between the west coast and east coast facilities, I opted for the area that was more familiar to me, the east coast school at Washington, D.C.

On the fateful day when we were to be given our first assignments, we were in formation, and Sergeant Williams called us, one at a time, to present us with the latest of the Army's whims. There were a lot of moans and groans and an occasional sigh of relief or joyful exclamation before my name was called. I stepped forward, confident that, because I had signed up for an extra two years and had scored very high on all the tests I had taken, I would get pretty much what I had requested. I was as right as I would ever be while in the Army.

"Arabic? There must be some mistake. I listed French, German or Italian."

"Well, you got Arabic, Private."

"But I don't know anything about Arabic. Is there anything I can do about it, Drill Sergeant?"

"Yeah: learn it."

It wasn't my first introduction to Army logic (nor would it be my last), but it may have been the most significant. Eventually, the training I was about to go through would change even the way I thought. Oh, well....I knew little about Arabic beyond what I had heard in the movie, *Lawrence of Arabia*, and that, of course, was precious little indeed. Then I read the next line. In my confusion I forgot myself,

"Excuse me, Drill Sergeant."

"What is it, Leeger?"

"I asked for the East coast language school, and they gave me West coast. Can I get that changed, at least?"

"Look, Leeger, let me give you some advice. You enlisted for four years in the Army Security Agency. You're not even out of Basic Training yet. The Army doesn't follow **your** thinking most of the time. And there's nothing you can do about it. It's easiest if you don't try to buck the system: go with the flow."

"Yes, Drill Sergeant."

"At least you made language school. Only one out of ten ASA troops ever gets to go. I think you'll enjoy California, son."

"Thanks."

Well, at least I no longer had to worry about being far away from my fiancee....

* * * * *

Finally, it was time to graduate. The only graduations I had attended until then included caps and gowns and diplomas. But, of course, this was not college. Or even high school. Graduation from Basic Training at Fort Jackson required the first official display of our dress uniforms. Creases and pleats were pressed to a sharpness suitable for a chef's knife. Gallons of Brass-O were consumed in the quest for the shiniest brass insignias possible. And every mouth was dry thanks to spit-shined shoes so shiny that you could shave in the reflections from them.

In preparation for our final inspection, our barracks was clean and neat enough to satisfy the most psychotic inmate in the land. Beds were made so tight that you could bounce a wallet on them, let alone a quarter. And the floor had been buffed to such a shine that we nearly had to wear sun glasses inside. Our rifles had been stripped, oiled, and reassembled: their stocks gleamed with wood oil. Everything looked better than new.

Inspection passed, we assembled in company formation about 9:30 a.m. Then we marched to the parade ground. There we discovered that our company was just one of many that were all graduating together. All our training paid off—we marched and we marched, this way and that. Then we stood at parade rest or attention for interminable periods of time before marching again. Eventually, we marched past the reviewing stand while the post band played various Sousa marches (what else?).

Soon, we were back at the barracks, and tickets in hand, were ready to embark on our next adventures.

MONTEREY

SERGEANT ANDERSON

For a fellow from cold, dirty Gary, Indiana, Monterey, California in November was difficult to believe. The sky was as blue and deep as the water in the bay: in Gary, both would be tinged, if not totally defiled. No wonder Steinbeck loved this place. I couldn't wait to see all that was already so familiar in my mind: the ramshackle beauty of Cannery Row, the loveliness of the Salinas valley. It was all there to be enjoyed. But first...

"My name is Sergeant Anderson. I am the Supply Sergeant here, and you men are assigned to me until your classes start. Pick up your bedding and stow your gear in barracks 2102. Report back here at 0800 tomorrow."
"Uh, Sergeant, do you know WHEN our classes start?"
"Check in the orderly room: they oughtta know."

With his stooped shoulders, and his perpetual frown, you just knew Sergeant Anderson spent the better part of every day bent over some sort of paper work. The man was the embodiment of his little domain. His sharply-pressed uniform helped disguise the unbelievable untidiness of his mind. His meticulous paperwork covered for the almost religious feeling of mystery and awe that resulted from someone managing to find what he was looking for in Sergeant Anderson's sanctuary. The Orderly Room wasn't much better.

"Excuse me, Specialist. Can you tell me when my class starts?"
"Lemme see your orders."
"I'm supposed to be studying Arabic."

"Oh yeah, that's the new Egyptian course. Let's see here, that's December first."

"December? But that's almost a whole month."

"Yeah: you'll like Sergeant Anderson. Hope you had a good time before you came here."

"What, in Basic?"

"No, your leave time."

"They didn't give me leave after Basic."

"You're kidding. Well you'll get a couple of weeks at Christmas."

"Super...."

After ten days of painting rocks and mowing lawns, even Arabic sounded good. I had discovered I was part of the largest company in the Army. Company B of the Defense Language Institute, West Coast at the Presidio of Monterey had more than 1,500 men assigned to it: most of them studying languages I had hardly heard of. In addition to Arabic, there were Chinese, Thai, Russian, Urdu, Hindi, Farsi, and of course, Vietnamese. We were due to begin a 47-week course in Egyptian Arabic: five days a week; six hours a day. But first, there were all those rocks that needed painting...

"You know, John, three months ago, no one could have convinced me I would be painting rocks in California."

"Do you think there's a marksman's badge for paintbrush?"

"We aren't going to find out today."

"Why not?"

"I hid the paintbrushes."

"C'mon, Carl. You're kidding. Aren't you? Don't you think he'll be suspicious?"

"Who, Anderson?"

"Well, we **were** using them yesterday."

"I'll lay you odds it doesn't occur to him."

Carl Stephenson was the zaniest individual I had ever met. He was from Wisconsin, and had the open-faced, curly-haired freshness common to that region. But he thought on more levels than I could imagine—all the time. Carl was always looking for the angles. **All** the angles.

"I'll also lay you odds we police the roads on the base."
"How do you figure that?"
"Figure it? I planned it. I've worked three weeks to..."
"Sh. Here he comes."
"All right you men. Fall in. Lessee....Yeah, you're all here. Now, uh, today we're gonna get all this crap off the shoulders. You four men'll be responsible for the East Road, and you four for West Road. Make sure you police ALL the roads up to A Company's area. Is that clear?"

Like a choir, came back the well-practiced antiphon:

"Yes, Sergeant Anderson."
"Well, get goin'. And don't let me catch any o' you screwin' around. You know I'll be checkin'."

I was tired of asking him how: he never told me anything. So this time I asked,

"Why, Carl?"
"Huh?"
"Well, assuming you actually engineered all this, why would you sooner pick up trash today than paint rocks? I could really give a fat, flying fuck in a rusty, rolling doughnut which of these pointless jobs we're doing, but you seem to have a need to pick up trash today. I want to know why."
"Well, that's easy. Right after lunch, I'm going to San Francisco."
"You are out of your mind. Anderson'll crucify you

when he finds out."

"How's he going to find out? I'm not going to tell him. Are you?"

"Well, no, but he's sure to notice you're missing, isn't he?"

"Today, he'll just think I'm where he isn't, and by Monday, he won't remember. Wanna bet?"

Well, of course I didn't. Carl had been on Sergeant Anderson's work detail longer than any of us. His Russian course had been due to start for so long that it was a standing joke. If anyone knew what Sergeant Anderson would do, it was Stephenson. So we picked up trash. There wasn't a lot of it. The Presidio swept up the side of the hill from the south side of the bay. From Company B you could see across the bay to Monterey, and even to the airport tucked in between the hills. Scoured by the sea breeze, it always looked fresh and new. It was so beautiful that even confirmed litterbugs were reticent about cluttering the place. And of course, the abundance of freshly-painted, white rocks would give anyone pause. True to his word, Carl left for San Francisco right after lunch. And true to his form, Sergeant Anderson never noticed. But I wasn't around to see it. Just before lunch, the unpredictable U.S. Army glitched again:

"Private Leeger?"
"That's me, Specialist."
"You're wanted in the Orderly Room."

Now what had I done? Had someone found out about Carl?

"Private Leeger reporting, Sergeant."

"Leeger, it has come to my attention that you had no leave after Basic. That right?"

"Yes, Sergeant."

"Well, your class doesn't start for two more weeks. Do you wanna take leave?"

"Do I? What's the hitch?"

"No hitch. Of course, you can't take leave and just lay around here on base, but I guess you'd wanna go home, right?"

"Uh, yeah. If I could afford it. Maybe my folks can loan me the money. Can you make out the papers, while I call home?"

"Sure thing, Private."

Now $90.60 per month didn't buy much, even in 1966. And it certainly would take a couple of months pay for a round-trip ticket to Chicago—even at military standby rates. Little did my folks know how many round-trip tickets they were going to front for me during that year in California. But just then, they really wanted to see me, what with Thanksgiving on the way. I don't think Sergeant Anderson missed me at all.

It was a wonderful month—full of surprises. My parents moved from the home we had lived in for 16 years. The new house was in Highland, Indiana. Close, but still a good 20-minute drive back to visit old friends and neighbors.

The day after I arrived, we had a phone call from my younger brother: his wife had just given birth to their first child! We rushed to Muncie, and found Bill looking bedraggled, but happy. It was exciting to become an uncle, and what a pretty little niece I had! Thanksgiving was extra special, but soon it was time to get back on the plane to return to California. It seemed like I had only been home a couple of days....

GAMEELA HADRANI

I made it back to the Presidio two days before my class was to start. Carl had pulled off his trip to San Francisco without any hitches. He had also started his language school—Russian. Boy, I thought, what I wouldn't give to be studying Russian instead of Arabic. I was to find out that no language is easy to learn, unless you have a gift.

Our class was lumped together with another, initially. The plan was to separate us, once we had the basics of the language, and make my half of the class Egyptian linguists and the other half Iraqi linguists. Two of the fellows in my section had known each other before the army got them. Tom McKinley was a short (about five feet, six inches), scrappy Bostonian. His friend, Tom O'Connor, was Jeff to his Mutt (about six feet, two inches and maybe 250 pounds). They were a sight together. Trying to talk to both of them at once was an exercise in frustration: eventually I learned to focus on a spot just over Tom McKinley's head and just under Tom O'Connor's chin.

Joe McDonald was a New Yorker. He really missed the hours he was accustomed to spending in the neighborhood bars. That level of camaraderie just wasn't available in Monterey—especially not for fellows who were obviously servicemen. Joey had an open way about him that made him popular almost anywhere, though. I don't think I ever saw him at a loss for the proper word to keep a conversation going. He, at least, had a gift for language. But he was to find that the gift did not extend to Arabic.

The last member of our section was John Wood. John was the only Marine in our group. He was from a little town in Georgia. Like most Marines, I'm sure John was a good man to have at your side in a fight. At least he looked the part. He reminded me a lot of Mike Nomad (Steve Roper's friend in the funny pages). John was easy to get to know, like most Southerners, I guess. Since my mother's family was from North Carolina, we got along quite well.

The Iraqi section of the class was made up of zoomies (Air Force types) from all over. Donald DiGiorno, Steve Kaplan and Mike Lewis were the names—and a more disparate crew, you couldn't imagine. Donald was from Chicago, fairly near my home, so we some things in common. He was honestly excited about the opportunity to study such an exotic language. All he ever talked about was getting to see such interesting, out-of-the-way places. Little did he know where he would spend the last two years of his hitch.

Steve was Jewish, and that was to cause some problems, as you can well imagine, if your recollection of history for 1967 is up to par. He was another typical New Yorker (but a different typical from Joe McDonald). He and Joe shared none of the same friends or watering holes.

Mike was a loner. He was probably finding it very difficult to adjust to life in the service. He always seemed to be withdrawn—a natural recluse. Since we were only together as a class for the first twelve weeks, my contact with the zoomies ceased rather suddenly, and they play a small part in this story.

Our little expedition into Arabic was to be a 47-week course: six hours per day, five days per week. If you add all that up, you will find that we spent a **lot** of time learning Arabic. I thought that my section of the class would have a very hard time: after all, everyone but me had very noticeable accents (I don't think I have an accent, of course). As it turned out, Arabic is so different from English, that the accents were little hindrance.

Our first day of class was typical of first days in classes anywhere. We were handed a mountain of books, as well as a mountain of tapes to accompany the books. The books all began at the back covers. My first feelings of inadequacy surfaced immediately.

> "Hey, is this for real? What are all these squiggles? I ain't ever gonna learn to read this stuff. And how come the books are backwards?"

Tom O'Connor (the big Tom, remember?) was the lumbering contradiction of the general rule that all Army Security Agency enlisted men were smarter-than-average college students who had dropped out for some insignificant reason or another. I'm sure Tom's reason was anything but insignificant—at least in the eyes of his college staff. But on the other hand, none of us could make anything out of the squiggles in the books. Mercifully, most of the books had some English which appeared to explain the squiggles, but at this point, "squiggles" was the perfect word for the other contents of the books.

> "Please, be seated. My name is Miss Gameela Hadrani. I will be your primary teacher for the first portion of the course, and will continue with the Egyptian students for the final portion of their course."

Things suddenly took a turn for the better. Gameela Hadrani was an Egyptian girl who was about my age, and quite attractive—short, a little plump but with lovely dark hair and eyes you could get lost in. She had graduated from Cairo University just the year before, and was living with relatives in Monterey. I wondered why Arabs made their women wear veils. She had a very noticeable accent, but seemed to know English pretty well—certainly much better than I knew Arabic. Maybe the next 47 weeks wouldn't be so bad after all.

> "The answer to your question, *Sayyed*, is that the books are **not** backward. Arabic is written from right to left, and **our** books begin at the front. It is **your** books which are backward."

And then again, maybe I had no idea of how bad the next 47 weeks could be...

> "After the first few weeks of class, we will try not to use English in the classroom as much as possible. You will speak Arabic, beginning today. But first, I must give you all Arabic names, to help you get accustomed to the language."

I was later to learn that my name, *Sayyed Looaee* (a reasonable transliteration), means Mr. Shining (or beaming). If she had explained the meanings the first day, I think we all would have felt like walking out. My name was not as silly as some of the others. But by the end of the day, we had already learned the first few words of Arabic. In fact, I don't think I will ever forget the first page of dialogue from that course:

هذا كتاب.	This is a book.
ذاك دفتر.	That is a notebook.
ما هذا؟ هذا كرسي.	What is this? This is a chair.
هل هذا فنجان؟ نعم هذا فنجان.	Is this a cup? Yes, this is a cup.
هل ذاك كرسي؟ لا، ذاك كتاب.	Is that a chair? No, that is a book.

Well, it was a start, anyway.

About two weeks later, we came to one of our favorite Arabic words:

> "Now, class, the next word we will learn is the Arabic word for "only." The word is *faqat*. Would you try, please *Sayyed Makram*?"
>
> "Fuckit"
>
> "No, *Sayyed Makram*, it is with a *qaf* from the back of the throat. Try again, please: *faqat*...."

"Fuckit"

"No, *Sayyed Makram*, that is not right. *Sayyed Mahmoud*, would you try, please: *faqat*...."

"Fuckit...."

Well, as you can imagine, none of us could say the word, and we all thought it was pretty funny. During the next class break, however, one of the other teachers must have told her what had been going on. When she came back into the room, Gameela was as red as a beet:

"I am ashamed of you, men: taking advantage of me like that. It is so difficult for me. Oh...."

And with that, she started to cry. Well, that hooked us all. We all apologized, and promised to do our best in the future: some of us even tried.

Later that night, one of the fellows in an advanced class told us the story about the Caliph, who woke in the morning, and went out on his balcony to look over the city. He looked down, and in the town square saw hundreds of beggars, plying their trade. Turning to his manservant, the Caliph said, "Oh what poverty, only poverty." That's not much in English, but in Arabic it's, "*Ya matha faqar, faqat faqar!*" None of us had the heart to tell Gameela that story, however.

BARRACKS

The barracks were two-story wooden buildings dating from World War II. They were divided into eight cubicles on each floor, four on each side of the center aisle, by wooden partitions that began about a foot off the floor and ended about six feet high. There were two squad rooms over the latrine for the platoon leaders. I shared the last cubicle on the right upstairs with a fellow named Dan Partridge. Dan was from Rhode Island, and was studying Vietnamese. It didn't take us long to determine that we had virtually nothing in common. He was very introverted, and an intense student. He spent most of his time at his little desk with his nose in his books. Now I did my homework, and memorized my dialogues, but I was usually done in a couple of hours. Dan would work until 9:00 or 10:00 nearly every night.

Each student had a little Ampex reel-to-reel tape player and a set of headphones to listen to the dialogue tapes. Right after class, the barracks was an eerie place. Most of the guys did their homework then, and when you walked down the aisle you could see 10 or 12 guys with their headphones on, mumbling their dialogue lessons. It was a modern-day tower of Babel.

A lot of guys would go to sleep listening to the dialogue tapes. The instructors assured us that your subconscious mind would retain those sounds if you played them while you were going to sleep. One of the fellows decided if one time through the tape was good, several times had to be better. So he came up with a system. He put the tape player on the floor and ran the tape around the legs of his bunk, his roommate's bunk, and the desk, then spliced the ends to make a loop.

"This way, the tape will keep playing all night."

"You don't really think this'll work, do you, Tom? What if the tape catches on something?"

"I've checked all the places the tape touches, and smoothed them out with some sandpaper. There shouldn't be a problem."

"I don't know.... This looks like a real Rube Goldberg idea to me...."

"You'll see. Tomorrow, I'll know this dialogue cold."

He didn't, of course. The tape must have broken early, so all he got for his trouble was a pile of mangled tape to clean up before class.

* * * * *

Ed Summers lived in the first cubicle on the right, upstairs. He was a stoolie, and universally disliked by the guys in the barracks. Whenever the NCOs wanted to find out who was responsible for anything that had happened in our barracks, they knew they could count on Ed. He went beyond being a good soldier to trying to be the ultimate soldier. You could read newsprint in the reflection from the floor in his cubicle (if you could read reflected writing, of course). His footwear was always so heavily-waxed it shone like patent leather. He kept his shoes and boots on his footlocker, so there would be less chance of scuffing the floor in his cubicle. The things in his footlocker were always in exactly the right position— I think he used a ruler to make sure they lined up perfectly. We called guys like him *pukes*, and he set the standard.

One Saturday night, a couple of the guys came back late, and very drunk. The next morning, Ed awoke early, as usual, and went downstairs to clean up. Then he came back up and got dressed. When he went to put his shoes on, however, his screams woke everyone.

"Somebody pissed in my shoes!"

That's what he said. We staggered out of bed and found that, sure enough, someone had filled his shoes and boots, and slopped some around on top of his footlocker as well. A lot of fingers were pointed. No one ever confessed, but we figured that one or more of the guys who had been drinking woke up in the middle of the night with a full bladder. Perhaps they were too lazy or too drunk to walk downstairs and back. Or perhaps they just did it out of meanness. But the odds were pretty high that one or the other of them had filled Ed's footwear.

* * * * *

Now, Don Jensen, another of the guys in our barracks, had a terrible crush on Vanessa Redgrave. When he saw that *Camelot* was opening in San Francisco and that she was starring, he got a group of us together to go up there one Saturday to see it. We managed to get tickets through the Service Club, so we would be assured of seats, and took the bus up early Saturday morning. It was a nice day. The weather was lovely, the movie was good, and the girl-watching was great. But that night, we were all awakened about 1:00 a.m. by Don's moaning.

"Vanessa....Vanessa....Ohhhhhhhhh....Vanessa...."

He went on long enough that one of the guys started taking notes. After about 20 minutes, we woke him up and sent him downstairs for a cold shower. Whenever things got dull, after that, Ted would retrieve the *Vanessa Notes* from their hiding place and read them with all the moans and groans in excruciating detail. Don never managed to find the notes or wrestle them away from Ted. And, of course, we never let him forget that night.

BLOOD DRIVE

One day at morning formation the sergeant said,

> "This Thursday there will be a blood drive. Those who donate blood will be given the remainder of the day off. The drive will be held at the clinic. Doors will open at oh-seven hundred hours."

I had already had enough Arabic that a day off sounded good. Thursday morning I fell in line at 6:15 a.m., thinking to beat the rush. I was the fifth one there. It's a good thing I got there that early: within 15 minutes there must have been 100 guys in line behind me! When I finally got inside and got through the preliminary paperwork, a nurse told me she was going to take a couple of drops of blood from my finger. She took her lancet and punched. Then she squeezed. Then she squeezed again.

> "I guess I didn't prick it deep enough. I'm sorry, but I'll have to try again."

So she punched again. Then she squeezed again; and again. Once more, not enough blood came out. After the fifth try on three different fingers, I said,

> "You know, I've played the piano since I was four years old. Maybe the calluses on my fingertips are too thick."
>
> "Oh! Why didn't you tell me? We can always take some from your ear lobe."

"It didn't occur to me. I've never done this before....My ear lobe?!"

"Sure. We do it all the time."

That worked, but I felt pretty much like a pin cushion. They decided that my blood looked red enough, so I got into the next line. Finally a sweet-looking little old lady came up to me and led me to one of the tables,

"Just sit on the edge of the table so I can decide which arm to use. Hmmmm, this looks OK. All right, just lie down like this, now....You're not nervous, are you?"

"Well, a little; this is the first time I've ever given blood."

"Oh! What a coincidence! You're my first patient, ever!"

Oh, boy! That made me feel good. Come to think of it, she didn't look much like a nurse, either. Oh, well, how bad could it be?

"All right, now make a fist around this block of rubber. Now, you'll feel a little prick...."

That was what the last lady had said! And sure enough, after the little prick, it felt like she was digging around under my skin and looking for buried treasure, or something. I gritted my teeth. After a couple of minutes, she stopped. I hazarded a look to see what was left of my arm.

"Oh, I'm so sorry. I couldn't find the vein. I'll have to try again."

Again she dug around. And again she stopped. Finally, on the third try, she struck pay dirt.

"There it is! Now wait just a minute until I hook up the bag....There! You're all set! Now, that wasn't too bad, was it?"

"I guess not...."

I lied. I laid there for what seemed like a long time. The little old lady was nowhere to be seen. Eventually she returned,

> "There, now. How are we doing?"

I thought I was probably doing not nearly as well as she was. She bent over to look at the bag. Her voice, sounding perplexed, came up to me,

> "Now, I wonder why it's filling that other bag. I thought it was just supposed to fill one."

I thought I had been worried before. **Now**, I was worried! I asked,

> "Uh....Is there something wrong?"
> "I don't think so, honey. You just lie there, and I'll go ask someone."

I didn't have much choice: I had to just lie there. Was I getting lightheaded from lack of blood, or just nervousness? Finally, she returned.

> "There's nothing to worry about. That other bag is just a little bag for sample testing. Everything is perfectly normal! And it looks like you are just about finished. Now let me see if I can get this thing disconnected...."

She wrestled with the apparatus (and my arm) some more. At last, she was done.

> "All right now, honey, let me help you over to the refreshment table. I feel so much better. Don't you?"
> "Sure."

I lied again. After sitting for the obligatory five minutes, we were told to drink plenty of fluids, take it easy, and avoid smoking and alcohol for the rest of the day. As I was heading up to the barracks, Don DiGiorno called after me,

"Hey, John! Where are you heading?"
"Back to the barracks."
"We're going to get some beer and head to the beach. Want to join us?"
"Well....Sure!"

The beach was wonderful! The beer was great! Of course, you couldn't drink much without passing out. At any rate, it beat the hell out of Arabic! I made all the rest of the blood drives, and I really enjoyed my day at the beach every couple of months!

SUSIE SCHROEDER

Suddenly, it was December 15, and a memo was circulated that informed us that those who did not take leave for Christmas would have their choice of KP or Sergeant Anderson's detail. I love Christmas time at home, but I had just been home, two weeks before, and I knew there was only so much leave time allotted to you during your tour of duty. Faced with the alternatives, however, I figured a quick call to the folks was in order. Sure enough, they wanted to see me, too, so I added another round-trip ticket to the tab.

I returned to Monterey late on New Year's eve, figuring no one would be traveling then, and that I would have an easier time getting a standby seat. Sure enough, the flight was nearly empty. I had brought my Arabic book with me, so I could study for the test I knew was coming as soon as I got back. I sat across the aisle from a pretty girl, not really thinking anything would come of it, just for the view. But there must be some truth in the old sayings about girls and uniforms because shortly after we were airborne, she said:

"What're you reading?"
"I'm studying Arabic," I replied, with as much composure as I could muster.
"Arabic! Why that's fascinating!"

I certainly didn't try to disillusion her. Her name, it turned out, was Susie Schroeder, and she was studying Psychology at Berkeley. We talked for a while, and then the stewardess came by and said:

"Happy New Year! Drinks are on the house."

We helped lighten their stock a bit, and talked some more. A little while later, the stewardess came by again and said:

"Happy New Year! Drinks are on the house."
I was a bit puzzled.

"I don't want to be a party pooper, but you already said that."
"Yup," she replied, "but we just flew over a time zone, so I'm saying it again."

We had New Year several times on that flight, and were pretty stewed by the time we arrived in San Francisco. I am reasonably certain that we went over more time zones than actually exist in the U.S., but I guess my memory could be a little hazy. I hoped that the folks up in the front room of the plane were going to wait until they landed us before **they** started celebrating. I was also beginning to wonder how I was going to manage when we got off the plane. Fortunately, the mother instinct saved me.

"Hey, how are you gonna get to Monterey tonight."
"I thought I'd catch a bus."
"Well, tomorrow's Sunday you don't have classes, do you?"
"No."
"Well, I was thinking, why don't you spend the night with me at my apartment. Then you could watch the Rose Bowl game and catch a bus to Monterey tomorrow afternoon. I could give you a ride to the bus station."
"Well...if it wouldn't be too inconvenient."

Not only wouldn't it be too inconvenient, but she took me to Chinatown, where we had New Year's eve one more time. We went to a night club where the Modern Jazz Quartet was performing, and caught their last set. Then it was back to her apartment.

> "This is really a nice apartment. How many roommates do you have?"
>
> "Well, just my boyfriend and I live here."

She must have noticed my expression, because she quickly added,

> "But he won't be back until Monday...."

Oh, boy. Just what I should have expected. From that moment on, I kept thinking, "**Now** is the time her boyfriend will show up and beat the crap out of me." Fortunately for me, her boyfriend kept to his schedule, and I got on the "dog" alive, but considerably the worse for the wear.

SAYYED AL-YAMANI

Meanwhile, Arabic training continued. By now we spoke only Arabic in the classroom area. This total immersion method was working wonders—even the two Toms spoke Arabic. And without a whole lot of Boston twang. We had begun to learn to write the language as well. This was fascinating to me. Making my hand write from right to left was very challenging. One evening I was writing a letter to my parents. I do not write letters easily. In fact, I seldom write letters at all. But it was prohibitively expensive to call, so write I did. This evening, in my haste to get the task over with, I started to write this sentence:

> The weather here has been very wet recently.

I wrote the word *very* at the end of the line, dropped my pen down and began to try to write the word *wet* from right to left, just under the word *very*. It looked like this:

The weather here has been very س

No, I hadn't been drinking, and I don't think I was acting any more stupidly than I normally do. My mind was so filled up with Arabic that my hand tried to write the Arabic letter *Siin*, which looks like this, س, and sounds like our letter *s*. Admittedly, this was not the correct sound, but as you can see, the first part of the shape was correct. After I had written the backward *w*, I sat, frozen, trying to comprehend what I was doing. My brain just could not force my hand to write the rest of *wet* backwards, but neither could it finish the letter *Siin*. So I sat there looking at my hand. When the message finally got through, I jumped up.

"What the?!...."

I couldn't believe it. I went downstairs to the bathroom and splashed cold water in my face. After a while, I finished the letter. But I left the weird letter with an explanation there for my parents. In her next letter, my Mom sounded more concerned about me than usual. Maybe she thought my mind was going at an early age.

We worked with dialogue tapes every evening. I had read about learning in sleep, so I regularly went to sleep with my headphones on, and Arabic growling in my ears. It may have helped, or I may have a knack for language, because I always did well in class.

One day, Matt Adams and I were returning to class from the PX where we had gone on break. As we walked toward the building, Sayyed Al-Yamani was coming toward us. He was one of the more popular Arabic teachers. About five feet five inches of rolypoly Iraqi, he always seemed to be smiling. Hi brown skin had laugh lines you could drive a truck through. He had a habit of rubbing his bald spot when he was perplexed. But he usually didn't let anything get beyond his sense of humor. I had never talked to him, but everyone who knew him loved him. He greeted us with,

"Marhabban."

I responded with,

"Ehelen wa Sehelen."

Then he hit me with the zinger,

"Kaif lounak?"

Now, *Marhabban* means *greetings* (or *hello*) and *Ehelen wa Sehelen* means....Well, *Ehelen wa Sehelen* means *Family and hearth* (Explanation to follow.), but it's translated as *greetings* (or *hello*). *Kaif lounak*, however, means *What's your color?* That's just what I was saying to myself—*What's your color?* I couldn't fathom why he would be asking me that. I finally decided it must be a pop quiz, so I answered,

"Ahbeyadh."

which means white.

"Ahbeyadh?"

Sayyed Al-Yamani asked, rubbing his bald spot,

"Ahbeyadh?"

And then he started laughing. Well, the line about the bowl full of jelly was very apropos. He laughed, and he laughed. He sat down on the stairs and laughed some more. He laughed until tears came out of his eyes.

I, in the meantime, thought I had really blown it. I had pictures of being kicked out of language school. I distinctly saw myself on the plane to Vietnam. I was not happy at all.

Eventually Sayyed Al-Yamani got control of himself and explained. In Iraq, when you asked someone how he was, you asked what his color was. The proper answer was *All right* or *OK*. What had struck him as hilarious was the fact that in all his 38 years, he had never thought of the literal meaning of *Kaif lounak*.

This increased my interest in etymology. I began to analyze everything I said, read, and heard—in English as well as in Arabic. And I learned a lot of fascinating things. One is the explanation for the term *Ehelen wa Sehelen* (*Family and hearth*). It seems that the old, nomadic Arabs were given to very flowery, euphemistic speech. I guess they had a lot of time for language in the desert. They also had a host of rules for behavior. And one of the most important things that one Arab could offer another was hospitality. After all, the desert is a very lonely, and very dangerous place. It was customary for Arabs to offer each other food and lodging when they met in the wilderness. And the customary phrase was,

> "The fellowship of my family and the warmth of my hearth are yours for as long as you care to stay."

(I won't bore you with the whole phrase in Arabic.) But as time passed, this became shortened to just *Family and hearth*, just as in English we have shortened *God be with ye* to *Goodbye*.

Sayyed Al-Yamani and I became friends. He told me of coming to the United States, and how fortunate he felt to be here in this beautiful area and be paid to teach the language he had spoken all his life. He introduced me to the music of Umm Kulthum and other Arabic artists.

One evening while I was practicing the piano, it occurred to me that he could help me translate the lyrics of some of the songs from the Broadway musical *Kismet*. I had bought the vocal score the previous summer when I was in summer theater at East Carolina University in Greenville, North Carolina. I already knew that *kismet* in Arabic meant *fate*. And that one of the big solos from the musical was called *Fate*. But a number of other Arabic words peppered the songs, and one song in particular, *Zubbediya*, intrigued me. In the play, the Caliph is looking for a bride. Lalume, his mother I think, has sent for all the eligible princesses from near and far to present to him for his approval. They dance and sing for him, and generally try to seduce him in front of the whole court. One of them is particularly brazen. She dances a very sexy dance, like a whirling dervish—removing scarves and assorted clothing as she whirls faster and faster. As she dances, the chorus sings a song in Arabic that sounds very suggestive—some shout things at her. In fact, the stage takes on the feeling of a strip show.

So the next day, I took the score with me to class. During the morning long break, I went to see Sayyed Al-Yamani,

"Ah, yes, Kismet. It means fate."

"Yes, I know, Sayyed Al-Yamani. And look, here is a song called *Fate*."

"Yes, well isn't that interesting?"

"And here is a song, *Rahadlakum*. What does that mean?"

"It is a candy, Sayyed Looaee. Yes, like the song says here, it is made with litchi nuts, yes, and kumquats....Oh yes, it is very good."

"Now this song, Sayyed Al-Yamani, *Zubbediya*. What does that mean?"

"Zubbediya! Oh....Zubbediya....Oh, Sayyed Looaee, that is very bad...."

"Oh? Well, what does it mean? And the lyrics. See, Sayyed Al-Yamani? What does Shabash mean, and these other words, 'E Zubbediya bala knizu, degnishbu yama naya, Y baba y baba dai!'"

"Oh, Sayyed Looaee....I cannot tell you these things. These are bad things, Sayyed Looaee...."

He was blushing! He was rubbing his bald spot. It was obvious that he was very upset by this. So I thanked him for his help. He was happy to get me out of his classroom.

But now I was really intrigued. I asked everyone I could what the lyrics meant. After lunch, Gameela Hadrani asked to look at the score. She didn't say anything, but she too blushed and became very embarrassed.

Eventually I learned what many of the words meant. I had always thought that Zubbediya was supposed to be the name of the girl, but *Zubbediya*, it turns out, means *the head of the penis*. I guess you can imagine most of the rest. To this day, I wonder how much of the Arabic lyrics the authors understood. I also wonder how shocked the Arabs who saw the play must have been. I don't remember ever reading about any negative reaction to the lyrics. Of course, in 1953 most minorities in the United States weren't organized the way they are now.

I wrote a letter to the girl who had danced the part of Zubbediya in summer theater that previous summer. I told her about the Arabic in *Kismet* and what Zubbediya meant.

She never answered my letter.

CARL STEPHENSON

School seemed to fly by. Even Carl Stephenson's Russian class started. He didn't seem to fit in, however. One day he asked me if I wanted to see something incredible. I went along, of course. We met for lunch at a little sandwich shop just off post, out the east gate. We sat at the bar and ordered sandwiches.

"Here he comes," said Carl.
"Who?"
"Godanov."
"Who the hell is Godanov?"
"He's my Russian teacher. See the little man just sitting down at the end of the bar?"

Professor Godanov was the picture of the Russian ex-patriot *intelligentsia*. He was about 55 years old, middle-height, stoop-shouldered and very thin, with whispy white hair. His skin was almost transparent. You could see the tracery of blue veins across his face and hands. His suit, though clean and well-pressed, was very old. It may have fit him at one time, but now hung upon him. The sadness in his eyes reminded me of pictures of Rachmaninoff.

"Watch what he does."

What he did was order and pay for a pint bottle of vodka and an iced-tea glass. He poured half of the bottle into the glass and drank it in about two swallows. Then he poured the rest into the glass and drank it almost as quickly. Then he got up and left.

Nobody but Carl and I paid him the slightest attention. In fact, it appeared that he had been doing the same thing for ages.

> "He does that every day," Carl said.
> "He must be very unhappy about something."
> "Well he's a pain in the ass in class."

Carl had a way of getting down to the things that were most important to him, quickly. It wasn't more than two weeks into his course when the end came. One day when Professor Godanov asked him to repeat a dialogue, Carl threw his books up in the air, fell on the floor and started kicking and screaming incoherently. Needless to say, the U.S. Army decided right then and there that Carl should do something else. Fortunately, there just **happened** to be the job of Company Clerk opening up, and Carl just slipped right in.

We had all made Private (E2), one step up from buck Private (E1—where you start in Basic Training), as soon as we came to language school. The minute they made Carl Company Clerk, however, they promoted him to PFC (Private First Class). I didn't think it was tremendously fair that someone who got himself kicked out of training should get promoted before me, but I figured, what the heck, Carl's a nice guy, and it was probably just another of the Army's screwups: little did I know.

Carl became invisible. His name was never on any duty rosters, and I seldom saw him anymore: he was a lot like Ensign Pulver from *Mr. Roberts*. It couldn't have been more than six weeks after he got the Company Clerk job when I saw him coming out from behind the stock room:

> "Hey, Carl, is that for real?"
> "Oh, hi John," he said, looking around, "Is what for real?"
> "That Spec-4 patch on your sleeve?"
> "Oh. Yeah, I made Spec-4 last week."

Well that floored me. None of the rest of us had even made PFC. Even cutting all the corners I had ever heard of, I thought you had to be in the Army at least a year before you could be promoted to Spec-4 (Specialist, 4th class). The timing wasn't the depressing thing, however, among other things, it meant Carl was making a good bit more money every month than we were.

"Well, uh, congratulations."

"Thanks."

"I hardly ever see you around any more. What happens when you get to be Company Clerk, do you forget your old rock-painting buddies?"

"No. Hey, I'm sorry. I'm just trying to keep out of sight. Uh, see, they tag almost any job onto the Company Clerk if they think you're not doing anything."

"Yeah. I guess that's right. You must be pretty visible in the Orderly Room all day long."

"That's the point."

That was at least one of the points. Carl stayed just at the edge of vision. It wasn't so much that he was hiding, just that no one knew precisely where he was at any moment. All the reports got filed on time, though, and that kept everyone happy.

And then one day it occurred to me that I hadn't seen Carl in quite some time.

"Where's Carl?"

"Carl who?"

"Carl Stephenson."

"Where've you been, John? Didn't you hear? He got himself transferred to the Presidio of San Francisco."

"What? You're kidding.... You're not kidding. That's so cushy, I can't believe it. Do you know he has relatives up there?"

"Yeah. I guess you also didn't hear that he made Spec-5."

Stunned again. I was speechless for a minute.

"You said he got **himself** transferred?"

"Yeah. Somebody told me Carl heard there was an opening there and cut himself orders. Got the CO to sign them when he was thinking about something else."

"Wow. That takes some nerve. What's his job in San Francisco?"

"Company Clerk, what else?"

I had visions of Carl slipping in and out of the fog around the San Francisco harbor: the Invisible Man. I wondered how long he would last in San Francisco.

I didn't have long to wait.

"Hey, John, did you see the card from Stephenson?"
"No. What card?"
"Wait'll you see this: it'll kill you."

It almost did. Carl had managed to become the ASA Liaison Officer on an island in the middle of the Pacific Ocean. If that wasn't enough, he was promoted to Spec-6. The card said that he was responsible for stamping as "OK" any classified documents that were transferred through the APO on the island. Now if that wasn't the cushiest assignment for an enlisted man in 1967, I didn't know what was. Just to put the icing on the cake, he had himself assigned there on what is called TDY (temporary duty) status with full quarters and rations allowances. That meant that in addition to his salary as a Specialist Sixth Class, he was getting about $150.00 per month in food and housing allowance—a princely sum in those days. He was renting a two-bedroom bungalow with hot and cold running maids and everything else for less than $50.00 per month and putting the rest, including just about all of his E-6 salary, in the bank.

Carl must have thought that he couldn't get any better either, because he stayed out there for one whole year: the maximum amount of time one could draw TDY quarters and rations. Then he managed to get himself an early out. That's right, while the rest of us were struggling through the last two years (plus a couple of months—I don't think Carl was even in for two whole years) of our four-year hitches, Carl was out of the service with a couple thousand dollars in the bank. One man's pain is another man's pleasure.

AL AND SUSIE DAWES

I had found the Service Club during my first months at Monterey. As soon as I found out there were several pianos there that we could use, I sent for some of my sheet music and started getting my fingers and voice back in shape: six months with little more than marching songs hadn't helped my musical ability at all.

The club was near the East gate on the Presidio grounds. It was an old, three-story building that housed all sorts of wonders. In addition to the pianos (which I quickly put to some heavy use) there were classes in drama, music, dance and just about anything else artistic you could think of.

Then, I discovered an awful fact: there were Army people who actually were allowed to work there, instead of learning unusual languages! "Boy," I thought, "this is for me!"

Wrongo. I tried again and again to get transferred into Special Services (the branch of the Army that ran the clubs), but was told, again and again, that my language skills were too valuable. Unfortunately, I couldn't bring myself to "pull a Stephenson" and get myself kicked out of language training. If I had, the rest of this book would have been quite different.

One day I dropped into an acting class that was going on. There, in the midst of all the Army nonsense was a **real** acting coach: I was impressed. His name was Al Dawes, and he had spent a good deal of time at the Tyrone Guthrie theater in Minneapolis. He was very well trained in virtually all aspects of theater and had an additional asset: his wife, Susie, was there helping almost all the time. I must admit I had a crush on Susie. She was a tall thin brunette who reminded me a lot of Michelle Philips in the Mamas and Papas, but with the loveliest brown eyes—she brought out the *protector* image in all the fellows around. She, too, had studied theater a great deal, and was a great deal of help to Al.

Like most of us, Al had been drafted when he dropped out of school to pursue a career (in theater, of course). Thin, about 30, and with chiseled (read "noble" if you are in theater) features, Al looked the part of the aesthete. He even acted the part, most of the time. I quickly signed up as a permanent member of his classes. He was a good teacher as well as a good actor (something most people can't pull off), but I think his strength was in teaching.

He and Susie had put on several plays at the Presidio, and a couple of them had received very good reviews from the local papers as well as the Post paper. One evening, while drinking a beer at his house, he said,

> "How would you like to write a musical?"
> "Sounds like fun," I said, "but I wouldn't know where to start."
> "Susie and I have written most of it already, John. What we need is someone to do all the arrangements and write the incidental music and possibly one or two more songs."
> "Could I see it before I commit myself?"
> "Sure."

It was a little gem, written using O Henry's *The Gift of the Magi* for the story line. I liked it at first glance. The music was good, but like they implied, they had only written the melodies and some of the chords. I spent every available minute of the next few weeks working on that score. It was something I had never done before, but the sort of thing I had always dreamed of. It went pretty smoothly, for the most part. But one evening I ran into a problem—sort of a composer's version of *writer's block*.

There was a place in one of their songs that needed a transition chord to get from one point in the melody to the next. For the life of me, I couldn't find the right chord. I sat in that little room with the door slightly ajar (driving the rest of the club crazy, I'm sure), playing those three measures over and over and over. No matter what I tried, I couldn't come up with the right sound. After a period of time that seemed like eternity, I was just about to throw in the towel. At that moment, the door was pushed open, and a heavily accented voice said,

"Try a second-inversion E-flat minor seventh."

I spun around to see Professor Godanov leaning in the doorway. I stared for a moment at this sad, old man, thinking, "What could he possibly know about it?" Then decided I might as well try it: it couldn't be any worse than what I had been doing. Lo and behold, it worked beautifully! You can imagine how dumfounded I was. I turned back around to thank him, but he was gone. I never had a chance to talk to him, and to this day wonder about his past: perhaps he had had a career in music in Russia before being driven out by the Revolution.

The performances went very well. We had a terrific time, and received favorable reviews in a number of local papers. Unfortunately, my name never appeared anywhere. A Presidio rule forbade troops from performing until they had been in class at least six months: the fickle finger of fame struck again!

MATT ADAMS

One of the other rock painters from Sergeant Anderson's crew was Matt Adams. He started Russian training about the same time I started Arabic. Matt was from Stamford, Connecticut, and was about as straight-arrow as you could imagine. About six feet one, he was thin, but athletic. His face was long, and he wore his light brown hair in a crew cut. Well, I guess right out of Basic many of us still wore crew cuts. But Matt was still wearing one four years later. He looked Scandinavian with thin, sharp features and clear, nearly translucent skin, but his eyes were piercing. When you talked to him, he looked at you so intensely that it could be disconcerting. You had the feeling that he was trying to draw more out of your head. I found him to be highly intelligent, and a fascinating conversationalist. Not only was he interested in just about everything, but he had considerable knowledge about everything I ever talked with him about.

Matt had gotten me interested in sports cars, and we had planned to go over to the Laguna Seca race track later in the year to see the races that were scheduled. One Saturday, while we were walking around ogling the girls in Carmel, I recognized a car that I had never even heard of a couple of months earlier.

"Hey, look Matt," I said, "It's a Type 35 Bugatti!"

It was not only thrilling to have seen one actually being driven on the street, but the thrill of knowing what it was made me pretty proud of myself. Matt looked closely for a minute and then said,

"Oh, yeah. That's chassis number 112. It was built in 1934. The first owner was Luigi Calibresi. He drove it in several races, placing well, and then crashed it in 1937. It was rebuilt and sold to...."

Well, you get the picture (even though **my** facts aren't right). He traced the entire history of the car from its construction to its present owner. I was flabbergasted! I had been excited just to know what it was, but here I found myself with a walking encyclopedia of automotive trivia. I asked,

"How do you know all that stuff?"
"Oh, I have eidetic memory."
"You mean photographic memory?"
"That's right. I'm sorry if I ran off at the mouth: the information sort of pops into my brain, and out of my mouth. If it bothers you, tell me, and I'll shut up."
"Well, how much do you forget? Any idea?"
"Not much."

As time went by, I found out that was a substantial understatement. He regularly amazed me with obscure trivial facts. And I do mean *obscure*! One day as we were walking through his barracks, we passed a group of guys who were quizzing each other on trivia.

"Hey Matt," said one, "I have one you can't possibly know."
"Ask away," Matt replied.
"Who was the sponsor of the old *Lone Ranger* radio show?"
"Quaker Oats," Matt shot back, "Who read the commercials?"
"Right again....What do you mean, *Who read the commercials*? Who knows who read the commercials?"

"I know," Matt said, "and I'm still asking, who read the commercials?"

"Baloney! I don't know who read the commercials, and I bet you don't either."

"Wrong again. It was Joe Daniels."

"You're full of crap—*Joe Daniels*. How do I know you didn't just make that up?"

"Go to the library, and look in a book called *That Was Radio*. At the bottom of page 137 you will find that Joe Daniels read the Quaker Oats commercials for the *Lone Ranger* radio show[1]."

Well, that shut him up. But I couldn't wait to get to a library. They had the book and, you guessed it, at the bottom of page 137 it said that Joe Daniels read the Quaker Oats commercials for the *Lone Ranger* radio show. I didn't often argue with Matt.

One day he said,

"Do you want to ride out and see the desert?"

"Desert?"

"Yeah. This guy in my barracks is letting me drive his car over the weekend. I thought I'd drive over the mountains and see the desert? Want to come?"

"Yeah, sure. Where'd you get a car?"

"A guy I know loaned me his for the day—it's a TR3."

"Definitely, then!"

I had never been in one of the little Triumphs, but they sure looked neat on the road. We left very early on Saturday. The TR was canary yellow, and made the nicest noises. Monterey was truly an amazing place. The weather was never too hot or too cold, but you could hop in a car and be swimming on the beach in a few minutes, or you could drive into the mountains in the winter and go skiing. Of course, if you continued over the mountains, you'd find yourself right in the middle of a desert.

I had never been in a desert before, but considering the language I was studying, there was at least some chance that I might find myself in one in the near future. We were sunburned by noon, and had to resort to hats, long-sleeve shirts, and plenty of lotion to keep from catching fire.

"Hey, Matt, what's that in the road?"
"A head?"
"Very funny. No, slow down. Stop! Look at that thing! I could see it from way back there!"

That thing was a tarantula—a **BIG** tarantula!

"Didn't I see a shoe box behind your seat?"
"I don't know—are you planning on catching that thing?!"
"Sure! See if you can find a rubber band to put around the box. I don't want it popping open with this monster inside."
"Matt, I'm not sure I even want to be in the same car with that monster—shoe box or no shoe box!"

It was a tight fit. I did manage to find a couple of rubber bands. We secured the box well. For a while our new friend tried to get out by springing up against the top, but the rubber bands held. I kept the shoe box on my lap to further guard against escape. I wanted to know exactly where that thing was at all times.

When we finally got back to the Presidio, we stopped off in the latrine in Matt's barracks. Matt put the shoe box on the shelf over the sinks, and we headed for the urinals. One of the other guys said,

"Hey, Matt, what's in the box?"
"Wait until I finish here....OK, check this out."

He carefully took the rubber bands off the box and sat it in the middle of the floor. Nothing happened. He reached out and tapped it a couple of times with his shoe. **BANG!** The lid popped a foot up in the air and the humongous spider hit the floor. It took a couple of seconds to check out its new surroundings. In the meantime, the level of human activity in the latrine instantly skyrocketed. A couple of the guys were trying their best to get toilet paper off the Army one-sheet-at-a-time dispensers with one hand while pulling up their pants with the other. Those who had been near the box got as far away as possible, and quickly sidled to the exit door, keeping the spider in sight at all times.

Before our eight-legged friend could get its bearings and find a good place to hide, Matt flipped the box over and recaptured it. Later that evening we set the poor creature free down at the wharf. Matt was roundly vilified for a while, but eventually things quieted down.

CANDY

One night I had gone to the Service Club to practice the piano. After a while, I stopped to take a break. Just as I stepped out of the room I glimpsed a beautiful vision in blonde, high heels, and red crepe. She took my breath away as she danced across the floor of the big room at the end of the hall. I stumbled to the doorway and tried my hardest (pun intended) not to stare. She really was a beautiful girl. And she had a figure that just wouldn't quit. Eventually I learned that her name was Candy, and she was doing an introductory dance lesson for the troops, courtesy of the nearby Arthur Murray Dance Studio. Well, I've always felt that I had two left feet, but I don't have to tell you that I stayed for her free dance lesson. Those who were interested (ostensibly in dancing) were given two free lessons at the studio. I signed up.

The free lessons came as soon as I could guarantee that she would be there to teach them. I learned all that I could about her while she was in my arms, and during breaks. She was from Los Angeles, and had moved to Monterey only recently when an assistant manager position opened up at the studio. We enjoyed the same kinds of music, and both had an interest in theater. She had lovely green eyes, but there didn't seem to be much behind them. I was willing to let that slide, if it was indeed the case. At the end of the second lesson, I asked her out.

"Well," she replied, demurely, "dancing is my life, you know. And I don't think I could be interested in anyone who wouldn't share that with me...."

The fish had obviously nibbled. Would he take the lure? Well, I had always wanted to be able to dance better: my mother thought that you had to be able to dance well to be truly civilized. (Sure, John, blame it on your Mom!) So the answer was—hook, line, and sinker. I signed up for $220.00 worth of dance lessons.

You probably think I was crazy. After all, those were 1967 dollars. And 220 of them were about two month's pay for a Private First Class in Uncle Sam's Army. But they did have a convenient monthly payment plan. And she was unbelievably beautiful! And she seemed willing....

The next Friday night, we went out for a movie and dinner. I walked down to the studio, and she drove from there. She was still lovely. There still didn't seem to be much behind her eyes. But late that night, parked overlooking the Pacific Ocean, she proved to be very willing indeed. As well as something of a contortionist. Her old Falcon didn't have reclining seats, and the back seat was full of Arthur Murray paraphernalia. Just as we were getting dressed again, a policeman drove up, sauntered over to the car, and asked all the typical questions. She was so embarrassed. She asked if I would mind coming to her apartment until she felt better.

No problem.

She had an efficiency apartment over the hill from Monterey, about halfway to Carmel. It was totally nondescript. The place had a double bed, a couch, and, over in a corner near the little kitchenette, a tiny table with two chairs. There was a little bathroom with a shower—no tub. It was very mundane, almost totally devoid of anything personal. A few pictures on the dresser and her clothes in the closet were all that indicated that this lovely creature lived there. No books. No hi fi. No TV. It looked like all she used it for was sleeping—or at least going to bed. She avoided talking about the people in the pictures. But she loved her clothes. She always dressed well for work. And she would change into something more casual before we left the studio. No jeans for her—everything she wore was soft, attractive, and definitely sexy.

We spent many nights in her bed, and I enjoyed it immensely.

Almost every Friday night I would meet her at the studio. We would go someplace inexpensive for a late dinner, and end up in her apartment. I never tired of looking at her. Her thick honey-blonde hair fell in heavy waves to her shoulders. Tawny, too, was her skin—not the dark sun tan that comes immediately with the image of the California girl, but a leonine, golden tan. Skin smooth as silk, she had the flawless complexion of a baby. Her face held the innocence of a preteen. She wore little makeup, just a tiny bit of eye liner to heighten the effect of those sea-green eyes. And her body.... Well, I had always liked well-shaped legs, and with all the hours she put in dancing, she was a leg-lover's dream come true. Holding her one night while we stood in her apartment, I was mesmerized by her reflection in the mirror on the bathroom door. She was gorgeous.

We often slept after sex, but she always took me back to the base early Saturday morning so that she could get ready to go to the studio for work. I never saw the place in daylight.

I talked to Matt Adams about her a lot. I respected his opinions, and had to share my incredible good fortune with someone. He had seen her in the club and agreed with me about her physical charms. But she was not the kind of girl he wanted. He was looking for someone more his intellectual equal. She was a very sweet girl, but very one-dimensional. That didn't bother me. Candy and I both seemed to crave the same thing, and neither of us seemed to want any permanent ties. In the end, Matt agreed that I wasn't using her any more than she was using me.

In fact, I enjoyed being used. There was something comfortable about her that went way beyond the sex. We had just finished making love one night when she said,

> "John?"
> "Yes, honey"
> "We're kind of special, aren't we?"
> "**You** certainly are."

...."We really...like each other, don't we?"

There was a plaintive note in her voice, but I thought she was being very honest. I liked her even more for that. Then she said,

"I'm going to be gone for the next couple of weeks."
"Oh....I'll miss you. Where are you going?"
"There's a statewide competition in Los Angeles. I'm going to stay with my parents."
"Oh....Well, I'm sure you'll do well. Your parents live in LA?"
"Yeah. I haven't seen them in a while. It should be fun."
"I'm sure it will be. Enjoy yourself, but remember, I'll be here thinking of you all the time."
"Me, too."

I did miss her, as it turned out. Not just the sex, but the companionship. She didn't demand anything from me. She was always there, and listened attentively. She was easy to like.

The day after she returned I called and asked her for a date.

"I'm not sure,"
"What do you mean?"
"Well, I'm just not sure, that's all."
"Oh....Well, I'd really like to see you again...."
"....Well, OK...."

That didn't sound too promising, and I grew curiouser and curiouser. The evening was a little strained, but we ended up back at her apartment. When we started getting passionate, she pushed me away. She said,

"I don't think we should."
"Why not?"

She started to cry quietly. I took her in my arms and said comforting things, and eventually, she stopped.

"While I was in Los Angeles I...uh...met...uh...a man...."

There was considerable silence. I just held her and waited.

"He's a photographer....And he wanted to feature me in a magazine spread he was doing....and....well, he wanted to take nude pictures of me."

There didn't seem to be anything to say, so I didn't.

"Well....I let him. And he....And I....He asked me to....I shaved it...."

This last was almost inaudible. I continued stroking her back and said,

"Is that all, honey?"
"....We didn't have sex. He just took my picture."
"I believe you."
"You do?"
"Yes."
"And...."
"I'm not upset about what you did. I'm sure you are just as beautiful without any hair there. In fact, I can't wait to see."
"Oh, John...."

She positively melted. She was very shy about getting undressed, but I did my best to put her at ease. We were both very tentative at first, but soon things seemed very much back to normal. Back at the base I couldn't stop thinking about her. I felt very protective of her. I couldn't wait for the next weekend when I could see her again.

About a week later, during a Monday-morning class, my groin started to itch. By late Monday night, it was driving me crazy. Tuesday morning I went on sick call. The medic at the Presidio thought it was an infection, and prescribed a salve. By Thursday, I was back. The medic decided perhaps I should see a real doctor, so he sent me across the bay to Fort Ord.

Doctor Huong appeared to be Vietnamese. And Doctor Huong was most definitely a woman. She was a short woman—in fact, she was tiny. A cast covered her left forearm and hand. I felt like I was in the wrong place. I had little confidence in the whole situation. She asked me the same questions the medic at the Presidio had asked, and a bunch more. I was uncomfortable talking about my sex life with her. When she told me to drop my trousers so she could see the infected area, I was very embarrassed.

"Ah, yes...."

She seemed to think she had found something significant. Taking a pair of scissors, she snipped a couple of my pubic hairs and took them into another room. She was only gone a minute or so. When she came back she had the pubic hairs between a couple of glass slides from a microscope. She said,

"You have *pediculosis pubis*."
"What's that?"
"Crabs."
"What? I can't have crabs! How could I get crabs?"
"Well, it is possible that you could have contracted them at the barracks. It happens all the time. They can live for a while on toilet seats, for example."
"Toilet seats!"
"Yes."
"Impossible! I can't have crabs."
"See for yourself."

She managed to extricate the pubic hairs from between the slides, and held them up for me to look at. Gingerly, I took them between my thumbnail and fingernail and held them close to my eyes. Sure enough, on the end of one of the pubic hairs was a little critter that appeared to be waving at me.

I was stunned. I was even more stunned when she told me what to do to get rid of them,

> "You can fill this prescription at the pharmacy down the hall. When you get back to the barracks, go into the shower and shave yourself from just below your rib cage to just above your knees. Then apply the ointment. It should kill any eggs that the shaving misses. Oh yes, and make certain to put all your clothes into the cleaner. Anything that you might have worn recently should be thoroughly cleaned as soon as possible. Continue to treat the area with the ointment for a week. That should take care of it. If there is a recurrence, the medic will be able to prescribe additional ointment."

Shaving myself was very difficult. But I got back early enough in the afternoon that I had the shower to myself. Most of my clothing went right to the cleaner, and I talked Sergeant Anderson into letting me swap all my bedding. I felt that I was going to get over this as quickly as possible.

Friday afternoon I thought for about ten seconds about calling Candy for a date. I couldn't do it, however. I was too embarrassed, and terrified of possibly passing crabs on to her. In the end, I called her with a story about a tough exam on Monday, but arranged to see her in a week. She was so concerned on the phone. She wished me luck.

Thursday, as Matt Adams and I were walking down to play handball I was bemoaning my fate,

> "God, Matt, having the crabs is one thing. Shaving is

another. But what's really killing me is having all these little hairs growing back. I can't be comfortable, no matter what I wear!"

"I guess that really is tough. But you only have to sit in class all day. Just think what it would be like for Candy teaching dance."

"Candy?!....."

I was thunderstruck! In my naivete it hadn't occurred to me until that minute that I might have gotten the crabs from Candy! Matt and I looked at each other for a minute, and then started laughing,

"I can't believe it! She gave me the crabs!"
"Toilet seats, indeed!"
"Photographer, indeed!"
....
"Well, are you going to date her again?"

Now there was the $64,000.00 question. I felt betrayed. She had lied to me! Or at least misled me. The fact that I hadn't been completely honest with her didn't enter into the equation then. I never saw her again.

Well, that may not be completely true. About two years later I opened the latest issue of *Playboy* magazine and there was Candy with a staple in her navel! All the breath came out of me in a rush. I couldn't believe it. It had to be her. The more I looked, the more certain I became. But when I got around to reading the text, I found that this playmate, Cheryl who was from Los Angeles, had a twin sister (whose name was not given) who lived somewhere in California. I tried to recall the pictures on Candy's dresser, but we never really talked about them. There were pictures of her there, though, now that I thought about it. And who had pictures of themselves on their dresser?

Was Cheryl Candy's sister? Was Cheryl Candy? I never found

out. But whoever she was, the playmate did turn up in the news again about a year later. She was convicted of smuggling drugs into the U.S....I hoped it wasn't her....or her sister.

SPRING BREAK

Lo and behold, Spring had sprung! And with it came Spring Break. We had two weeks of freedom! Did I say freedom? At morning assembly the top sergeant said,

> "Pay attention, men. As you know, Spring Break begins two weeks from Friday at the end of class. Those of you who are not taking leave will spend your two weeks working for the Army. Some of you will work with Sergeant Anderson, and the rest will pull KP."

Sergeant Anderson? Could I take another two weeks of the good sergeant? More to the point, did I want two weeks of KP? With the Christmas Break and the trip home before class started, I really didn't have any leave time. But considering the alternatives, I decided to see if anything could be done,

> "Excuse me, Sergeant..."
> "What is it Specialist?"
> "Well when Sergeant Johnson told us about Spring Break this morning, I wondered if I could put in for leave?"
> "Sure thing. Let me get the forms....Now, why don't you sit down at that desk and fill these out: I'm sure we can have your orders cut in a few minutes."

It truly was a hard thing to believe—the Army getting something fixed that quickly. Cutting corners for a PFC? Well, either Sergeant Adams really loved his troops, or I was missing something....
See how it gets to you? I hadn't even been in the service for a

year, and already I was suspicious about anything that looked good. I filled the papers out, reading all the fine print carefully, but couldn't see a catch. As much as I didn't want to spend two weeks with Sergeant Anderson—or worse yet, on KP—I had to take the chance of blowing what looked like a sure thing. Something just didn't seem right:

> "Excuse me again, Sergeant....Here are the papers."
> "Ummm....Just let me look through these first."
> "Uh....Sergeant Adams...."
> "Yes?"
> "I really want to take this leave, but I have to be honest with you: I don't think I have enough leave time credited to cover two weeks."
> "That's no problem, Specialist. You can loan yourself leave, up to a point."
> "Oh...."
> "And we'd be happy for you to take it. See, there's only so much stuff that needs to be done around here. If we have too many guys, we have to dream up things for them to do."
> "Oh, I see...."

And I thought I did. But what I missed was the "company store" aspect. Later that night while I was studying, the light bulb came on: I was going into hock with my leave time. Eventually, if I didn't cut down on the amount of leave I was taking, I would owe Uncle Sam a whole lot of days.

Suddenly, it didn't seem like such a good idea after all. I had borrowed money from my parents for the two trips home, and of course, I still owed some for the dance lessons. Where would I come up with enough money to go home again?

> "Hi, Mom!"
> "Hi, Johnny! It's been a while since you called. How're you going in school?"

"Oh, real well, Mom. In fact, we have two weeks break coming up."

"Are you coming home?"

"Well....I can't really afford it, Mom."

"Oh....That's too bad....I guess we could lend you the money?...."

"I've been thinking about it, Mom. I would borrow the money, if I could work at the mill for the two weeks I was home. That way, I could come home and pay you and Dad back at the same time."

"Oh, that's a wonderful idea! I'm sure your Dad can find you a short-term job in the mill. Just tell me when you'll be home and what days you want to work. When your Father comes home, I'll have him set it up."

And it was as easy as that! Well, almost that easy. You see, I **did** have to work. My Dad was captain of an ore freighter for Inland Steel, and was, indeed, able to find me a job. But a steel mill in June is no fun. It was hot and dirty. And I had to work the swing shift. But at least I didn't have to work for Sergeant Anderson. And I didn't have to pull KP. And, yes, I made enough money to pay my parents back and even have a little bit left over.

LAGUNA SECA

Just north of Monterey, nestled in the hills near Fort Ord, is a lovely race track. No, this isn't a high-speed oval like the NASCAR racers run on. It's a twisty, turny, up and down road course. I went to my first race in June with a bunch of the guys, and I was hooked! The Can Am Challenge cars ran there several times that year. What an experience! Most of the cars were powered by big-block American V-8 engines. They made deep, guttural roars when accelerating and decelerating. By contrast the few Porsches and Ferraris that ran whined like banshees.

    I was lucky enough to see some incredible cars and drivers. The Penske team with driver Mark Donahue was my favorite: those immaculate, royal blue and gold cars were easily the best-prepared on the course. And Mark Donahue was the consummate driver/engineer. It looked like he had a line drawn on the course that only he could see: lap after lap he was on the same line, shifting and braking at the same points. But I had a soft spot in my heart for the maverick machines that Jim Hall fielded. The Chaparrals were always outrageous. Some with huge wings that flipped up or down. Some that used motors to create a vacuum and suck the rear wheels down to the pavement. The expression, "it corners like it's on rails," was made for these suckers. Then there were the adobe-orange McLaren cars with Denis Hulme leading that team. The cars were huge and reminded me of earthbound fighter planes.

    As the resident sports car expert, Matt Adams showed us to watch how the drivers maintained (or didn't maintain) the proper line through curves. How they were able to work the track to keep marginally faster cars from passing. And how the cars that were considerably faster just drove around the track hogs. It was quite an education. And I didn't miss a race for the rest of the year.

Just as interesting were the private cars that people drove to the races. Such an assortment of exotic cars added fuel to the fire of my growing interest in cars and racing. People showed up in Ferraris, Porsches, Mercedes Benzes, Aston Martins—just about any of the premier cars imaginable. We even saw a Rolls Royce or two.

There were other attractions, too. Beer flowed freely, as did other beverages. The weather was glorious, albeit a little dangerous: sunburns were common. Walking around the course on one occasion I ran into a friend who had one of those paper toilet seat covers around his shoulders, and one folded up on his head. He had left his shirt at the blanket we brought. Half way around the course when he realized he was burning up, the only shelter to be found was one of the porta-potties. He knew he couldn't stay in there forever, but he couldn't bear to go back out in the sun. Hence, the impromptu clothes. He looked so silly, I wasted a picture on him.

And, of course, it was a great place to meet girls. One Saturday in early August, standing in line to buy a soda, I struck up a conversation with a lovely young thing. Carol, it happened, was majoring in music and home for the summer. We found that we had a lot of things in common, and she asked,

> "Would you like to come over to my house this evening for dinner? My folks are out of town, but I could whip up something for us."
> "I'd really like that!"
> "Great!"

Yes, it was. We spent hours talking about music, literature, art, and almost everything else. By the time I got back to the base Sunday night, I thought I had died and gone to heaven. Unfortunately, she had to go back to school the next week. Although we exchanged a few letters, I never saw her again.

MONTEREY POP FESTIVAL

Everyone who was anyone in rock and roll was coming to Monterey. In June the hills would be alive with the sound of **LOUD** music. As I read the ads, I became more and more excited—most of my favorite groups would be there. And then I came to the show stopper: *Proceeds to benefit the Diggers*....Hey, wait a minute. Aren't those the people who run soup kitchens and flop houses for those hippies in San Francisco? Can I stand to see a month's pay used for that? It was a hard question to answer. While I was hoping to avoid Vietnam, nonetheless I had felt enough of a sense of duty to answer my country's call with a four-year enlistment. And at my tender age, four years seemed like an eternity. I had nothing against hippies *per se*, but the thought of spending a month in uniform so that I could afford to send that much money to people who were pouring it down a drain (or a vein) was too much to stomach. I decided I would file my protest by not attending.

I knew that my carefully-reasoned logic should have made me feel good about myself, but the thought of missing all that good music kept grinding down my resolve. Friday night, while the rest of the young people on the West Coast headed for the hills, I headed for my favorite bar. Mike's on Fisherman's Wharf in Monterey was just the ticket. It was quiet and dark, with lots of glass lit by ethereal blue light to resemble the ocean's depths. I sat at the bar, and wallowed in self-pity (and Scotch).

After a while, I noticed a group of people at a nearby table whom I had originally taken to be some hippies down from San Francisco. Now, I am normally very reticent about approaching celebrities. I try to put myself in their place, and feel that in their position I would appreciate being left alone. But I just had to say something. Leaving my drink on the bar, I approached hesitantly,

"Excuse me, but you're the Mamas and the Papas, aren't you?"

"That's right."

"I hate to bother you, but I just have to say one thing. I've studied music all my life, and you are the greatest vocal group I have ever heard."

"Thanks. Why don't you join us for a while?"

I managed to not say anything foolish (I think). But on the other hand, I don't remember much of what was said. I nursed my drink, and when it was gone, I left them alone. On the walk back up the hill to the barracks I thought that if I had gone to the festival, I wouldn't have had the opportunity to meet them. I was glad I had decided not to go.

Now, although I still cherish those few minutes, a tiny part of me regrets not having shared the much larger experience of the first Monterey Pop Festival.

MOTORCYCLE

One day in the mess hall I noticed an odd sight,

"Hey, Matt, what's the story with that guy?"
"Which one?...Oh, that's Bill Chambers. You haven't heard about him?"
"No. What the heck kind of cast is that?"
"Well, he's in Vietnamese, and about three weeks ago he bought a new motorcycle. The day he got it, he ran it into a tree and broke both collarbones. He just got released from the hospital yesterday."
"Ow! That's gotta be miserable."
"Worse than that. See the guy feeding him? Think about it. With both arms in casts like that, he can't do much of anything for himself. There are three or four guys in his barracks that help him with everything."
"Oh, man! You mean everything, don't you?"
"Yup. Not only do they dress and feed him, but somebody's got to help him go to the bathroom, wash himself—yeah, everything is just about right."

Well, once I had seen him, it was hard not to notice him all the time. There would always be someone with him, helping do whatever he had to do. Then one day it occurred to me that I hadn't seen him for a while. I looked for him at lunch for a couple of days, and finally asked Matt,

"Remember the guy with the broken collarbones? I haven't seen him around lately. Did he get the casts off?"

"Oh, yeah, Chambers. Well, in fact he did get the casts of last Thursday. The same day, he got on his rebuilt motorcycle and drove it into a bridge abutment. This time, no one has to help him."

"...He killed himself?"

"I don't know if it was on purpose, or an accident, but it sure seems weird, doesn't it?"

"Didn't you say he was in Vietnamese? Maybe he just couldn't face going to 'Nam."

"Yeah. Maybe."

....

"I feel sorry for him."

"For him?! No, man, you shouldn't feel sorry for him. You should feel sorry for the guys who followed him around for four weeks, dressing him, feeding him, helping him pee, wiping his ass. Those are the guys you should feel sorry for."

"Boy, isn't that the truth."

I never met anyone who knew him well, so I can only guess at how he could have managed two such spectacular wrecks. Nonetheless, I still feel sorry for him.

He didn't even get his name on the Vietnam Memorial Wall....

RE-QUALIFYING WITH THE M14

We were into our second year in the Army. This meant that we needed to re-qualify with the M14 rifle. Our entire company was scheduled to spend a day at Fort Ord proving that we hadn't forgotten everything we had learned in Basic. Accordingly, we were all bused over at what is affectionately known as *Oh-Dark-Thirty*. About the time we arrived, the sun had risen to the level that I remembered as *morning* in the civilian definition of the term. We were issued rifles, and marched out to the firing range.

It was midmorning when we finally fell into the bleachers for the re-familiarization course. It was good to sit in the shade for a while. A short Hispanic sergeant walked out in front of the bleachers and waited for us to settle down. When everyone was seated, and most of the commotion had died down, he began:

"Jou men are goin' to re-qualify wi' de M14 raifle...."

There were a lot of gasps. Not only did Sergeant Fernandez *look* just like Bill Dana, but he *sounded* exactly like the character he had created, Jose Jimenez. He went on and on in his oh-so-familiar voice. He even had the same mannerisms. I looked around to see how many other people had the same reaction—it was unanimous! While a few people looked bored or totally inattentive, most of the guys were doing their best not to laugh out loud.

Well, you should know that no one did laugh out loud or otherwise embarrass Sergeant Fernandez (or themselves). But for me, at least, it was an all-day struggle. Later I wondered whether

Bill Dana had been stationed at Fort Ord and had been inspired by Sergeant Fernandez to create Jose Jimenez. At any rate, it sure helped turn an otherwise boring day into an experience not soon forgotten.

THE GLASS MENAGERIE

Late in the summer Al asked me if I would like to direct "The Glass Menagerie" for him:

> "I'm afraid I've committed myself to too many things, John. If you could take this over for me, I would be very grateful."
>
> "I've never done the play, but I've loved it for years. I'd be happy to direct it for you. How far along are you?"
>
> "Well, I've cast all the parts. You know some of the people: Mike Collins will be Jim, the gentleman caller."
>
> "Oh, sure, Mike's in the Techniques Class."
>
> "Yes. And Renee Burkhold will be Laura. Do you know her?"
>
> "No. I don't think I've never met her."
>
> "Well she's perfect for the part...."

That assessment turned out to be far truer than I could have imagined. I pitched in with enthusiasm and soon thought that I had everyone doing very well. I was astonished by Renee. She **was** perfect for the part. Everything about her was medium—height, skin color, hair color, eye color, voice. I noticed that people sort of looked past her when they looked at her at all. It was as if she were so inconspicuous that your eyes just couldn't focus on her. When you did see her, your reaction was to protect her: she was too innocent for the real world. In fact, she appeared to be the essence of the old-fashioned, stay-at-home girl.

Her reading of Laura was so honest and true-to-life that I never had to ask her for anything: her performances were always just right.

I found myself wondering about her career: she must have done a lot of acting to get that level of sincerity without being gushy or overacting. I never had a chance to talk with her socially, though: Sarah Somers, the woman who played her mother in the play, always drove her to and from the rehearsals, and she was very protective about Renee. I assumed it was because Renee was very young.

One night, after a couple of weeks of rehearsals and just about two weeks before we were due to open, I thought I had an idea that was, if not better than, at least as workable as what Renee was doing in one of the last scenes in the play.

> "Renee, I like what you're doing there, but if you were just to sort of turn away from Jim, and address that line to the wall, I think it would be a little bit more effective."

She just stared at me.

> "Here, let me show you what I mean."

I walked over to Mike and did the encounter the way I envisioned it. Then I turned to Renee and asked,

> "Can you do it like that?"

Renee looked like her favorite dog had just been run over. She started taking big, sobbing breaths, her face melted into tears, and she spun around and ran out of the room. I stood in shock for a minute, and then ran out after her. I found her kneeling in the grass crying her eyes out. Between sobs, she was crying, "I'm sorry. I'm so sorry. It's all my fault...." over and over again. I tried to comfort her, but she seemed to be inconsolable. Sarah came to us and started stroking Renee's back and soothing her like she was a child, "It's all right, baby. Don't cry, honey. It's not your fault...." she whispered.

After a long time Renee quieted down enough for Sarah to

take her home. When I returned to the rehearsal room, the rest of the cast and crew sat stunned and silent. I sent them all home, promising to call as soon as I could figure out what was happening. As soon as I could get to a phone, I called Sarah's home number over and over until I finally reached her.

"Sarah? This is John."

"Oh, hi. I'm sorry about tonight."

"What in the world happened?"

"I apologize. Renee's parents thought that she was beyond this. She has been home from the...hospital for more than a year. No one would have thought she would relapse like this."

"What do you mean, hospital? What kind of a relapse?"

"Well, John, Renee spent a year and a half in a...rest home for schizophrenia. I've known her parents for a long time, and they assured me she has not had any episodes since she has been home. They were certain that this level of exposure would be good for her."

"But surely, Sarah, to have a schizophrenic play the part of an emotionally disturbed young woman, someone must not have been thinking too clearly. I think we should call the whole thing off. We don't have an understudy for her, and I think it would be criminal to try to have her go through with this. Don't you agree?"

"I guess so."

I became even more incredulous when I spoke to Al, later.

"I was hoping this wouldn't happen," he said.

"What do you mean, **hoping**? Are you telling me that you **knew** she had been schizophrenic?"

"Sure. But I was told she was over it."

"Al, I can assure you she isn't. I'm going to call off the performance."

"We can't do that, John. It has already been announced."

"Well un-announce it then. I insist that you call it off, unless you know of someone else to step in and do the part on such short notice. I won't continue with Renee in as Laura."

He finally agreed, and the performances were canceled. We all breathed a sigh of relief.

The next week, Mike Collins and I went over to Carmel to see the movie of *The Persecution and Assassination of Jean-Paul Marat as Performed by the Inmates of the Asylum at Cherenton Under the Direction of the Marquis de Sade* (I just love the sheer bulk of that title, don't you?). As we were looking for a seat, Mike nudged me and said,

"Look! Over there."

"That's not Renee, is it?"

"Sure it is."

"Who let her come to this? This can't be good for her. What do you think we should do, Mike?"

"I guess we should sit with her, in case she needs someone."

"Oh....I guess you're right....Hi, Renee. May we sit with you?"

"Sure."

She was very quiet throughout the movie, but at a couple of points where I was gripping the handles of the seat, I noticed she was smiling as though this was the loveliest story she had ever seen. It seemed as though all of her reactions were diametrically opposed to mine. Her behavior coupled with the insanity portrayed on the screen had me very uneasy.

When the movie was over, Mike and I suggested that Renee might like for us to walk her home. Her parents weren't home when we arrived, so she invited us in until they came back. While we were waiting, she told us a bit about her family. Her father was a German-born physicist who was **very** strict, and her mother was a concert pianist (also on the strict side). She had been left alone a lot when she was young, but, at the same time, had been constantly pushed to perform better in all aspects of her life. The pressure must have been intense.

She turned on the television, and there was "Wuthering Heights." She was so excited. She said it was her favorite movie. I couldn't believe it. So we all sat and watched the end of that, too! Mike and I were both near the limits of depression, and Renee was smiling—again. By the time her parents returned, I was a nervous wreck. We made our way out of there as quickly as possible, and found the nearest bar, posthaste!

SERGEANT BAKER

Suddenly, things started going sour. We started having inspections every weekend—and they even expected us to have the floor shiny! The culprit was easy to spot—we had a new top sergeant. After doing a little research I discovered that Sergeant Baker was not just what the Army ordered. He had flunked out of one of the Vietnamese courses just before the old top sergeant was due to be rotated. Unfortunately for us, he was put into the top spot. No one knew if it was temporary or permanent, but it was definitely not a welcome change.

Sergeant Baker was one of the Special Forces, Green Beret, soldiers. Everything was spit-and-polish and by-the-book for him. Previously the Army had gone easy on us. Sergeant Johnson, the old top sergeant, had realized that these courses required an inordinate amount of time for studying. Under him, everything was sensible. The barracks had to be kept clean and neat, and your uniform had to be clean and neat as well, but no fanaticism. That had all changed with Sergeant Baker's arrival in the Orderly Room. His first day on the new job, he addressed the troops as we stood lined up in the early morning mist,

> "All right! I want you men to understand: this is the Army! And I'm sick and tired of the lack of discipline that I see here every day! From now on I, personally, will carry out complete inspections every week! You men remember how the barracks looked in Basic Training?! I want the same here! Floors will shine! Boots will shine! Your lockers will be set up according to SOP! The first inspection will be at 07:30 hours Saturday! You WILL be ready!"

"And another thing: I will not put up with this spotty attendance at morning roll call! Starting tomorrow I want to see every man at formation! Do I make myself clear?!"

Yes, he was certainly clear...and loud. All his sentences ended in exclamation points. He sounded just like the Drill Sergeants in Basic Training. Maybe it came from jumping out of too many airplanes.

As much as I dreaded the thought of going back to shiny floors and boots, I had to admit that he had a point about the morning formations. No one took the morning formations seriously. Although everyone was "required" to be at the formations, often there were only five people to represent a whole barracks. The platoon sergeant was usually a Spec-4 or Spec-5 who had been prodded into taking on what little responsibility went with the job. Then there were squad leaders for each of the four squads per barracks. Many of the barracks only had those five people show up for the formation. Before reporting to the top sergeant, the platoon leader would begin this little ritual:

"First Squad; report!"
"First Squad; all present or accounted for, sir!"
"Second Squad; report!"
"Second Squad; all present or accounted for, sir!"
"Third Squad; report!"
"Third Squad; all present or accounted for, sir!"
"Fourth Squad; report!"
"Fourth Squad; all present or accounted for, sir!"

Notice the word **or** in the squad leaders' reports. We had been told that as long as the squad leaders could see everyone in their squads, they could report like that. (We took that to mean if the squad leader **had** seen everyone in his squad.) At one formation, the company next to mine showed up with just the platoon sergeant and one squad leader. After reporting for the first squad, the squad leader took one step back and reported for the second squad.

Then he did the same for the other two squads. It was pretty ludicrous. Out of 1,500 men, 200 or 300 would be in the formation.

I have always been an early riser, so I had no problem being a squad leader. We lined up all down the *company street* which stretched from the upper gate nearly to the bay down the hill. Some mornings the fog from the bay covered the first four or five platoons entirely: disembodied voices would come from the bottom of the hill,

> "First Platoon reports all present or accounted for, sir!"
> "Second Platoon reports all present or accounted for, sir!"
> ....

When the seals were active down at the bay side, it was often hard to hear what anyone was saying. Their barking carried through the fog up that asphalt street so well that you would swear they were just 10 feet away.

At any rate, everyone started turning out for formations the next morning. What he got was still not what he wanted, however. Many of the guys thought that just being up and standing outside at that time of the day should be enough. Wearing the correct uniform, shaving, putting on boots—those things were just too much. I could see at least two guys who had decided that any clothing was too much. They had put on was their field jackets for warmth, but that was it—no shoes, no shirts, no pants, and certainly no hat.

> "I've never seen such a disgusting-looking group! You men WILL be in complete uniform tomorrow morning! And you WILL be shaved, neat and clean! I will make you remember what STRAC means!"

Well, I still don't remember what STRAC means, if I ever did. But things definitely continued sliding downhill. The first Saturday inspection was a disaster. Nobody remembered what the SOP was for arranging a locker or foot locker. And, of course, the floors hadn't been really shiny for years. On top of that, many people's areas had taken on a sort of academic clutter—books, tapes, headphones, and writing paraphernalia were scattered all over most of the cubicles. Many of the guys had made little or no effort to straighten things out. Sergeant Baker was furious! He had been told that he could only put people on extra duty for severe infractions. Naturally, he thought that these were severe infractions. The folks in the Mess Hall and Sergeant Anderson didn't know what to do with all the extra help they suddenly had.

For several weeks, things continued to get worse. People were getting desperate. One day at break several of us were talking,

"I don't know about you guys," said Tom McKinley, "but I can't stand that son of a bitch! It really pisses me off that someone who was so stupid that he flunked out of language school should make life so miserable for the rest of us!"

"Yeah," said Tom O'Connor, "I'd pound that little bastard, if I thought I could do it and stay out of the brig!"

"Or stay alive," John Wood continued, "I heard he has a black belt in Karate."

"Well, he ought to have a black belt upside his head," Tom continued.

"There must be something we can do to get back at him," I said.

"Yeah, but what?" said Tom O'Connor.

....

"I had a professor once that got on my nerves," said Tom McKinley, "I arranged for *Playboy* to be delivered to his office."

"Oohh! That's a good one!" I said, "But for Baker, we should do something worse than that....How about subscribing to the *Berkeley Barb* for dear Sergeant Baker?"

"Yeah! That's the ticket!" said O'Connor. "We could order him some furniture or something, too...."

Well, everyone had their ideas, but when it came time to actually do something, no one did. I kept reminding the other guys about their plans for the next couple of weeks, but everyone was just too busy to take the time. And things kept getting worse,

> "You men look like a bunch of candy-assed faggots! I think you have forgotten that the Army has rules governing hair and sideburn length! By this Saturday's inspection, you had all better be trimmed right!"

Well, that was the straw that broke **this** camel's back. That night when I should have been studying, I started making plans for Sergeant Baker. The next Friday morning, during the 9:00 class break, I called the local phone company,

> "Uh, I have a problem. I've just been told that my father died suddenly this morning."
>
> "Oh, I'm sorry to hear that, sir...."
>
> "I'm stationed at the Presidio of Monterey, and I have made arrangements to fly out today with my family. I don't know how long we will be gone. Could you have my phone turned off today? I'd like to have it done this morning, if possible."
>
> "Certainly, sir. I'm sure we can have it done before noon. Now, if you'll please give me your name and number...."

I gave her what she wanted, and headed back to class. At the lunch break, I made some more calls. I turned off his electricity, his water, his gas, and stopped his mail and newspaper delivery. At 10 cents per call, I thought I had made a pretty good investment.

I found out later from a couple of the guys in the orderly room that when he arrived home, his wife was waiting with their bags packed,

> "Where are you going?" he asked, "and why is it so dark in here?"
>
> "I'm so sorry about your Dad," she responded. "The phone man told me."
>
> "Told you what? And what about my father?"
>
> "Well, that we were leaving for the funeral this afternoon....Your Dad's funeral...."
>
> "What do you mean, my Dad's funeral?! There's nothing wrong with my Dad that I know of...."

And that was the start of an interesting weekend for Sergeant Baker. Monday morning at formation, Sergeant Baker went ballistic!

> **"Some of you bastards think you're cute! Well, we'll find out who's cute around here! And when I find out who was responsible for last night, they will regret it for a long time! No son of a bitch is going to do that to me and get away with it!"**

He had a lot more to say. He ranted and raved for a long time with his eyes bulging out and the veins on his forehead in danger of instantaneous aneurysm. Only one of us knew what he was referring to, and that one wasn't about to say anything to anyone. But reports of his tantrum got back to the Captain. And soon, Sergeant Baker found himself transferred away. I'm sure he was more at home in Vietnam. And I wouldn't doubt that he was one of those who were "fragged"[2] there.

CONCOURS

Every year the Pebble Beach Golf and Country Club hosts a *Concours d'Elegance*. Judges award prizes to cars in various categories, according to how closely they resemble the original issue. People come from all over the world to show off their beautifully-restored automobiles. When I was in Monterey, three or four of the cars where exhibited at the Service Club at the Presidio a couple of days before the event. I was enraptured. These cars looked better than they had when they rolled out of the factory! I went to the Concours with a couple of other automobile diehards. Matt Adams went, of course. As usual, he was a walking compendium of information about most of the cars we saw.

The exhibition was held between the Country Club itself and the eighteenth green. It was easily the most well-kempt place I had ever seen. Situated right on the rocky California coast, the grass was so perfect it looked artificial. Craggy cypress trees stood here and there sharing their home terrain with palm trees and other exotica. The day was perfect. The sky was so clear you could see halfway to Hawaii with only a few wispy clouds high above. The breeze off the ocean provided relief from the warm sun. And the cars.... Well, the cars littered the greensward like precious gems. All colors of the rainbow, all shapes and sizes. It was an amazing display.

In 1967 you only had to be rich to be a member at Pebble Beach—billionaire status was required much later. But the wealthy were there in abundance. The women rivaled the cars with their designer clothes and jewelry. We wandered for hours, taking it all in.

We made our way to the awards stand and watched a few of

the cars receive their prizes. A ramp had been erected, and the cars were required to be driven up the ramp to stand proudly about three feet above the ground so that people could see them better.

We had just walked a few feet away from the stand when they announced the winner of a production sports car prize: it was an early Ferrari Testarossa. We had seen it while making our rounds. The Ferrari red was so bright it was almost lurid. Just then, we heard the car start up. It had little or no muffler, and made an incredible noise. People were startled by the roar. We rushed over to see it. The car had been designed for racing, and the owner had raced it in club events. It had a competition clutch and huge tires. The owner revved the engine for a few minutes to spread oil through the engine and warm things up. Then he steadied the engine and let in the clutch. "Rrroowwwrr! Rumph rumph rumph." The car wanted to fly, but of course, there was no room. Quickly, he depressed the clutch again. Then he steadied the engine again as the car slowed down, and again he let in the clutch. "Rrroowwwrr! Rumph rumph rumph," went the car again. And then, I saw it. Each time he let the clutch in, those great big tires threw up huge pieces of that gorgeous turf. Every 50 feet or so that Ferrari left twin patches of naked earth about 10 feet long. I hoped that the driver would go back and replace his divots, but I didn't see it happen. I think that was the last time owners were required to drive their cars to a reviewing stand.

CHRISTMAS BREAK

In early October we were told that we would be getting our next assignments by the end of the month. Everyone was at least a little worried. Despite the expense of the language training we were getting, the word was that graduates in many languages were nevertheless being sent to Vietnam. Matt Adams, however, thought he had an inside track to where he was going. He was studying Russian, and one day he chanced upon an advance notice,

"Hey, John, look at this."
"That looks like Russian to me, Matt."
"Yeah. It's the latest issue of *Pravda*. We just got it today."
"Well, you'll have to translate whatever that says."
"Sure. Basically it extends congratulations to the members of the Defense Language Institute, West Coast, Russian course who graduate in November."
"That's pretty neat."
"No, wait until you get a load of this. It goes on to list our assignments!"
"Get out of here!"
"No. I'm not kidding. It says I'm going to be stationed in Saporro, Japan."
"Japan?"
"Yeah. We have a field station there, I've been told."
"You don't think you are actually being assigned there, do you?"
"Well, it's not beyond the possible."
"Where do you think they got this information—assuming it's accurate?"

"Who knows? Spies. Wherever it came from, I can't wait to find out if it's true."

As it turned out, it was true. In fact, all the assignments listed in that article were accurate. Somebody sure seemed to have all the answers a long time before we did. In Matt's case, however, they weren't entirely accurate. The Army decided to have an advanced course in Russian, and Matt was chosen. So he got to spend an extra 24 weeks at Monterey. But in the end, sure enough, he was sent to Saporro.

Then we got our assignments. All the Army people in our section were to proceed to Fort Devens, Massachusetts, on January 2 for Radio Traffic Analysis School,

"Radio Traffic Analysis? What's that, Sergeant?"
"Well, Specialist, you'll find out when you get there, won't you?"

Another answer that didn't tell me anything. I was really looking forward to Massachusetts in January. After a year of California's non-climate, I was ready for winter again. As it turned out, I wasn't nearly ready for what Mother Nature had in store for us in January. But that was still some time in the future,

"I guess you're happy, Tom. You and O'Connor are from the Boston area, aren't you?"
"Yeah. And Fort Devens is only about an hour drive from home."
"Must be nice. What's it like there?"
"Well, in January it's pretty bleak. But it's pretty country. Do you ski?"
"Never have."
"There are a lot of places nearby where you can take lessons."

"Thanks. I'll keep that in mind."

Our graduation date was November 30, the Thursday after Thanksgiving. And once again we were given the dreadful choice—take leave, or do KP from then through New Years. I couldn't believe it. The Army was happy to advance me the leave time, but by doing that I would nearly use up all the days I would accumulate over my entire four-year hitch. I didn't think that was too wise. On the other hand, four weeks of KP didn't sound too good, either.

I decided to take the leave. The opportunity to be home for Christmas was impossible to pass up. And, provided no emergency came up, I should just barely have enough leave time accumulated to not owe Uncle Sam anything when it was time to get out. What's more, for a change, the Army would pay for this trip home, since it could be considered one leg on the trip from San Francisco to Boston.

I hit the books harder, hoping to be granted a slightly better position when I finally was assigned some place where I could use the Arabic.

GRADUATION

By the time November rolled around, we were definitely getting the hang of Arabic. Most days, we didn't use any English in class. And we were allowed to read Arabic newspapers and magazines as part of our classroom training. This was often very confusing. Although we had studied Egyptian and Arabic culture, it was difficult for us to remember how restrictive the society was compared to America in the sixties.

Gameela and Sayyed Al-Yamani decided to have a party for all the Egyptian and Iraqi sessions. It would be held in the meeting hall on Thursday afternoon during class hours and several of the teachers would cook authentic Arabic food. Everyone was enthusiastic. Gameela and her mother and Sayyed Al-Yamani worked half of Wednesday night preparing delicacies that most of us had only read of. At noon we went back to the barracks and changed into civilian clothes, then at 2:00 we all met at the meeting house.

Gameela and her mother were trying to get the oven in the little kitchenette going to warm up some of the dishes. We students set the tables and milled around, generally enjoying ourselves. Then Gameela came up to me and said,

"Sayyed Looaee, I cannot make the oven to light. Would you please help me?"

"Sure, Miss Hadrani....Do you have an instruction manual or something for it?"

"This paper for the building is all we have...."

"Well, let me see. It says the pilot light is all the way in the back of the oven. I see it. Is that where you have been trying to light it?"

"Oh, no, Sayyed Looaee, that must be our problem. We have been trying to light the bottom jets."

"Well, let's just see if it will light. I guess we don't have to turn the gas on; it smells like there is some in there already. Hand me some matches."

"Here, Sayyed Looaee. Yes, we have had the gas on...."

"BOOM!"

No, I didn't say boom. The oven exploded. I was knocked heels over head.

"Oh! Sayyed Looaee! Are you all right?!"

"Uh...."

Momentarily stunned, I took stock. Yep, all fingers and toes were there, but I had lost my eyebrows and the hair on the back of my right hand. My ears were ringing pretty badly. And the right sleeve of my sweater looked considerably the worse for wear.

I was alive, however. All the excitement certainly had not lessened my appetite. We got the oven started and eventually sampled some incredible things. Gameela was justly proud of her hummous bi tahini. We had dolma, couscous, shish kebab, falafel, and a dazzling variety of sweets. The exotic tastes were scrumptious. It sure beat the Mess Hall!

When the dishes had been cleared, Tom McKinley stood on one of the tables and said:

"On the Saturday after graduation, Pammy and I are getting married. You are all invited to the ceremony. I have announcements here to pass out."

Married? I hadn't even known he had been dating someone until I had met Pammy at this party,

"Hey, Tom," shouted Tom O'Connor, "What's the matter? Are you too cheap to mail the things?"

"Oh, yeah? Let me find yours first so I can tear it up!"

Everyone laughed. Then we surrounded Tom and congratulated him on what we all assumed was his good fortune. When I read the announcement, I leaned that the wedding was to be held at the Post Chapel. But the reception that followed—that would be held at the Pebble Beach Country Club. Obviously someone wasn't too cheap to mail the invitations.

* * * * *

The gradation ceremony was held the Thursday after Thanksgiving. The auditorium was packed—several classes shared the occasion. We all filed up, shook the CO's hand, and were presented with diplomas mounted in leatherette cases. They made it look like we had actually accomplished something. Some sergeant had said that the course was sanctioned by the University of California, but as hard as I searched, I couldn't find anything on that piece of paper that said it. Oh well, hopefully whatever college I went to after I finally got out of the Army would honor the work. Time would tell....

We returned to the barracks and spent the next day packing our bags and getting ready for a return to civilian life—at least for a month or so. It was amazing to me to see how much junk I had accumulated in a year. Friday night, most of us met at a bar on Fisherman's Wharf to celebrate with a few drinks.

After the morning mist burned off, Saturday's weather was perfect. We had to wear our uniforms to the wedding—there was a lot of good-natured grousing about that. The Post Chapel was filled. Aside from his parents, we were all the "family" that represented the McKinleys. The bride was beautiful. The music was just right. In fact, everything was about as perfect as a young couple could wish for. We lined up to kiss the bride. Then we rushed back to the barracks to change and pack the few things left that we weren't wearing. We piled ourselves and our luggage into a couple of the limousines and were taken to the reception. Inside, the Pebble Beach Country Club was just as luxurious as you would expect. There was a large band, an open bar, and a buffet table piled high with goodies. Pammy's parents seemed to be nice folks. It looked like little Tom had really married well. The champagne was terrific. One of the ushers said,

> "Would you like a refill, sir?"
> "Why, sure. In fact, do me a favor and keep an eye on this glass, will you? I intend to drink a lot of this stuff."
> "Certainly, sir."

True to his word, I never emptied my glass that afternoon. He managed to find me every time I was getting low. I don't know how much champagne I had, but it must have been a significant amount. Finally, Tom and Pammy announced that it was time for us to go. In a moment of weakness weeks earlier, Tom had decided it would be a great idea for us all to share the same flight from Monterey to San Francisco. So, we all trooped outside and back into the limousines.

At the airport we headed straight for the plane. Once aboard, I corralled one of the stewardesses:

> "See that guy over there? The ecstatic one with the cute blonde?"
> "Yes."
> "Well, he just got married, and we are escorting him on the beginning of his honeymoon. I know this is such a short flight, but could you bend the rules, and serve drinks?"

She looked at them with tenderness and what looked like envy.

> "Well....Sure!....Don't they look happy?...."

When we arrived at San Francisco, we all headed for the airport bar. We commandeered a few tables and set about trying to embarrass the hell out of Tom and Pammy. The toasts got more and more ribald. I guess Pammy had been inured to this sort of thing by being around Tom—none of it seemed to faze her. And Tom, of course, joined right in. Eventually, we all tottered down to their gate to see them off. Then we returned to the bar.

By this time, everyone was pretty stewed and very maudlin. We made pledges to stay in touch, drank each other's health, and generally made fools of ourselves. One by one, we escorted each other to our flights. Finally, just John Wood and I were left. I don't remember much of our conversation. Let me be totally honest: I don't remember any of it.

I do remember watching John get on his plane. I found my way to the boarding area for my flight, and sat there feeling like I had just gone through a rite of passage. I was pretty sure I would never see any of the zoomies or John Wood again. Or, other than the guys from my Arabic class who were going to be at Fort Devens with me, any of the other people I had called my friends during the last year.

On the plane, I had dinner and a couple more drinks. By this time, the stuff in my bloodstream could have passed for anti freeze. It was 4:00 in the morning when we landed at O'Hare. I staggered to a pay phone and called home, waking my mother,

"Hello."
"Mom? Izzat you? Ish me, John."
"Oh. Are you sick, honey? You don't sound like yourself."

I knew I didn't **feel** like myself—I hardly knew who I was. I slept through most of the day.

The month away from the Army was not what I had expected. I saw a few friends, and spent most of my time organizing a 25th Anniversary Party for my parents. They were married on Christmas day in 1942, so getting everyone together was a formidable task. The hardest one to bring along was my Dad,

"Dad, Bill and I would like to take you and Mom out to dinner tonight to celebrate your anniversary."

"We don't need to go to dinner. We can celebrate here at home."

"Sure we can....But we really want to do something special for you two."

"You can't afford to take us out to dinner."

"Yes we can, Dad. We have been putting some money aside for this."

"Well, save your money. Your Mom and I would sooner stay home."

"I think it would be nice for us all to go out to dinner," said Mom, who had happened to come into the room, "We wouldn't have to go someplace real expensive."

Dad, however, was adamant. We were NOT going to go out to dinner. Eventually, I had to corner him away from Mom,

"Dad, you and Mom are cordially invited to your Silver Wedding Anniversary Party. The other 100 guests have already accepted. What do you say that we manage to surprise Mom, at least?"

"Damn it!"

It was one of the few times I ever heard my Dad swear. We went upstairs together.

"Mom, I've managed to convince Dad. Bill and I are going to take you two out to dinner."

"No, I don't think that would be a good idea. Your father doesn't really want to go."

"Uh—yes, dear, I think we should."

"You're just saying that. You'll be grumpy all evening."
"Oh, for crying out loud."
"I won't be grumpy. Let's go."

Eventually, Mom was convinced. She was also totally surprised. I was happy that so many people had taken the time right before Christmas to help celebrate. It was a great party.

In less than a week, it was time to get on another plane, and head for my next duty assignment. I would finally find out what Radio Traffic Analysis was all about. Once again, I left on New Years eve. This time, however, no one offered me a nice place to spend the night, and my destination was not warm, sunny California, but cold, snowy Boston.

AYER

COLD

Now, growing up in Gary, Indiana we had cold weather, and it was certainly winter when I left. But, notice the word at the top of this page....Yes, cold definitely took on a new meaning that winter in Boston. I got off that plane and when I left the airport, I realized that I had never really known cold. There I was in my dress khaki uniform—short sleeves! The only thing I had to keep me warm was a field jacket, but we hadn't been issued liners for them in California. Here I was, right at the beginning of the coldest spell ever recorded in the Boston area with the wrong clothes. I found my way to the bus to Fort Devens, and rode there, shivering.

The guest quarters were not very warm, either. But the next day was unbelievable. I made my way through the cold and snow to my new unit. The sergeant told me how to get to the barracks, and told me to go and unpack my duffle bag and report back by 1300 hours (1:00 p.m.). Lo and behold, when I got to the barracks, there were some of my old classmates from Monterey: Tom McKinley, Tom O'Connor, and Joe McDonald. Tom McKinley was living off post in a little apartment he and Pammy had rented. He had reported for the winter clothing issue and had wandered over to the barracks to get out of the cold. Because of my experience as a squad leader at Monterey, I was assigned to one of the squad rooms in our new, but old, home. The barracks were of the same design as those in Monterey. Built during World War II, the frame construction was in great need of repair. Our barracks looked like it would probably remain standing for the 24 weeks of our course, but you couldn't be too sure. In the mild weather at Monterey, buildings like these were adequate protection from the elements. But here, in frosty Massachusetts, they didn't seem to be enough to shelter us from the elements.

Our class was to start Monday, January 8, so we had nearly a week for Uncle Sam to find something for us to do. First things first—we were to be issued winter gear. I was ecstatic! With the wrong clothes, I had already had enough of Boston's idea of winter. We lined up in the company street. There must have been about 100 of us, and everyone was cold. The wind was blowing steadily with occasional howling gusts. I found out later that for the first two or three weeks of 1968 the temperature averaged between 10 and 20 degrees below zero, and the wind averaged about 20 mph. The average wind chill factor was about 40 degrees below zero. It felt like about 100 degrees below zero!

We marched about a mile to the supply room, and then, unbelievably, they had us stay in formation while they took about five people at a time inside to issue warm clothes. It took most of the rest of the day. I thought my fingers and toes would drop off before I was finally granted entrance. At least we were allowed to bundle into our new great coats and hats as soon as we got them. We marched back to the barracks feeling considerably warmer.

Later, we assembled in the company street again. (Maybe they wanted to test our new winter clothes.) The company commander came out to give us the official welcoming speech. He beat a hasty retreat, leaving us to the mercies of our new NCO in charge. By the time Sergeant Johnson finally finished speaking, I was convinced that he was a displaced Eskimo. The cold didn't seem to affect him at all. Although he was wearing a regular uniform cap, no gloves, and a field jacket, he droned on and on for about half an hour. He explained that since our class didn't start for a week, the Army had decided we should perform some sort of fill-in labor to earn our keep.

There was so much snow that the powers that be couldn't find any rocks for us to paint. Then again, maybe that was a uniquely west coast way of marking time. At any rate, they fell back on the favorite old standby, KP. We were to show up in uniform and ready for work at the mess hall the next morning at 0500 hours. Yes, that's right, 5:00 a.m. Oh, joy—more KP!

Then we got our next bit of Army-style good news. Because there were so many people to train, our class would be held in the evenings, from 6:00 p.m. until 1:00 a.m. Night school! Now this was going to be a bit different.

Finally, we were given the rest of the day off to straighten up our barracks, and to get plenty of sleep before our 0400 (ugh! 4:00 a.m.) wake up call. Instead, the ex-Monterey, Arabic-speaking contingent piled into Tom McKinley's used car and headed for the nearest bar. We spent the next several hours getting up to date, and filling our systems with anti freeze.

As it turned out, you couldn't get drunk enough not to notice the cold. I turned in about 10:00 p.m. Normally, I slept in just my underwear, winter or summer. But after an hour here, I started putting on more clothes. Eventually I reached what would be my nightly sleeping outfit for the next couple of weeks. From the inside out, here is what I wore to sleep in:

> Underwear
> Long underwear
> Fatigue uniform (long-sleeve shirt)
> Two pairs of socks
> Field jacket with liner
> Hat with ear flaps down
> Great coat with liner
> Cotton shells from gloves
> Sheet
> Two blankets

That sounds like a lot. I felt like a mummy, but I was still not warm. In the morning, I found out why. When my alarm went off, I opened my eyes and saw that my blankets were covered with a liberal dusting of snow. The walls of the barracks were so porous that snow blew right through them! Fortunately we had hot water and plenty of it. Few things in life compare with digging your way out of that frigid bed, shivering your way into the shower room, and stepping into that hot, hot water! In fact, even KP was pleasant—it was always warm in the kitchen. And though not as warm as the kitchen, the mess hall was another wonderful place to be.

RADIO TRAFFIC ANALYSIS

At Fort Devens, we were to learn more about what Mickey Mouse meant when used as an adjective. Here at the home of the Military Intelligence group, the requirement to salute officers was expanded into Army Security Agency propaganda. Previously when we saluted, we were required to say,

"Good morning, Sir,"

(or afternoon, or evening), and officers were supposed to respond in kind. But at Fort Devens we were told that when we saluted an officer, the greeting and response should be as follows:

"ASA, Sir!"
"All the way, Specialist!"

Now that was just a bit too hokey for me. I never had a problem with saluting officers, but I couldn't bring myself to recite that doggerel every time I saw one. Only one or two of them called me up on it. Whenever that happened, I pleaded ignorance, listened to the inevitable lecture, and eventually was allowed to go on my way.

Even with that, however, we were all interested to learn how one performed radio traffic analysis. It turns out that this arcane art concerns tabulating data from intercepted radio traffic to determine troop dispositions, chains of command, and that sort of thing. In 1968, many countries still relied on Morse code to communicate from place to place. Voice radio was rarer in the Arabic-speaking countries. We found that a lot about our new skill was classified. In fact, from this time forward, we were never supposed to tell people what we did in the Army. And we were to be exposed to code words and other Captain Billy Whiz Bang things like that.

Our class was one of many held in a compound of three-story brick buildings. It looked like a quadrangle from an ivy league college had been dropped into a field on the top of a little hill. The courtyard of this quadrangle, however, was fenced off with chain link topped with barbed wire. Flood lamps kept it brightly lit all night long. And armed MPs were posted inside each of the doors. These were serious young men. They took their jobs seriously, and their 45 caliber side arms were not just for show: they were fully loaded. This was probably, at least partially, intended to impress upon us just how serious this schooling was. It certainly impressed me!

Our class was held on the top floor. There were no elevators, of course. And at break time, the sound that we made thundering down three flights of stairs to the little room full of vending machines just by the outside doorway was truly impressive. The subject matter was interesting. It was amazing to find out how much information could be gleaned from radio messages that were supposed to be secure. Our instructors always had an interesting illustration from their service in the field. We dutifully memorized all the current code words, and learned which ones were used for what. We were even taught the rudiments of deciphering encoded messages. It was fascinating stuff—certainly far more interesting than KP duty!

We quickly grew acclimatized to our unusual schedule. And we found ourselves actually looking forward to each night's class.

GHOST

One part of our evening routine happened during the 9:00 p.m. class break—the nightly rush to use the pay phone. We were one of only two or three classes that met in the evenings, but even that small number of guys make quite a line when there is only one pay phone to share. At that time, the long distance rates went down significantly at 9:00, so everyone whose family lived in the eastern part of the country wanted to call as soon after 9:00 as possible. Thus, there were always at least two or three guys trying to use the phone at once.

    One night, I had a brainstorm. The buildings were not only three stories high, but they had three entrances. We used the one at the right of the building, near the canteen. But it occurred to me that night there just might be pay phones at the bottom of the other stair wells also.

    An MP stood just to the right of where we entered the building, and the doors to the canteen were next to his station. Under the stairs was the phone booth. The corridor leading off to the left wasn't used during the evenings, but the lights were on down there. It just stood to reason that, as methodical as the Army is, there should be another stairway and another phone at the middle entrance. So that night at the 7:00 break, instead of going down the stairs with most of the rest of the guys, I went farther down the third floor corridor to test my theory. Sure enough, there was the stairwell. I hurried down to the ground floor.

    The arrangement at the ground floor was the same as at the far end of the building, except for the canteen. The phone booth was there, as I had expected, as were doors out to the front and rear of the building. The doors that exited out to the front of the building were solid, high-security affairs. But the ones leading out to the back were those that have nine panes of glass arranged in three rows of three in the top half of the door. I figured they weren't too worried about any unauthorized person coming in from the courtyard, what with all the flood lights and barbed wire. I picked up the telephone to make certain it worked—everything seemed to be in order. Now, if no one else had figured this out, I would have this phone to myself at 9:00.

When the 9:00 break finally started, I lagged behind in the class room for a few minutes, then headed straight down the third floor corridor to the middle staircase. As I ran down the stairs, I realized that the lights on the ground floor must have gone out since I was there earlier, but I knew that I could tell which coins in my pocket were which just by feel, and I was determined to use that phone. When I got to the ground floor, I groped my way over to the phone booth. It was pitch black, and the heat must have gone off as well—it was very cold. And quiet. Although it didn't occur to me just then, I couldn't hear the guys down by the canteen, but I had been able to hear them earlier. It also didn't occur to me that there should have been light from the courtyard streaming through the nine-pane window in the door next to the phone booth. But it was as dark as the bottom of a mine shaft at midnight on an overcast night.

I felt my way into the phone booth, and put my change on the little shelf under the phone. Then I sorted it into nickels, dimes, and quarters. I picked up the receiver, put it to my ear, and inserted a dime in the coin slot. The phone responded with the expected, "ding ding," and I waited for the dial tone. But instead, after a little silence what I heard was slow, gasping, almost tortuous breathing. It sounded like a pneumonia patient getting ready to shuffle off this mortal coil. I listened for a moment. It didn't stop, and the dial tone didn't come on. I found that my hands were starting to shake. I decided I wanted out of there—NOW!

Scooping the change off the shelf, I ran down the dark corridor toward the canteen and light. It looked and felt like a mile.

When I finally burst out of the corridor, Joe McDonald looked at me and said,

> "What the hell is the matter with you? You look like you've seen a ghost."

I stammered quite a bit before I could make myself understood,

> "I didn't SEE a ghost, but I think I HEARD one."
> "Where? What did you hear?"

The MP walked over,

> "What happened, Specialist?"
> "I was down there earlier, but all the lights were on then,"

I said, pointing down the corridor. To my surprise, all the lights were on again,

> "What the?..."
> "Well, what happened?"

the MP asked again. I told them, trying to convey the terror that had grabbed me in that phone booth. Then the MP said,

> "It sounds like you've seen our ghost."
> "What ghost?"
> "Well, about three months ago, some guy broke out of the brig down the hill from here. Guards were chasing him, but he had a good lead on them. He ran up here, and looking for a place to hide, ran in this door. The MP on duty hollered at him, but he kept running. He turned down the corridor. The MP, meanwhile, had drawn his pistol, and shouted at the guy, 'Halt! Halt, or I'll shoot!' he said. When

the guy kept running, the MP fired once and killed him. Ever since that day, strange things keep happening down there. Lights that should be on, suddenly turn off, and vice versa. Doors that should be locked and closed are found open, and vice versa. We think he's haunting the building. You see, he died right at the foot of the middle stairway."

Later, I asked several of the instructors, and other regulars in the building, and they all had stories to tell. I hoped I had heard the last of him, but about 10 days later, I saw him. I had just called home (from the phone booth in **our** stairwell!), and was walking from the phone to the doorway into the canteen. As I passed the corridor, I glanced to my right. There, in the middle of the hall, was a silhouette. The lights between me and him were out, but the lights behind him were on. Just as I went past the hallway, it occurred to me, that I should have seen a shadow on the floor coming toward me from the figure. I stopped, took two steps back, and looked. No one was there, and all the lights in the corridor were on. Gingerly, I walked down the hallway testing the doors. They were all locked. There was no way that someone standing in the middle of that corridor could have disappeared that quickly.

That was the last time I went down that corridor. I kept looking to see if I would see him again, but I never did.

BOB LAWRENCE

Despite the fact that the Radio Traffic Analysis class was a full-time job, Uncle Sam required each of us, from time to time, to serve in the orderly room—this was the reception area and nerve center of each company's building. One afternoon, just before we were to fall in to march to class, I went into the orderly room to make certain I didn't have duty the next weekend. For some reason I happened to glance at the name of the Officer of the Day (the OOD—don't you just love Army anagrams?). The name was Second Lieutenant Robert Lawrence. No—it couldn't be Bob, could it? Just for grins, I looked into the office. It was Bob Lawrence, indeed. I stepped into the office, snapped my heels together, saluted, and in my best official Army voice said,

"Specialist Leeger reporting, **Sir!**"
"Huh? Leeger!? Well, I'll be damned! It *is* you! How the hell are you, John?"
"It's great to see you, Bob. When did you get here?"
"Day before yesterday."

I had met Bob at language school. He was studying Russian. Both of us had applied for admission to the Officers Candidate School program. We were both accepted and assigned to Fort Benning, Georgia. I was to start six weeks after Bob did. We were excited about getting out of the enlisted ranks, and making more money as officers. He left for OCS, and the next week, the Army changed its requirements for admission—from that time on you had to have an undergraduate degree, not just two years of college. I would be an enlisted man, after all.

"You know, John, the only thing that kept me going for the first six weeks of OCS was the knowledge that you would show up, and I could put you through the same crap that I had gone through. The morning that your class arrived, I was there, waiting. I watched all the guys getting off the bus. And YOU weren't there! I was so pissed, I almost lost it!"

"Well, that almost makes this enlisted stuff worth putting up with."

"Hey, Friday night I'm going up to Boston to see what I can pick up. Want to come along?"

"Sure. Uh....But what about the business of officers and enlisted men fraternizing?"

"Oh....Forget that! We'll meet off post, and of course, we'll be in civvies."

"Yeah. That's great. Hey, I have to get to class."

"OK. See you Friday. What say we meet at the Ayer Post Office after your class?"

"That's great! But even though we get out early Friday, we don't get out of class until 10:00."

"That's OK. I'll see you at what, 10:30?"

"OK. See you then."

Friday, I hurried to Ayer, and we took off for Boston. Bob knew some people who knew some people who knew....Well, you get the idea. At any rate, we were headed for party central—an area where the sororities were thick, and the girls were, supposedly, easy. There were plenty of sororities and girls, but as it turned out, they weren't interested in even talking to a couple of short- haired GIs. We found several parties still going strong after 2:00 a.m., but the message was always the same—thanks, but no thanks.

About 2:30 a.m. we gave up and decided to go downtown. Boston itself, though, was closed up tight. We got on the expressway and headed home. Or so we thought. Pretty soon, it was apparent that we were not headed the right way. We took an exit that appeared to be the one we wanted, but were still not on the right road. We went an exit or two, and found the one that just **had** to be right. A mile or two later, I began developing a bad feeling about this particular trip,

"Uh....Bob. Doesn't this look familiar to you?"
"I was just thinking that."
"This looks like the first road we were on. Haven't we gone under this bridge?"
"I think you're right."
"I know I didn't drink **that** much tonight."
"Me too."
"Take the next exit...OK. Slow down. Let me read this sign. That looks right. Doesn't that look like the right road?"
"Yeah. That's gotta be it."

We turned onto the new road. This must be it! A couple of minutes later, it became apparent that something weird was happening,

"Wait a minute. Wait a minute! We're back on the same road!"
"That's impossible!"
"Yeah, but look ahead—that's the same bridge we went under before!"
"You mean **twice** before!"
"God, this could be a *Twilight Zone* episode! Don't take the next exit. That's the one we took before."
"OK, but what do we do?"
"Go slowly. Let's be sure this time. Damn! The map just doesn't correlate to these roads. No....Wait....This looks right. There! Take that exit!"
"OK. This looks different. Yeah....I think we've got it."

....

"Huh? No...**no**....**NO**! That's the same damn bridge! What the hell is going on here?"

"We're going around in circles!"

"Pull over....Here, look at the map. I don't see any circles, do you?"

"No. What's going on?"

"I sure as hell don't know. Let's just stay on this road this time, and see where it takes us."

Well, it took us back to the same place we had already been several times before. We were getting desperate! We tried two or three other exits—they all took us back to the same stretch of road! Finally, after an hour of coming back to the same underpass, we found ourselves on what seemed to be the right road.

"Bob, look! I think we're finally on the right road."

"Yeah....It sure looks right."

....

"I'm sure this is it. Aren't you?"

"Yeah. This is it. In another hour we should be back at lovely Fort Devens."

....

"You know, Bob, a couple of years ago I read a book on Irish folk stories—leprechauns and that sort of stuff."

"Yeah?"

"One of the things they talked about was leprechauns playing tricks on people—making them get lost in places they had lived all their lives."

"You don't think leprechauns have been playing tricks on us, do you? Come on, get real!"

"I don't know what the hell has been going on. But I do know that we kept taking different turns and ending up on the same stretch of road. How do **you** explain it?"

"Well....I guess I don't know how to explain it."

"I don't either. So I guess leprechauns are as good an explanation as anything—particularly in an Irish town like Boston."

"This is crazy!"

"I'll certainly agree with that!"

We made it back to Fort Devens about 4:00 in the morning.

MARCHING TO CLASS

At Fort Devens, we were not to be trusted to straggle over to our classes like some kind of college campus. No, siree! We marched. Maybe this, too was a matter of temperament—even under Sergeant Baker, I couldn't imagine the Presidio of Monterey mandating marching to class. Perhaps the authorities at Fort Devens were afraid we would get lost in a snow storm. At any rate, every weekday evening we formed up at 5:30 p.m. and marched to class. For the first month or so, we looked pretty hilarious. The snow on the route we took was packed solid as ice, and no matter how much they salted and sanded, we slipped and slid most of the time. Marching in step was pretty much out of the question, but we tried. Oh, how we tried!

In its wisdom, the Army had determined that the most gung-ho among us was Corporal Adams. He was designated platoon guide, and was in charge of us as we marched to class. Well Tom Adams was a total disaster in interpersonal interaction. He embodied the Army's credo that expected obedience under any and all circumstances. The trouble for Tom was that most of the rest of us hadn't come from infantry training school, but were, instead, language school graduates. Having been (relatively) coddled in Monterey, we didn't think we should have to put up with having someone shout orders at us—particularly not someone who was the same rank us we were. So we were less than enthusiastic about our marching.

In fact, we were pretty rebellious. We walked, instead of marching. And, as the weather improved, we talked, and hummed, and sang, and did pretty much whatever we felt like doing. Tom didn't like that one bit. He screamed and hollered at us constantly, when he wasn't counting cadence. We all ignored him. Then one day, he complained enough to the First Sergeant, that he was told he could report the worst offenders, and they would be punished. The punishment was KP duty. Now, we had enough to do trying to absorb the arcane intricacies of radio traffic analysis. No one wanted to pull KP under the best of circumstances. So we cleaned up our acts—on the surface, at least.

We concentrated on developing other methods of circumventing Tom's petty authority. I worked out an insidious plan of my own. I taught myself to march with my legs and arms out of step with each other. Try it. As you walk, when your left foot goes forward, make your left arm go forward, instead of your right. It's unbalanced, sure, but then we were pretty unbalanced by then, too. I worked on it until I could walk like that so naturally that it looked normal. Then I tried it one night as we marched to class. While Tom was looking elsewhere, I began my unbalanced marching. Pretty soon, Tom started marching right next to me. He looked, and he looked. Then he said,

"Leeger, get in step!"
"I am in step, Adams."
"No you're not, damn it. I said get in step!"
"Look at my feet. I'm in step with your cadence, aren't I?"
....
"Well, goddamn it, you're doing something wrong. Now I said, **get in STEP!**"
"And I said, I am in step."
"You quit doing that!"
"Doing what?"
"Whatever in the hell you are doing. **GET IN STEP!**"
"I **am** in step, asshole. Go bother someone else!"
"I'm going to report you, Leeger!"
"For what?"
"For deliberately marching out of step!"
"Who'll believe you?"

"Sergeant Dohlman will believe me, that's who!"
"Hey guys! Am I out of step?"
"No."
"You're in step with me, John."
"Lookin' good here, man."
"Well, Adams, who's going to believe you?"
"You son of a bitch. I'll get you for this."
"For what?"

Well. it provided endless amusement. For the rest of the time we were there, I would march unbalanced at least once a week. And Adams never figured out what I was doing. It drove him nuts!

One Friday night, however, he got me back. I had planned to go into Boston that night to another one of Lawrence's unproductive parties. Just to make sure, before we lined up to march to class, I checked the duty roster. My name was on it for CQ (Charge of Quarters) duty for that night! It wasn't there the day before: someone else had been scheduled then. I knew immediately who had put me there. I waited until I saw him go around the back of the building, and then I followed him.

"Adams!"
"What?"
"You put me on that duty roster at the last minute. You knew I had plans for this weekend! Now you are going to get me off that duty!"
"Fuck you, Leeger!"

I grabbed his shoulder, spun him around, and slammed him up against the wall.

"You slimy son of a bitch! You put me on that roster. Now I'm telling you, take me back off or I'll break your face."

I pulled back my fist. I guess he thought I would really hit him.

"All right. All right! Just leave me alone, asshole."
"Call me whatever you want. Just get me off that roster!"

I didn't think I could really hit him—I've never been a violent person. In fact, I was surprised at my behavior. But it worked. He walked into the CO's office, and in a few minutes, the duty roster was switched back to the way it had been before.

Adams never did figure out what I was doing while we were marching to class.

NEW YORK
(JUST LIKE I PICTURED IT?)

When I had had enough of the cold weather, I started looking for a car. All I could afford was a 62 Corvair four-door. It had more than its share of rust. It burned oil. But it ran, and the heater worked! I suddenly found myself more popular. On a break one night, Joe McDonald made a suggestion.

"Hey, John, how'd you like to see New York?"
"Sure, Joey. I've never been there before."
"Really?"
"Really. But I'd like to go there some day."
"Why don't we go down there Friday after class for the weekend? I'll give you a guided tour."
"Yeah. Sure. I'd like that."

I had visions of Broadway musicals, the Empire State Building, the Statue of Liberty—even Grant's Tomb. Friday after class my suitcase was packed, and I was ready to go. Joe had suggested that Tom O'Connor (from language school) and Bob Simpson (a classmate at Fort Devens) go with us. I agreed. But I started to suspect that my weekend in New York wouldn't be quite what I had in mind.

At 11:00, after class, we all piled into the Corvair. Joe grew up in Brooklyn. As we drove into New York in the wee hours, Joe said,

"Just a couple more blocks, and we'll be home. Mom will be glad to see us. Hey, look, Angelo's is still open. Pull in over there."

We pulled in and unfolded out of the little car. The minute we walked into the place, the bartender recognized Joe.

"Joey! Hey, Joey, you back in town?"
"Just for the weekend, Timmy."
"Yeah? Well welcome home, Joey. You and your buddies are welcome. First drinks are on me."
"Well, all right!"

In fact, after the first one, we only paid for alternate drinks. Joe must have been pretty popular at Angelo's. We had several drinks, then piled back into the Corvair. About a block later, Joe said,

"Hey! Tony's is still open. Pull in there."

Once again, Joe was recognized. Once again, every other drink was on the house. After three bars, we finally made it to Joe's house. The sun was coming up. I couldn't enjoy the sight. In fact, I could hardly see—between the alcohol and the lack of sleep, I was done in. It was a good thing that all three bars were within a two-block radius from the McDonald house. I didn't feel drunk, just exhausted.

Mrs. McDonald welcomed us with open arms. She didn't seem surprised at the hour, or our condition. I got the impression that this sort of behavior was expected from Joe and his friends. She offered breakfast, and I forced myself to eat something. I hoped to keep myself from getting sick.

We slept on the floor in the sun room. By noon, everyone was awake. Mrs. McDonald offered us lunch. We ate again, then Joe proceeded to give us our New York tour. The radius of our tour expanded by one block. This provided four more bars. And four more bartenders who knew Joe on sight. Once again, we paid for only half our drinks.

By 6:00, it was starting to get to me. And I was drinking about half as much as the other guys. It was time for dinner. Joe guided us back to his house where his mother had dinner ready. We ate again. I'm sure his mother was a good cook, but I don't remember much about the food.

At 7:30, we resumed our tour. Our tour radius expanded by another block or two, which was enough to keep us in bars until 2:00 a.m. Sunday morning. It was amazing how many bartenders knew Joe by name. And remember, he had only been home on leave a couple of times in the last year and a half.

I nursed my drinks, trying to stay sober. This may have been the smartest thing I had done in my whole life until that time. When we finally collapsed in the sun room early Sunday morning, I was exhausted, but reasonably sober—well, at least not totally drunk like the other guys.

At 9:00 a.m., Mrs. McDonald served breakfast. We read the paper and then, about 11:00, we headed back to Fort Devens. Mrs. McDonald packed sandwiches for us to eat on the road. We hadn't driven two blocks when Joe said,

> "Hey, look. Marty's is open already. Pull in there."
>
> "No, Joe. I think I've seen enough of New York for one weekend."
>
> "Oh, come on. Pull in."
>
> "No. I have duty tomorrow morning. I would like to be able to see."
>
> "Oh, all right....Hey, look up there. Charlie's is open...."
>
> "NO, Joe!"

Tom O'Connor and Bob Simpson were pretty trashed, so I got no argument from them. We made it back to Fort Devens in time to get a good night's sleep—something we all needed. I was sure there must be more to New York. After all, I had seen the pictures and movies. I had read the books. But I certainly hadn't seen any of **that** stuff during Joey's guided tour.

But my interest had been piqued. That week, I bought tickets to two musicals for a weekend about a month later. I went by myself, and I had a great time. One of the musicals I saw was *The Man of La Mancha*. It was even better than I had heard. And the performance I attended was the last performance ever in the old Anta theater. The next day they began tearing it down to make room for a parking lot for the City University of New York.

Before the show began, someone came onto the stage and asked the people in the audience who had seen the play once before to stand up. I felt pretty alone—nearly everyone in the audience had seen the play before. Then he asked people who had seen the play twice before to remain standing. Still, nearly three fourths of the people were standing. When he asked that only those who had seen the play five times or more to remain standing, the number dropped to about one fourth of the audience!

It was an incredible performance! Many people in the audience were sobbing, and many in the cast were also crying. I don't remember how many standing ovations we gave them, but my hands were sore the next day.

Yes, New York definitely **could** be *just like I pictured it.*

WORCESTER GIRLS

"Hey, John, you wanna go to Woostah? I heard about a pahty happenin' there tonight. Supposed to be a lot of girls."

Now Tom O'Connor wasn't the brightest of guys, and he didn't speak too clearly under the best of circumstances (and since he hadn't been drinking, this *was* one of the best of circumstances), but Woostah was a new one to me.

"Are we going to a...rooster?"
"Nah, you dumb shit. I said Woostah.... Woostah.... There's a pahty in Woostah tonight."
"How do you spell that?"
"W O R C E S T E R. Woostah. Whatsa mattah with your ears?"

I won't continue to try to transliterate Tom's version of English. Since he was from Boston, however, I thought he might have actually found a lead to some women. So I signed on.

"Sure, Tom. I think that would be great."

Of course, one of the principle reasons I was invited, aside from my stunning good looks, my marvelous physique, and my amazing wit, was the fact that I was the only one of our group who had a car.... We found the apartment about 9:00 p.m., just as things were beginning to get lively. And, sure enough, there were a lot of girls there. With our too-short hair, and our out-of-town ways, we were treated with some curiosity and a great deal of aloofness. We browsed for a while, and then I discovered a young lady who not only was attractive, but seemed willing to talk. And despite all the braggadocio about our sexual prowess, we would all have been satisfied to just have an intelligent woman to talk with.

Her name was Karen, and she was from New Hampshire. She was a sophomore studying art history, and wanted to teach after she graduated. She had lovely brown eyes that were so large that she looked constantly surprised. I was enjoying our conversation, and she seemed to be beginning to think of me as something more interesting than a third cousin just in from the country.

"And where are you from, John?"
"I'm from Gary, Indiana."

I cringed as I admitted it. The movie version of *The Music Man* had been out for several years, and most people started singing "Gary, Indiana, Gary, Indiana, Gary, Indiana let me say it once again..." as soon as I told them where I was from. Not Karen, though. I was still more impressed with her.

"Where's that? What's it near?"
"It's close to Chicago."
"Oh....How's the surf there?"
"The what?"
"The surf....You know...."

Well, actually, I didn't know. Lake Michigan has some waves, certainly. In fact, in the middle of the lake during violent storms, there are some huge waves. But they usually peter out before they get too near the shore. Since Gary is on the eastern shore, the prevailing westerly winds mean that it gets more waves than cities like Milwaukee that are on the western shore. But surf? No, the one-foot waves Gary gets could never really be considered surf.

"Actually, we don't get surf in Gary—just some little waves. I think the biggest waves I ever saw were about two feet high, and that was when a major storm system came through."

"But you have to get surf....How close are you to Big Sur?"

"Big Sur?"

"Yeah. You've been there, haven't you?"

"Well, sure, I've been there, but..."

"Well don't they have heavy surf at Big Sur?"

"Sure, but Gary isn't anywhere near Big Sur. Big Sur is on the west coast."

"Yeah. How far away is Gary?"

"About 2,000 miles."

"Huh?"

"About 2,000 miles. Gary is in Indiana."

"Oh. Isn't that on the coast?"

"Uh....No....Uh, would you excuse me, I've got to find the bathroom."

"It's right over there."

I stood in the bathroom for a minute, thinking. After all, she was only studying art history. Maybe they weren't required to know geography. But surely, she must have had **some** geography, **some** time....

Maybe not. When I came out of the bathroom, I found Tom waiting for me.

"Let's get outta here."

"OK with me. What's the matter? Aren't you enjoying yourself?"

"Nah....These broads are too stuck up for me."

"Yeah....I know what you mean."

The ride back to the base was a quiet one.

DITTY BOPPERS

Each night on the march to class we were witnesses to a strange ritual—the training of the Morse code interrupt operators. These poor devils were learning Morse code so that for the next couple of years they could spend eight hours each day listening to it. They taught Morse by sheer volume. The instructor stood at the front of the class and shouted a code symbol, and the students screamed back the phonetic name of the letter.

"DIH DAH!"
"ALPHA!"
"DAH DIH DAH DIH!"
"CHARLIE!"
"DIH DIH DIH!"
"SIERRA!"
"DIH DAH DAH DIH!"

On and on it went. We could hear them faintly from about half a block away. Then, the sound would crescendo so that as we marched past the converted barracks they used for a classroom, it seemed as loud as thunder. Then, gradually, the noise would fade away.

Charlie Riggs was a ditty bopper. Although most radio traffic analysis people considered themselves too elite to associate with ditties, Charlie and I got along well. I met him once when we both pulled KP. He was a black guy from south side of Chicago. I guess we felt some bond since we had grown up within about 30 miles of each other.

We talked sports and politics—politics for us, of course, meaning the Democratic machine that ran northern Illinois and Indiana—and found that we had a lot in common. It didn't hurt that I had lived downstairs from Cazzie Russel, Bill Buntin, and Oliver Darden for my Freshman year at the University of Michigan.

Eventually we even got into race relations. It was amazing to discover how ignorant I was about people of other races. Although I had grown up in a city that was nearly 50% black, I hadn't really spoken with a black person until I met Charlie. I found myself becoming cynical about the country I had thought was so wonderful. But Charlie wouldn't hear any of that stuff:

> "What the hell are you talking about, man? I know that things aren't perfect here, but c'mon, get real. What do you think things are like any place else for blacks? Man, I've got more opportunities here than I would have anyplace else I know of."
>
> "Yeah....I guess that's right. But I've lived in the south, and I'm telling you, blacks don't have much to hope for there."
>
> "Maybe it's tougher, but I guarantee it's going to get better."
>
> "What makes you think so? It sure as hell didn't seem like a good place to be for a black man a year ago when I lived in North Carolina."
>
> "Maybe so, but we're getting organized, now. Dr. King is **doin' things** down there."
>
> "Who's Dr. King?"
>
> "**Man!** You really **don't** know anything, do you?"

And so I learned about the civil rights movement only a couple of months before its leader was assassinated. I also learned about black people's pride in their African heritage:

> "Man, I hope I get to go where you're going."
>
> "Yeah. Ethiopia has to be better than Vietnam."
>
> "No, not that. I mean **Africa**! I would love to go to the

home land."

"But I thought you were so solid on America."

"I **am**, man. But to get to go back to the home land—wouldn't that be cool?"

"Yeah. I guess for you it would be extra special."

"Now you're talking, man!"

It occurred to me that there weren't many blacks at Fort Devens. I guess the military still thought that blacks couldn't handle jobs that required more brain than brawn. When I thought about it, I realized that I hadn't seen many blacks in language school, either. And Ayer Massachusetts certainly didn't have much of a black community....

"Hey, Charlie. Don't you get lonely?"

"Yeah, man. Don't you?"

Well, that was it in a nutshell, I guess. We are, all of us, lonely, unless we make an effort not to be. He might have found someone to talk to, but I had found someone to listen to. It worked out pretty well for both of us.

CODE WORD FUNNIES

Part of the arcanery we were required to master at Fort Devens was the system of code words and security classifications. In addition to *Classified*, *Secret*, and *Top Secret*, there were *Classified code word*, *Secret code word*, and *Top Secret code word*. Even the code words themselves were classified. We were not to divulge them to anyone under threat of the direst punishment. The code words were all five-letter words that most people had never heard of. I looked them up in the dictionary to make certain they weren't just so much gibberish.

Some of the things that were classified seemed funny at the time. They seem even funnier now. A lot of the *intelligence* that we pored over was gleaned from the UPI and AP wire services. Stories from those sources that appeared in daily newspapers around the country were routinely classified.

The buildings we studied in were highly secure. In addition to the barbed wire and security lights that I mentioned earlier, the buildings were well within Fort Devens—out of earshot of the most sophisticated listening devices of the day—and constantly tested to make certain that some devious spy hadn't managed to infiltrate this very bastion of security to ferret out information that would cause us to lose the cold war.

In addition to a paucity of blacks at Fort Devens, I don't think I ever saw a woman attending any of the security classes there. There were certainly some women in the military stationed at Fort Devens, but I never saw any in our classroom building. Things were simpler then, you may remember. For instance, because there were no women students, the Army only had to have one type of bathroom. It wasn't even labeled as a bathroom, but in typical military jargon, the door was emblazoned with the legend *TOILET*.

Now it happened that the top secret code word at that time was *TOILE*. This word emblazoned the most secret documents of the time. The only place this word was supposed to occur in the Army was on documents that were so classified. Well, one of the guys realized that bathrooms in the Army were nearly decorated with this forbidden word. So he took it upon himself to procure a little can of paint exactly the same color as the door and painted over the final *T* on the door, at once exposing the proscribed word.

Once you have gone to the bathroom at your office or school how many times do you actually read the word on the door? I don't know how long the word had been altered when I finally noticed it, but it must have been done after our class started—at least I **think** it wasn't that way the first time I entered. The night I noticed it, I stopped dead in my tracks, and stared in wonderment. I checked to see if the paint was fresh—it wasn't. I was still staring at it when Tom O'Connor came up behind me.

"What's the matter? Is it out of order?"

"No....Look."

"Look at what?"

"Read the sign."

"Huh?...Hey! That's cool! Did you do that?"

"No. And I don't think I would like to be the person who did when one of the instructors finds out."

"Yeah....Somebody's gonna get nailed for this."

Well, sure enough, someone noticed it. But it took three more days before the subject was brought up in class. Sergeant Thomason was furious! The guilty person (whomever it was) was threatened with everything imaginable. The threats went on for weeks, but I don't think they even figured out whether the deed had been committed during the evening or the day. At least we never heard of anyone being charged with the transgression.

In an organization not known for its efficiency, the top secret codeword was changed in short order.

KENNEBUNKPORT

Spring had sprung, and summer was fast approaching. One day Bob Lawrence and I were talking:

"Have you ever been in New England before, John?"
"No. Ayer is just about it for me."
"I've never seen any of it either. You know, there's no class next week. Why don't we clear out of here and go up the coast?"
"What a great idea!"

Bob had things to do, so it was Monday before we left. We went out to Cape Cod and checked into the cheapest place we could find—it wasn't that cheap. We found a number of nice clubs and some terrific restaurants. Danced a little. Drank a lot. It didn't take us long to go through the larger portion of the funds we had available.

Thursday we drove north to see more of New England and, hopefully, to find an area that wasn't so expensive. We wound up in Kennebunkport, Maine. At that time it was a quaint little fishing village that had just begun to gradually give way to the kind of trendy, artsy shops that eventually litter most of the desirable places in our land.

We walked around most of the afternoon, and then looked for a place to sleep. We found a little inn that had a vacancy (and that we could afford), and checked in. After dinner and a good bit more exploring, we returned to the room and turned on the TV.

We were stunned to find that Dr. Martin Luther King had been assassinated! We sat in silence watching the scenes of unrest unfold across the country. There in Kennebunkport, one could have been forgiven for thinking that it hadn't even happened. We hadn't overheard anyone make any mention of the event all day long. Indeed, no one looked any different the next day either. I wondered if this sort of complacency had been the order of the day in Kennebunkport a few years earlier when JFK had been gunned down. But then, I really hadn't seen any blacks there at all....

What had begun as a good time turned into a somber experience. We drove back to Fort Devens the next day.

ASSIGNMENTS

Once again it was time to move on. Radio Traffic Analysis school was over, and now it was time to put what we had learned into practice. We awaited our assignments with an air of complacency. After a year and a half of what we had been told was very expensive training, we knew there weren't many places where we could use all that we had learned. None of us had ever been to the Middle East. In fact, most of us hadn't even heard of Ethiopia (the country we were likely to be stationed in) before we were assigned to study Arabic in Monterey. Language school seemed a million years ago. When we started talking about it, we realized that in just six short months, our Arabic ability had already decreased dramatically. We were sure, however, that after a little exposure to the language, we would once again feel comfortable with it.

Uncle Sam hadn't quite made up his mind about us, however. We were told that upon graduation we would be assigned to a holding company in a new barracks to await assignment. The graduation assignment was even less impressive than the one at language school. Basically, they just handed us our certificates, and that was that.

We reported to the new barracks, and to our surprise, it was a *new* building. It had been built in the mid fifties, and was a welcome change from the World War II buildings we had been in to date. Of course, the Army couldn't leave us idle while we waited for our assignments, so we went back to the kitchen.

"Jeez, KP again. I almost wish they would ship us to 'Nam. I'm really tired of looking at these potatoes."

"Speak for yourself, O'Connor. I, for one, have no desire whatsoever to see Vietnam."

"Yeah, watch what you wish for: you just might get it."

"Well, yeah, me too. But I am **tired** of looking at these potatoes!"

Soon it seemed like we would never stop looking at potatoes. We pulled KP for two solid weeks. I was beginning to feel like I really knew Idaho....

As usual, things **could** get worse:

"All right, men, the Base Commander is going to inspect this barracks at 09:30 Saturday morning. That gives you just three days to get this place spotless. I want you to know that the CO **always** scrapes the floor with a pen knife to see if there is wax build up. Your job is to clean it down to the tile, and then re-wax it so that it is as shiny as it is now. Use steel wool, where necessary. Got it?"

"Yes, Sergeant!"

"Then get on it! When we come through here Saturday, I expect to see this floor perfect!"

"Yes, Sergeant!"

After he left, we got to work. Well, sort of....

"Can you believe that? We have to scrape this entire floor! This room must be 50 feet by 20 feet—that's 1,000 square feet of floor! How can we possibly scrape and re-wax the entire floor by Saturday morning?"

"Yeah! It's not enough that we have to pull KP every day! This sucks!"

"Wait a minute, guys. I have heard something about this CO that may be worth a gamble."

"What is it, Bill?"

"Well, I've heard that he really does scrape the floor with a knife..."

"What the hell good is that? We already know that!"

"Would you let me finish? What I heard is that he almost always scrapes right along a wall, or in a corner."

"Why?"

"Yeah, why should it matter where he scrapes the damn floor?"

"Well, he knows that the buffers don't get into corners very well, so that's where the wax build up is worst."

"Oh...."

"If he holds true to form, we could get away with just scraping about a foot around the outside of the room."

"Yeah. Yeah! That sounds good!"

"It would sure cut out a lot of work!"

"Let's do it!"

"Wait a minute! Remember, if he doesn't scrape around there, we could be in a world of hurt."

"Yeah...."

"Possible...."

....

"Oh, what the hell! If he scrapes somewhere else, we'll just have to do it later. I say, let's scrape around the wall, and call it quits."

"Yeah! When's the last time you saw an officer break a habit."

So we scraped down to the tile around the outside of the room, and then waxed the whole floor. Sure enough, when the CO came through, he actually got out a pen knife and scraped the floor looking for wax build up. And as Bill said, true to form, he scraped in one corner. We got commended for the superior job we did on the floor.

Then one day at morning formation,

"I got assignments for the following men. Step up when your name is called: Adams, John. Brown, Amos."

I always got a kick out of the Army way of calling first name last. Amos happened to be brown, however.

> "Carpenter, George. Kingsley, William. Leeger, John. McKinley, Thomas. McDonald, Joseph. O'Connor, Thomas...."

What? Back up there a minute. That was me! Oh, boy! Finally I was getting out of KP. I walked forward and took the envelope. On my way back to formation I opened it. Just as I had expected, I was going to the United States Army Security Agency Field Station in Asmara, Ethiopia. The bad news was that I would have to endure two more weeks of KP.

I looked up to see the two Thomases and Joe heading my way: they were white as sheets.

> "Hey, what did you guys get?"
> "'Nam...."
> "Yeah....Me, too...."

Joe's face said it all.

> "'Nam? That can't be?"
> "Didn't you get 'Nam, Leeger?"
> "Uh....No....I got Ethiopia."
> "You lucky stiff. I can't believe you're going to Ethiopia and we're going to 'Nam."
> "Me, too! There has to be some mistake, guys. What the hell good will you do in Vietnam?"
> "Yeah. There has to be some mistake. I mean, how many Vietnamese do you suppose speak Arabic?"

But there wasn't any mistake. Out of our whole Arabic class, I was the only soldier who got stationed in the Middle East. I guess the Army really needed radio traffic analysts in Vietnam. I didn't know what to say to Joe and the Thomases—especially McKinley. He was going to have to leave his new wife behind. And of course, although no one ever said it, a lot of guys didn't come back from Vietnam. We said what we had to say that evening over a great amount of beer at McKinley's house. We promised to stay in touch, but that turned out to be an optimistic promise. I haven't heard from any of them since we left Boston.

My parents rejoiced at my good fortune, and made plans to come to Boston to say good bye before I had to leave. I was happy to see them when I got off the bus in Boston. We had made plans to tour the warship Constitution, known as "Old Ironsides" which was docked in Boston Harbor. As we were approaching the car, I asked,

"Do you want me to drive, Dad?"
"No. I'll drive. This Suburban takes some getting used to, you know."
"Yeah, but the drivers in Boston are crazy."
"I can handle it."
"OK."

We drove over to see the Harvard campus, and then we had to cross the river. Dad turned into the far left lane of a one-way bridge. About halfway across, we saw a car coming toward us, the driver blowing his horn. Dad swerved into the next lane to the right to avoid a head-on collision. As he passed us, the driver yelled out of his window,

"Get outta the way, you jerk!"
?????!!!!!
"Did you hear that?!"
"Dad, I told you the drivers here are crazy."
"Maybe you'd better drive, after all...."

The remainder of our visit was uneventful, but great fun. Although I had lived just a stone's throw away from Boston for half a year, I hadn't really seen much of it. The bus ride back to Fort Devens was a lonely one.

The Army glitched again a couple of days later, and told me that I could have a week of leave at home and leave for Ethiopia from there. I was enthusiastic about avoiding KP, but once again, Mom and Dad paid for my flight home. It was a wonderful visit. I guess it just seemed extra special in part due to my relief at not having to go to Vietnam and in part because I knew I wouldn't see any of my family or friends for another year and a half.

One day some family friends were visiting. I was answering their questions about my new assignment based on what little about my job I was allowed to tell, and on what little knowledge I had about Ethiopia, and that was precious little indeed. I didn't know much about Ethiopia beyond some basic facts, such as:

Location	—	East Africa, on the Red Sea
Capitol	—	Addis Ababa
Emperor	—	Haile Selassie
Principle Language	—	Amharic
Province I Will Be In	—	Eritrea
City I Will Be In	—	Asmara

Ron Newman, one of Mom and Dad's friends, listened for a while, and then just as seriously as you can be asked,

"So, are you going over there to help Highly Sell Assy?"

I thought it was one of the best puns I had heard all year. The visit was far too short.

Soon it was time to leave for the airport and the long ride back in time to feudal Ethiopia.

ASMARA

FROM THE 3RD CENTURY...

Considering that I would spend the better part of the next day there, the interior of the Pan Am 707 didn't look so large. My flight would take me to Athens with brief stopovers at Boston and London's Heathrow Airport. After spending a night in Athens, I would board an Ethiopian Air Lines 707 for the flight to Asmara with a short stop in Cairo. I had been cautioned not to even get off the plane in Cairo. According to Uncle Sam, I was now the possessor of knowledge that the evil empire would like to have, and that Arabic-speaking countries were also interested in. In fact, after leaving the Army, I would be prohibited from visiting any Arabic-speaking or Soviet Bloc countries for seven years. After that, I would have to get approval from the State Department before visiting any of those places.

When we took on passengers at Boston, one of them turned out to be Charlie Riggs, the black Morse Code intercept operator I had known at Fort Devens. As the flight was not full, we managed to sit next to each other. He was really excited.

"Man, can you believe this? I get to visit the Mother Continent!"

"Yeah. You've got to be happy."

"I mean, I'm gonna get to see the lands where my ancestors came from. I can't wait to meet my brothers!"

He was so effusive, it was difficult not to be happy for him. We talked a lot on the trip, reestablishing and deepening our friendship. I don't have the shortest of legs, and Uncle Sam certainly wasn't about to fly me first class, so I got up often to stretch my legs. I chatted with some of the stewardesses, and was amazed at how blasé they were about the cities that they spent so much time in. To me, London, Athens, and Cairo were magical places. I couldn't wait to explore even the airport at London, and to hear all the people speaking the Queen's English. Although my schedule would not permit any time for visiting London itself, I was eager to see Athens. I envisioned myself standing in the Parthenon, looking over the remains of the ancient city. I was as excited as Charlie. We talked about ancient civilizations. Neither of us knew much about Africa beyond what we had been taught about Ethiopia, and our scant knowledge of ancient Egypt came mostly from old mummy movies!

Eventually, the conversational well dried up, and we retreated to writing postcards, reading, and sleeping. We crossed the Atlantic in the dark, and I didn't get to see even a tiny fraction of Heathrow. We were restricted to a small international terminal while the plane was refueled. Nonetheless, there were quite a few people awake, and the accents were lovely. I eavesdropped as much as I could without being too obnoxious, trying to assimilate as many of the different versions of English as I could.

And then we were in the air again. I tucked myself into the cramped seating area, consoling myself with the knowledge that we would soon be in Athens. We were to arrive in the late afternoon, and had reservations in a hotel preselected by Uncle Sam. I napped off and on, and spent some time trying to guess which countries we were flying over. I knew our route, but as the young Arthur discovered in T.H. White's *The Once and Future King*, it was impossible to tell from the air where one country stopped and another started.

Eventually we landed in Athens. A shuttle bus was standing by to take Charlie and me and a few others to the hotel. It certainly wasn't a four-star hotel, but we hadn't expected that. It was about 5:30 p.m. Charlie and I agreed to meet in the lobby in a half hour to see about dinner.

My room was certainly not *a la* Holiday Inn. It had a tile floor, an armoire in place of a closet, a lovely old bed with matching night stand and desk. Behind the French doors, there was a little balcony overlooking the street below. I stepped out and savored the air. The aromas were unlike anything I had encountered in the U.S. I couldn't see the Acropolis, or much of anything else, from my balcony, but the thought of being so close to such wonders was very exciting.

I shaved and threw some cold water on my face to try to wake up some more. I hadn't expected jet lag to happen to me, but I was pooped! We decided to try the hotel restaurant. Since Uncle Sam had already paid for it, it was particularly appealing. In addition, we spoke no Greek, and couldn't imagine how we would get around in town. The waiter spoke very little English, but tried to make us feel at home. The menu was not bilingual, so we had to ask him what to eat. He suggested the house special for the night, which seemed to be some sort of sea food. His English wasn't good enough to tell us exactly what, but we figured we would go with his suggestion. And that is how I first came to taste octopus. Simmering in its sauce, I couldn't tell what it was, but I knew it didn't look like any fish I had ever had before. Neither of us were very keen on it, but we were hungry, so most of it disappeared. The wine with the meal pretty much killed any excursion I might make to Athens. I told Charlie I was just going to bed, and he thought that was a good idea. I went to the front desk to see if they had a wake up service.

"Certainly, sir. What time would you like to be awakened?"

"Six o'clock ought to do it."

"Six o'clock it is, sir."

"By the way, can you tell me what I had for dinner? Our waiter said it was the special for the evening—some kind of sea food."

"Oh, that was octopus, sir."

"Octopus?"

I felt myself turning a little green. Charlie looked a bit pale himself.

"Yes, sir. It is one of the chef's specialties."
"Oh....Well tell him it was...very good."
"Thank you, sir."

Bed seemed even more appealing, now. Swearing to myself that I would find a way to visit Athens as a tourist, I quickly fell asleep, and slept like a rock for 10 hours. We had time for breakfast—again in the hotel restaurant—in the morning before the shuttle bus took us back to the airport.

And there it was—an Ethiopian Air Lines 707 waiting to take us to Africa. The bright colors on the tail seemed to foretell an exotic land with adventures just waiting to be experienced. We climbed the stairs and entered another world. Our stewardesses were the first Ethiopian people I had seen. I was immediately stricken by their appearance. The brown skin I had expected, but I was totally unprepared for the Caucasian features. I assumed that they had picked these women for international service, but was soon to discover that it was a common trait. We were to find that most Ethiopians looked like dark-skinned Europeans. I thought the stewardesses were lovely, but I could tell Charlie was a little bit disappointed.

We took off, and only then did I get a glimpse of the Acropolis. Once again I swore to return and spend some time as a tourist. The Mediterranean looked much like Lake Michigan from 35,000 feet. The flight to Cairo wasn't too long. When we landed, we remembered not to get off the plane. We tried to see something of Egypt from the little windows, but modern airports all look much alike. I had hoped to see the pyramids from the air on our approach or as we left, but even that wasn't to be. The Nile, however, was impossible to miss. We could see it for some time after we left Cairo. After a while, we could see the Red Sea off to the left.

Airplane food turned out to be much the same, even on an

Ethiopian airliner. Many of our fellow passengers, however, looked a lot different from those we had encountered before. Some wore long robes, some wore sandals, few wore the traditional western business suit and tie. And of course, there were several languages being spoken. I recognized several, but many were totally unfamiliar to me. Charlie and I had noticed a cloying odor when we boarded this plane. I thought at first that the plane just had stale air, but I was soon to learn otherwise.

At last, the stewardess announced we would soon be landing in Asmara. She said it several times in different languages including English, Arabic, and French that I recognized and others that I didn't. As we lost altitude, the ground rose to meet us. Did I mention that Asmara sits on a plateau some 7,800 feet above sea level? As we approached the plateau, the mountains came up so swiftly that I hoped we wouldn't run into them. And then we landed.

The airport terminal looked modern, but it was tiny, about the size of an airport in a small American city. When we stepped out of the 707's door, the source of the odor in the plane was immediately apparent. The air smelled, how shall I say this, *different*. Actually, it smelled like a very pungent barnyard. Fertilizer was one of the first thoughts that came to mind. No, actually, excrement was more like it. I thought it would take a long time to become accustomed to this. We were ushered inside. Everything looked modern and new. And then I saw the soldiers. As soon as I saw the first one, I noticed that there were many of them throughout the terminal. They were all in well-pressed battle fatigues, and all were armed with submachine guns. None of them looked too happy. The understanding of what a military dictatorship actually meant began right there and then.

As we were picking up our duffel bags and other luggage, we were greeted by a soldier who said there was a bus waiting for us. We went through a cursory customs inspection (leaving the country was another matter, indeed) and lugged our gear outside. Where you would expect to find cabs lined up in an American airport was an assortment of tiny Italian sedans, even tinier three-wheeled motorcycles, and garry carts. Now a garry cart is the typical Ethiopian taxi. It consists of a crude two-wheeled cart with automobile tires, a broken-down horse, and an Ethiopian with a horsewhip. You throw your stuff in the back, and sit on the single seat with the driver, hoping he doesn't have fleas or lice. This was all explained to us by the soldier who escorted us through the beggars, vendors, and taxi and garry cart drivers to the bus.

Most of the taxis weren't what you might expect. They were three-wheel motorcycles with a tiny enclosure made of canvas. They looked for all the world like little motorized tricycles. The passenger enclosure had flimsy canvas doors with metal rod frames. Although the garry cart horses farted a lot, the smell in the little taxis was considerably worse. And the noise was nearly unbearable. I only rode in one once.

The bus took us to the post, a large, walled compound at the outskirts of the city itself. On the way we passed swarms of people looking like extras from a National Geographic Special. Nearly everyone was dressed in just a piece of cloth wrapped around sort of like a toga, with sandals, and not much else. Many of the men had walking sticks that were often taller than they were. They reminded me of the quarter staffs that had been used in England during Robin Hood's days. Our escort chattered on as we rode in.

"Ethiopia is one of the poorest countries in the world. The average yearly income here is $47.00."

"Wait a minute. Did you say $47.00 per **year?**"

"That's right. And good old Haile Selassie is rumored to be one of the wealthiest people on earth. No one knows exactly how much he is worth, but it's said to be in the billions of dollars."

"You mean millions, don't you?"

"No, I mean billions. The U.S. Government pays quite a lot for his friendship, you will find. Look up ahead on the right. See the man squatting on the curb with his back to the street?"

"Yeah...."

"He's taking a dump. Many of these people come here from the sticks, and don't know any better. Get used to it. You'll see a lot of it. Oh, and watch where you step."

That proved to be good advice. We saw herds of sheep and goats being driven down streets that also had vehicular traffic. The drivers of the cars were screaming at the drivers of the beasts, who screamed right back at them. No one seemed very happy.

KAGNEW STATION

We were taken to our different companies and dropped off. Charlie and I promised to keep in touch. I made my way into the orderly room, and talked to the company clerk.

"Hi, I'm Spec 4 Leeger, just arriving."
"Oh, yeah, we're expecting you. Give me a minute to finish this and I'll show you where to drop your stuff."

I looked around, and found that things looked pretty much as expected. The big difference, as far as I could tell, was that these barracks were masonry. None of those old, wooden buildings here. That made sense, I realized, considering that the post had certainly not been around as long as the other places I had been, not to mention the fact that at 7,800 feet, lumber was probably pretty scarce. The outside door was open, so I stood there and looked some more. The sky was a brilliant, almost-brittle blue with very few clouds. What scant vegetation there was around the company area didn't look too unusual. Across the street was another masonry barracks just like the one I was in. It had two stories and was painted robin's egg blue—a most-definitely non-army color! The paint had faded a bit. The buildings were considerably longer than the wooden ones I was accustomed to.

"OK, Leeger, let me give you a hand with this stuff."
"Thanks."
"You're in the building across the street. You've been assigned to the lower squad room on the right side—over there."

ONE IN A HUNDRED

We crossed the street and entering the door on the right end of the building found ourselves in a large squad room. The room had 18 bunks arranged in three rows of six separated by lockers, with an aisle down the middle. My bunk was right in the middle. I was shown my foot locker, bunk and locker. This was to be my home for the next year and a half—less space and less privacy than I had had since Basic Training.

"Well, make yourself at home. You've been assigned to the day shift. The bus will pick you up tomorrow morning at seven o'clock just at the end of the sidewalk at the end of the building where we came in."

"Thanks. Hey, where's the Mess Hall?"

"Oh, I forgot. Come with me back to the Orderly Room, and I'll give you a New Arrival's Packet. It has a map, and all. Most people don't eat in the Mess Hall. They go to the Club."

"Is the Mess Hall all that bad?"

"See for yourself."

"What's the Club?"

"Oh. We have an Enlisted Men's Club as well as an NCO Club and an Officers' Club. You'll probably eat most of your meals there. Well, here's the packet. Nice to meet you."

"Nice to meet you, too. Thanks."

I unpacked my duffel bag, found the bathroom, splashed some water on my face, and brushed my teeth. I looked through the New Arrival's Packet, and found the map, a booklet, a bunch of mimeographed sheets, and a starter book of chits for the Enlisted Men's Club. Then, map in hand and chits in pocket, I determined to get the layout of Kagnew Station. The first thing that I learned was that all the company areas were at one end of the post. Right down the street was a softball field. I took a left at the field, and headed for the main post area. I walked by the Mess Hall, swimming pool, movie theater, Special Services building, Post Headquarters, NCO club, bowling alley, PX (Post Exchange—the Army's version of Wal Mart), commissary (the post grocery store), Officers' Club, and at last came to the Enlisted Men's Club. It was called the Oasis Club, and like the fellow in the Orderly Room said, I would spend some time there.

I noticed that almost no one was in uniform. The post was clean, but barren. There was little greenery. Almost all the buildings were masonry—some paint was faded more than others, but all were painted in pastels. And, after what was not a very long walk, I found myself somewhat tired. This was the first indication I had that, indeed, there wasn't as much oxygen 7,800 feet above sea level. I went into the Oasis Club to look around.

On the right was a sort of club with a bar and dance area. On the left was a dining room with tablecloths on the tables. The floor was linoleum, but clean and attractive. In fact, it wasn't such a bad room. At some of the tables, guys were playing cards and drinking. At others, people were having dinner. I sat down, and soon a young Ethiopian man in a white jacket came over,

"You want menu?"
"Uh, yes. And bring me some iced tea, please, with no lemon and lots of ice."

He was back quickly with the tea and a menu. The menu presented a variety of old standards, and the dinners I had noticed as I walked in looked pretty good. I decided to go ahead and order. After all, it was late afternoon, close enough to dinner time, and I didn't feel like trying the Mess Hall first thing. I ordered roast pork with dressing, and was pleasantly surprised. It tasted good, and there was plenty of it. I took my time with dinner, watching the people, and just relaxing. By the time I got back to the barracks, the day shift was just arriving from work. I met most of my roommates, and was invited to join a group of them at the Club for dinner. What the heck, I tagged along, just to get to know them.

No one, it seemed, ate at the Mess Hall except for breakfast (the walk to the Club at breakfast was just too much, first thing in the morning), unless they were flat broke. And with the prices as low as they were at the Club, it wasn't too much of a financial strain.

Evan Lowrey was from Connecticut. He was about six feet four inches, and thin, sort of rangy. Blonde hair, soft-spoken, and very intelligent, his face was open and honest. He asked if I played Bridge. When I told him I did, he said,

> "That's great! The guy who used to be my partner just transferred back to the States. If you're up to it, there is a game tonight, after dinner."
>
> "Well...what the hell. Sure. I'll play."
>
> "Terrific! Oh, by the way, are you any good?"
>
> "I guess I play pretty well—not tournament level, but OK."
>
> "Good. No one would put up with someone who was really good."

Ralph Boswell was from Cleveland. He was about five feet 10 inches. Kind of stocky with dark hair, and an athletic build. He didn't play Bridge, but told me about the Club.

> "Wait'll you see Saturday nights at the Club. They send the pussy wagon downtown and bring back a busload of Ahtees to dance with. And, of course, they're all available."
>
> "Not all, Ralph."
>
> "Well, OK, Evan. Occasionally they get a couple of Caffolattis, but that's awful rare."
>
> "Hold it, guys. You're talking Greek, and I left Athens this morning. What's an Ahtee, and a Caffolatti?"
>
> "Oh, sorry. Ahtee is Ethiopian for girl, and Caffolatti is from the French *café au lait*. It means a person who is half Ethiopian and half European."

"Usually Italian. There's a large Italian population that stayed here after World War II. And, by the way, Ralph, Ahtee is Amharic, not Ethiopian."

"I've been meaning to ask, what is the local language in Asmara?"

"Well, you should use the plural, John. The official language in Ethiopia is Amharic, from the Amhar tribe that Haile Selassie belongs to. They also consider English as a national language, although not too many Ethiopians speak it. Italian is spoken a lot in Eritrea, but you'll primarily find the natives here speaking Tigrinean, the language of the Tigre tribe that principally inhabits Eritrea."

"What about Arabic? After all that school, doesn't anybody speak Arabic?"

"That's a touchy subject, John. See, the Eritrean Liberation Front guerrillas want to cut Eritrea out of Ethiopia. They are primarily Muslims, and form a near-majority in Eritrea, while the rest of Ethiopia is Coptic Christian."

"Yeah, there's a guerilla war going on here. Mostly off the plateau, but getting closer and closer. The guerrillas are known as Shifties."

"You should pronounce it Shifteh, Ralph."

"What's the difference? At any rate, you don't want to run into them. They haven't killed any Americans yet, but if you get ambushed, they'll take everything you have."

"He means everything."

"The last guys they left in just their underwear—took their car, clothes, cameras, money. Well, you get the picture—everything."

"Where shouldn't I go?"

"As long as you stay in or close to Asmara, you'll be all right. It's the trip down to Keren or Masawa where they might get to you."

"Keren? Masawa?"

"Those are R&R places. Keren is about half way dow n

ONE IN A HUNDRED

the mountain. It's a little town with a villa, like a hotel, run by the Army for GIs to unwind in. Masawa is Ethiopia's principle port on the Red Sea. There is a larger hotel there. You'll like it, if you like hot, that is."

"How hot is hot?"

"Oh, anywhere from 90 to 110 or more."

"Get out of here! Does it ever get cool there?"

"Nope."

"Well how far away is it? It's not anywhere near that hot here. I'll bet it wasn't 80 degrees when I got here this afternoon."

"It's not how far away that counts, here. It's how far down. See, we're only about 5 degrees north of the Equator, so it should be hot here. But being way up here on the plateau keeps it cool. I don't think it ever gets above 85 or so here, and it never gets below 50 or so at night."

"Tell him about the monsoons, Evan."

"Yeah. You're just in time for the monsoon. About the end of August it will start raining here every day. And when I say rain, I mean rain. It's like stepping outside into a waterfall. It rains every day like that for an hour or so in the morning and for an hour or so in the evening for a couple of months."

"What about winter?"

"Winter isn't much different here. Although they say that in the early fifties it snowed once. I'm told that hundreds of Ethies died of shock. They had never seen snow before, and thought the world was coming to an end."

"You're putting me on, right?"

"That's what I heard."

"Yeah, me too."

Well I watched them eat dinner. By the time I had walked all the way back to the Club, I had worked off some of my dinner, so I had dessert with them. Then Evan and I joined a couple of other guys to play bridge. Ralph retreated to the bar. Ron Hartwell was one of the other players. He was dark-haired, about six feet tall, and heavily built. He looked like a bear, with the sort of shambling strength that can be deceptive at first glance. He sort of scowled out from under bushy eyebrows most of the time. But when he smiled, his face softened. Maybe Teddy bear would be more accurate.

"Hey, I know you, Leeger."

"No, I don't think so."

"As a matter of fact I know who you are. You are assigned to my section. I'll walk you around tomorrow."

"Hey, that's great. I'll be working for you?"

"No, we'll both be working for the larger-than-life Sergeant Thornton."

"Do I like the sound of that?"

"Sergeant Thornton may be the fattest NCO in the Army. His butt is so fat that when he sits down in one of those swivel armchairs, he has to force his butt between the arms of the chair."

"I don't believe that."

"You'll see for yourself, tomorrow. You'll also meet Phil Silverman—and a bigger jerk you may never meet. Oh, I'm sorry. I shouldn't be prejudicing you about these guys. I'll let you form your own opinion. Not another word out of me until tomorrow. Let's play cards."

Ron's partner was Neil Billingsley. He was there with his wife, but she didn't play Bridge, she just watched and talked—and talked, and talked and talked....Mostly she sat at another table with some other wives and talked to them. Neil talked with a little lisp. In fact, if he hadn't had his wife there, I would have sworn he was gay. His hair was always in place, and looked like he had stolen it from Dick Clark. He was thin, and kind of soft-looking. His wife, Betty, on the other hand, was as tall as he, loud and brash.

She wore her hair in a beehive and looked like a lady wrestler. What a pair! As we played and talked, Neil said,

> "With that voice, you must be a singer. Am I right?"
>
> "Sure. That's what my major was in college."
>
> "Oh that's just wonderful! I direct the chapel choir, and I also direct a secular choir. You must be a bass. Would you like to sing? We can always use good men's voices."
>
> "Sure. I love choral singing. When do you meet?"
>
> "Well, the chapel choir meets Thursdays at 7:00, and the secular choir meets Saturday mornings at 10:00. Why don't you come, and see if you like it?"
>
> "Yeah. That'd be great. Well, I'm assuming I don't work weekends. What about it, Ron?"
>
> "Nope. You'll be on straight days. Monday through Fridays from 0730 until 1630."
>
> "Are there people working around the clock, then?"
>
> "Yeah, there's someone there all the time. But there are fewer people evenings and just a skeleton crew nights."
>
> "Well then, sure, I'd be happy to come to rehearsal."

We talked and played until way too late. It was a nice start.

TRACT C

When I got back to the barracks, some of the guys in my squad room were already asleep. I introduced myself to those I hadn't met earlier who were still awake. We talked briefly, and turned in. I set my clock for 5:30 a.m., and had a hard time getting to sleep, and the jet lag didn't help any. This was my first real duty station, and I couldn't wait to see what it would be like. In the morning I showered quickly, and made my way over to the Mess Hall. The fellow in the Orderly Room hadn't exaggerated too much. While the breakfast certainly wasn't worth writing home about, it wasn't any worse than the other Mess Halls I had been exposed to. I ate quickly to make certain I would be on time for the bus.

I felt like a kid waiting for the school bus. I tried to remember all the new names and faces, but knew it was a hopeless task—I had never had that knack. The bus looked like a school bus, but it was painted the traditional Army color—olive drab. I found that the place I was working was called Tract C. No one seemed to know where Tracts A and B were. The site was a few miles away from Kagnew Station. I got to see more garry carts and little Italian cars as well as farmers working their fields. Everything looked pretty primitive to me. I didn't see any mechanization—not even a tractor. We passed by several groups of men who just seemed to be talking. There were few trees, and nothing to sit on, so they squatted, flat-footed, around little fires.

"Are they cooking something there?"
"Yeah, they're making breakfast."
"What do they eat?"

"Usually they eat pretty much the same thing whenever they can get it. The national dish is a stew called Zignie. It's a stew, usually with a tomato base and whatever meat is available. They eat it by dipping a sour dough bread called Anjara into a common pot."

"What do you mean by, *whatever meat is available?*"

"Just that. Don't ever eat Zignie unless you get it in a good restaurant. You never know just what you'll get."

"Yeah, but most of the *good* restaurants in town are Italian. You probably won't find Zignie on a menu at any of them."

"Well, I think you are much too picky. I've eaten Zignie out in the fields, and have never gotten sick..."

This last was from Tom Haslip. He was one of my roommates who had really gotten into the native scene. As I found out later, he must have had the constitution of an ox—an Ethiopian ox, at that. He regularly spent weekends in country, living in mud huts with natives he had befriended. He often brought them food from the base, but in general, he shared whatever they had to eat. Tom was certainly one of those people who are in another world.

"...In fact, I can't think of anything better than a good Zignie served with warm Anjara, and washed down with some Muhs."

"What's that?"

"Oh, Muhs is the local beer. It's basically a fermented honey—very tasty."

"Yeah, Tom, if you like lumps in your beer!"

"I don't see anything wrong with Muhs. You guys are just too fussy."

The thought of lumps in beer didn't set too well with me, either, but I was determined to keep an open mind about all things Ethiopian.

And then, we went by a scene that could have been lifted from the Old Testament.

> "Are they doing what I think they're doing?"
> "Over there?"
> "It looks like they're winnowing wheat!"
> "That's exactly what they're doing."

An ox was walking around a pole he was tethered to making about a ten-foot diameter circle. As he walked, women poured wheat in front of him on the rock-hard earth. After a few turns around the circle, the wheat was swept up and placed in flat trays. Baskets, actually, they were about four feet in diameter with about an inch-high rim. The women would throw the wheat up into the air repeatedly and then catch it as it fell, letting the wind separate the chaff from the grain.

> "They did that in the Bible!"
> "That's true. You'll see a lot of other things here that haven't changed much since those days."

Some months later, my Mother sent me an article about Ethiopia she had cut out from a newspaper. One of the sentences ran something like this:

> "In the years since he became Emperor, Haile Selassie has managed to drag Ethiopia from the Third Century into the middle of the Twelfth."

By then, I had even more evidence of the truth of that article.

We passed by a veritable forest of antennas. They were tall, spindly things with a multitude of guy wires. They stretched far into the distance on the right side of the highway. Crops were planted right up to them, and underneath the guy wires.

> "How do they harvest underneath the antennas?"

ONE IN A HUNDRED

"By hand, of course, just like they harvest everywhere else. But you know what? Uncle Sam pays rent for all the land around the antennas, and if we have to service one of those things, don't you know the Ethiopian government charges us for the crops we damage."

"You're kidding, right? We pay rent, they farm, and we pay for the crops?"

"That's about right."

"No wonder our pay checks are so big!"

At last we could see the site. A high, double chain-link fence surrounded the place. There was the guard shack, and a chain-link gate. We got out outside the fence, and were checked in. As we passed through the gates, Ron asked,

"You know why there's a double fence, don't you?"

"No, why?"

"At night they put some killer Doberman Pinschers in there to encourage people not to try to get in."

"That would certainly do it for me!"

"Yeah, me too."

The site was a large, masonry building with one door, and no windows. Popular music was playing loudly from speakers situated so as to provide a continuous din, regardless of where you went within the site. This *cover music* was supposed to make it impossible for enemy intelligence agents to eavesdrop on the goings on inside the building. High-power lights were also positioned to light the site grounds. There were a couple of outbuildings, but no trees, bushes, or anything else that would restrict sight lines.

There was a sign, however, that I didn't notice until I had been working there for a long time. In typical Army fashion, it was all upper case and totally devoid of punctuation. The sign read:

CAUTION

BURIED TELEPHONE

CABLE BEFORE DIGGING

IN THIS AREA CALL

321-3212

After I finally noticed it, I looked forward to reading this sign every day. Read each line separately, and you too may wonder why they buried a telephone, or where the telegraph office was, should one actually want to send a cable. Perhaps I'm too picky, but it tickles me to this day.

The lighting inside was just this side of harsh. Ron took me on a quick tour, pointing out the Colonel's office, the Communications Center, the rest rooms, the rooms where the ditty boppers (Morse Code intercept operators) stayed, and the voice intercept rooms (where he worked). At last we came to the room where I would work for the next year and a half. To get to it from the hall, we first passed through a long, narrow room. Only about ten feet wide, it was about thirty feet long, running along one of the walls of the room where I would work. In this *bowling alley*, Morse and voice intercept traffic were separated, sorted and placed in an array of boxes stacked above the sorting table along the long wall that faced the room I would be working in. There the traffic would picked up and processed by the various groups inside.

The room where I was to work was about thirty feet square. About 25 men shared the room with a plethora of gray, military-issue desks, chairs, and bookshelves. There were a few partitions, but you could see across the room from most positions. In the middle of the wall at the right end of the room was an opening about six feet wide. Inside, Ron explained, is where the officers worked. And in front of the opening were two desks. The men who sat there were the senior NCO and the Warrant Officer for the shift. On the day shift, the Warrant Officer was Mr. Smith, and the NCO was Master Sergeant Farnsworth. Ron introduced me, and they confirmed that I would be working in his section,

> "Saudi? But I was trained in Egyptian Arabic."
> "Egyptian, Saudi, what's the difference?"
> "Well, actually Sergeant, there is quite a lot of difference."
> "You'll cope, Leeger."
> "I suppose so, Mr. Smith."
> "Don't worry, Leeger, most of the men here are in languages they weren't supposed to be in. You'll be just fine."
> "Thank you, Sir. I hope you're right."

Then Ron took me to meet Sergeant Thornton. No, he hadn't exaggerated—Sergeant Thornton must have been the fattest NCO in the army. While Sergeant Farnsworth was definitely overweight, Sergeant Thornton was the walking, or should I say waddling, definition of an endomorph. He really did have to force his buttocks between the arms of the chair he sat in. The buttons on his khaki uniform shirt looked like lethal weapons, just waiting for one more Twinkie before they would be blown through some poor soul who might happen to be in the way. His skin was an unhealthy, crepuscular white, and looked like it had just been basted with some sort of cooking oil. The wispy, baby-fine hair that still managed to cling to the top of his head never stayed in place for more than a few minutes. And he jiggled when he walked—actually, he looked like a walking series of seismic after shocks when he moved. I immediately thought of Santa's bowlful of jelly. To top it all off, he had a nasal, whining voice that irritated me immediately.

> "Glad to meet you, Leeger. We can use some help here.

"This is Fred Silverman. He is my other worker bee here in the shop. Ron, of course, works in voice intercept."

"Hi. What do I do?"

"Well, clean out that desk. Barkley left it kind of messy."

Actually, the whole area bordered on chaos. I spent the next hour or two getting organized, without knowing precisely what I was organizing for. While I sat waiting for Sergeant Thornton to put his new-found worker bee to work, Ron came by.

"Come on. It's break time."

"Already? I haven't done anything, yet."

"Neither has anyone else. But your turn will come. Right now, it's time for a break."

I followed him out the door, and around the back of the site. One of the outbuildings turned out to be a snack shop. You could buy doughnuts, sandwiches, drinks, and other things to keep the hunger pangs from interrupting your work. It turned out that most of the guys skipped the mess hall, and just got a doughnut from the snack bar for breakfast. As we munched, Ron asked,

"Well, what do you think, so far?"

"You were certainly right about Sergeant Thornton. I can't recall too many people who were more offensive than he is."

"He's also a mental midget. Saudi reporting is a shambles. He managed to get a second tour here."

"Because the duty is easy?"

"Probably because he hasn't had to take a physical fitness test."

"I wondered how he got away with being so fat as an NCO."

"Anyway, he's married—can you believe **that**?—so he's going on five years here. The big question is, will he manage another rotation here, or will he get transferred when this tour runs out next February?"

"Let's go back to *he's married*. To what?"

"I've never seen her, and don't know anyone who has. But I pity the poor bastard who ends up running the Saudi show when he finally leaves. Nothing is up-to-date. Wait'til you try to make sense of the reporting."

"What has he done?"

"It's not what he **has** done, it's what he **hasn't** done. I don't think half of the call signs are associated with the right groups. Troop strengths and dispositions are all in his head. While the Saudis have moved things around in five years, Thornton hasn't kept up."

"Doesn't anyone check him?"

"I guess not. If they do, they don't know what the hell they are doing either."

He was right again. As the months wore on, I pointed out discrepancies to Thornton again and again, to no avail. He insisted that he was right. Eventually, I got tired of arguing.

The daily routine seemed pretty boring. First thing in the morning we would check on what had happened over night. Then we would get the morning's traffic from the bowling alley, and get to work. The traffic came to us on quintuple, pin-feed sheets. The first thing that had to be done was to remove the carbons (we switched to carbon-less copies about halfway through my tour in Ethiopia) and separate the copies. Then the copies were distributed to various agencies for their use back in the U.S. We analyzed ours on the spot. It's pretty methodical stuff, usually, but every once in a while you would find something out of the ordinary. The difficult part was translating everything twice.

That's right. The Morse code intercept operators weren't Arabic linguists—they just knew Morse code. As they listened, they typed on ancient typewriters that only had upper-case letters. These were known as *mills* and the Morse intercept room sounded like the clicking and clacking of an ancient weaving factory. To the operators, of course, what came out on paper looked like gibberish. The letters were English, but the words were nonsense. A typical phrase might look like this:

AKCAR MN A:RIN SIARAT

We had to translate that into the Arabic characters which looked like this:

اكثار من اشرين سيارات

If you knew how to read this, it would sound sort of like this:

AKTHAR MIN ASHREEN SAYYARRAT

And then we had to translate that into English. The final result would be:

More than twenty automobiles...

Then, of course, we had to decide if what we had translated was worth including in the report. After a while, you skipped the step of translating into Arabic characters and went directly from the Morse intercept output into English.

Some messages, however, were encoded. The intelligence operations in the Arab countries weren't too sophisticated then. The codes they used consisted of two- to five-digit substitutions. That is, each character in the message would be replaced with a two- to five-digit corresponding code. Although they can look pretty intimidating, codes like this are fairly easy to crack. I hadn't been trained in cryptanalysis, but before long I was breaking codes with the best of them.

The voice intercept stuff came to us in dribs and drabs all day long, but it was already translated. If we wanted to check, we could go back and listen to the tapes ourselves, but in general, we trusted the voice guys. About once an hour or so, we would pick up more traffic of both varieties. We generally filed our report in the early afternoon. It was checked by a couple of civilian consultants who usually just rubber-stamped it and sent it along. But every once in a while, they would want something changed. It seemed to us that the changes they wanted were more in the line of job security for them, rather than anything meaningful. We didn't much care—especially in the Saudi section where things were screwed up anyway. They never seemed to notice the inconsistencies in Thornton's view of the Saudi situation.

PREVENTIVE MEDICINE— ARMY STYLE

One of the facts they didn't tell us before we left the States was that in Ethiopia we had to have a Gamma Globulin shot every few months to prevent hepatitis. Way back in high school, a kid in one of my classes got hepatitis. I had a Gamma Globulin shot then, and didn't much like it. So when I reported in for my first shot in Ethiopia, I thought I was prepared for the worst. Unfortunately, Gamma Globulin dosage is computed by patient weight, and I had grown quite a bit since 10th grade.

"OK, Specialist Leeger, on the scale. OK, let me see...hmmm...all right, now, which would you sooner not be able to use tomorrow, one of your arms or your butt?"

"My butt, I guess. I had one of these in my arm when I was in high school, and it really did slow me down."

He went to a small refrigerator and started to fill a syringe.

"That's a pretty big syringe...."
"Well, we do these by weight."
"I know....Don't you warm that stuff, first?"
"No. That's part of the charm. Now, turn around."

It felt like he was using a toilet plunger to put that stuff in me. Not only did it seem like a lot, but it felt syrupy. At last, he managed to empty the syringe.

"Yow! That made a lump on my butt...and it's cold!"

"Yeah, it'll be there for a day or two, and it'll be sore and stiff for a couple of days, too."

That was an understatement. The lump got warm in an hour or so, but it was still there two days later. And I could still tell where he had given me the shot nearly a week later! From then on, I could always tell when one of my fellow workers had just had his GG. He would sit in very strange positions, and often he would get up and walk around, rubbing the sore spot.

* * * * *

I was in Ethiopia nearly a year before Army Dentistry caught up with me. In the Army, we were required to visit a dentist on a regular basis, and since I couldn't go to my own who was back in the States, Uncle Sam was happy to provide one for me. The dentist's recommendations, however, didn't make me very happy. He proclaimed that the X-rays he took revealed several cavities and a tooth that had to be pulled. I told him that I had visited my dentist in Indiana before coming overseas, and had been told that I had no problems.

The Army dentist did his best to persuade that my oral health had changed since I left the States, and I really needed this work done. I refused. My mouth felt just fine, and I had no plans to be a guinea pig for him—especially since I was so far away from what I considered to be competent care.

The dentist implied that I was refusing a direct order from an officer, and told me I was required to have a little talk with my company commander. Lieutenant Graham, looking very uncomfortable, tried to explain to me what my best interests were, but I had other ideas. I politely told him what he could do with his dentist friend. Eventually they stopped trying to persuade me.

When I got back to the States, I went to my family dentist who told me there was nothing at all wrong with my teeth. I wasn't in the least surprised.

NEIL BILLINGSLEY

Chapel choir rehearsals were Thursday evenings at 7:00. Neil had me stand up and say a few words about myself during the first rehearsal I attended. When I mentioned that I had studied piano since I was four, the accompanist's eyes lighted up. After rehearsal that evening, she quit (I found out later that she couldn't stand Neil, but had continued for the sake of the group). Neil asked if I would accompany, and I didn't feel I could leave them without an accompanist, so I agreed. She also quit as the chapel organist, so I found myself volunteering for both jobs. There really wasn't a choir for the chapel services. I just played an introit, some hymns, and responses, and a postlude for chapel. I liked Lieutenant Colonel Vaughn, the chaplain, however, and he appreciated having someone to play during services.

Neil wasn't the greatest director I've ever worked with. No, let's be honest: he wasn't very good at all. There were a number of reasonably good voices, however, and they carried the day. The secular choir, the Kagnew Singers, were not bad. We didn't sing anything too difficult, which made the group sound better still. Even though it was a secular choir, they were rehearsing for a Christmas Concert to be given in early December.

After that first rehearsal, Neil's wife Betty asked me if I would like to help celebrate Neil's birthday. It just happened to fall on the next Thursday, so she had arranged for a bunch of us to meet at the club for dinner and drinks, then after rehearsal we would resume partying back at the club.

When the next Thursday came along, we all got together for dinner at the appointed hour. Betty had ordered a couple of bottles of champagne to kick off the evening. Then there were drinks for more toasting and wine with dinner. By the time rehearsal came along, everyone was feeling pretty jolly indeed.

After rehearsal, everyone resumed drinking as though there was some kind of contest. I had never been drunk before, and thought I held my liquor better than most people (ah, the ignorance of youth!). By now I was enjoying my favorite drink, a Rusty Nail. That's a shot of Scotch and a shot of Drambouie on the rocks. It's pretty potent stuff, as I found out that night. I had drunk many Rusty Nails on many occasions, but hadn't counted on the altitude. When the waiter placed the eighth (!) Rusty Nail in front of me, I still felt in control. I took a sip or two, and then Ron said,

> "Hey, John, I'll buy your next drink, if you drink the rest of that one in one shot."

Well, the drinks weren't very expensive, but I thought that sounded like a good deal. So I swallowed the whole thing. True to his word, Ron ordered another one for me. When the waiter brought it, Ron held it out to me and said,

> "If you can drink this one in one shot, I'll buy you another."

By now, the old thinking machine wasn't working too well, so I gulped number nine. Now I felt like I **was** getting drunk. Ha! In fact, my blood alcohol level approximated an automobile cooling system after a recharge during a Minnesota winter. He made the same offer for my tenth drink, but somewhere enough gray matter kicked in to keep me from ossifying my entire liver in one evening.

It was nearing midnight, and the party was breaking up. Only a few of us were still drinking. I finished my last Rusty Nail as we were getting up to leave. Someone noticed there was still a little wine in one of the bottles, and looking for the nearest sewer to pour it down, offered it to me. Sad to say, I drank that, too. Ron said,

"Hey, man. I could use a cappuccino. How about you?"
"I could certainly use something. Where are we going to get a cappuccino at this hour?"
"I know a drive-in downtown."
"Get out of here, Ron! A drive-in in Asmara?"
"Come along, laddy, and I'll show you."
"Lead on MacBarf...."

Now Ron was one of the few single enlisted men to have a car. It was a Fiat Topolino—an automobile in the literal sense of the word, and that's about all. It looked like a toy car—a tiny little thing with Spartan accommodations for two adults in the front and two consenting midgets in the back—a lot like the car Mickey Mouse used to drive in the old black and white cartoons. It was of indeterminate age, and considerably worse for the wear. The outside was rust red—I think it might have been paint, but I wouldn't swear to it—and the inside was musty brown. The engine looked like something out of an old lawn mower. But it beat walking.

We shoehorned ourselves in, and Ron headed the little econobox toward town. He steered through the maze of Asmara's streets while I sat with the window down trying to clear my head. Clearing your head in the cloying Ethiopian air turned out to be an impossibility.

Finally we pulled into a head-in parking space in front of a row of shops that looked like all the other shops in Asmara.

"Where the hell are we, Ron?"

My speech was getting slurred by this time. I won't try to reproduce it in print. Just imagine the worst comedian's imitation of a drunk, and you'll be close.

"We're here."

Ron couldn't speak very well either. God truly watches out for drunks, it seems.

"Where the hell is here?"
"The drive-in."

As he spoke, a little Ethiopian man dressed in black Bermuda shorts and a mostly white waiter's jacket sauntered up to Ron's window.

"What you want?"
"Two cappuccinos."

He strolled back to a doorway, and in a couple of minutes came back with two cups of steaming cappuccino. The idea had been great, but I never really liked coffee, and the more I sipped, the queasier my stomach became. Finally, I couldn't face it any more.

"Ron, I can't drink this stuff. I think I'm getting sick."
"Yeah, me too. Let me get the waiter to take the cups, and we'll get out of here."

He tapped his horn, and the waiter eventually came and took the cups. As we were driving back, Ron said,

"I know where the little peckerhead lives. Let's drive by and wake him up."
"Who, Neil?"
"Of course, Neil, who do you think?"
"I don't think I'm up to knocking on doors."
"Who said anything about knocking on doors. Here we are, now."

He started blowing his horn and shouting,

"Happy birthday, you little prick! Hey, Neil, I'm talking about you!"

"Yeah! Happy birthday!"

We shouted, and he blew his horn until half the lights on the block went on and some people were shouting back. We drove back to the barracks with the windows down, drunker than skunks.

When I started getting ready for bed, it all hit me at once. I knew I was going to throw up big time. I ran down to the bathroom and let fly. While I was at it, I realized that I had developed a major case of diarrhea as well. I didn't know whether to kneel or sit. I held out in the kneeling position as long as I could, and then sat down and lost everything I had eaten and drunk since I had arrived in Ethiopia. Well, that's what it felt like, anyway.

I spent most of the night alternating between kneeling and sitting. By the time my alarm clock went off, I knew I wouldn't be good for anything that day. I managed to get dressed, and went to sick call. The doctor examined me thoroughly, and finally said,

"You're new here, right Leeger?"

"Uh, yes Sir."

"Well, what you have is a major case of what we here call Asmaraitis."

"What's that, Sir?"

"I guess you haven't had time or haven't bothered to read the packet of information you got when you arrived here. When you go downtown, you should only eat at approved restaurants. Otherwise you'll get a major case of diarrhea and the sweats, like you have. I'm writing you up to take today off. You should be OK by Monday."

"Thanks, Sir."

"Just be careful in the future."

"Yes, Sir."

I learned that Asmaraitis was also called Eritrearrhea, a name I preferred. I also learned that you can get some serious parasites by eating or drinking in the wrong places. What I never did figure out was whether the doctor really hadn't been able to smell the alcohol that was oozing out my pores, or whether he just took pity on me.

LIEUTENANT GRAHAM

Our company commander arrived a couple of days before I did. Lieutenant Graham was fresh from Officers Training School. How he managed not to be shipped to Vietnam was a puzzle to us all. He looked insecure about something (or everything). He seemed to be uncomfortable with other officers and tried to be friendly with the enlisted men. It's hard for someone who hasn't been in the service to understand what a gulf there is between enlisted men and officers, but it's certainly there. Enlisted personnel are all too aware of the awesome power that officers have over their lives. An officer can increase the misery factor geometrically for an enlisted man who happens to fall in disfavor. Graham never understood that, and tried to ingratiate himself with his troops, to little or no avail.

Bob and Nancy Johnson were two of the people who played bridge on a regular basis at the club. Nancy had arrived on the same plane I came in on. I met her and Bob that night with the rest of the card players. She was a large, but well-proportioned woman—my mother would call her *big-boned*. Strikingly attractive in a large sort of way. Very outspoken, she never held back an opinion in all the time I knew her. They were both from the Atlanta area, and had charming southern accents. Bob looked like a good old country boy. A bit taller than his wife, with a sort of shambling gait, his appearance and his mannerisms reminded me of Gomer Pyle. I got along well with both of them—it wasn't difficult to do. The next Tuesday on the way out to the site, Bob said,

"Did you see that *2001* is playing tonight at the theater?"

"No. That's a great movie. I saw it in Boston a couple of months ago. How long is it here?"

"Tonight's the last show."

"I think I'll go see it again, then."

"Nancy and I are going. Why don't you join us for dinner at the club, then we can go together?"

"That's a great idea!"

After dinner, we headed down to the theater. There, in the lobby was Lt. Graham.

"Do you mind if I sit with you all?"

"'Uh, no...."

"Uh...sure...."

We sat in the middle of the nearly empty theater. We had come early, thinking there would be a crowd, but there were only about a dozen others there. After a few minutes Nancy said,

"Bob, I want some popcorn."

"Oh, honey...I'm tired. I've been working all day. Why didn't you think of that while we were in the lobby?"

She increasingly poured on more and more of the sweet young thing charm, dripping with her Southern accent, as she tried to get him to do her will.

"I just don't know why. Go get me some popcorn, please honey."

"No. I'm too tired. You're a big girl. You can get your own popcorn."

Right about then, Lt. Graham made one of the biggest mistakes in his young life. Trying to be cute, he said,

"Specialist Johnson, as your commanding officer, I order you to get your wife some popcorn."

It got very quiet in the theater. But only for about three seconds. Nancy's mouth dropped open. Then she turned on him,

"You candy-assed little faggot!"

she said, in her brassiest voice,

"Don't you dare tell my husband what to do, you jerk!"

Now it was **definitely** quiet as a tomb in the theater. Everyone sat as though carved from Ethiopian granite. Mercifully, the projectionist turned the lights down, and started the movie.

* * * * *

Some months later, Bob was suddenly scheduled for duty on a weekend that he and Nancy had planned to go to Masawa, a city on the Red Sea that was used as an R & R (Rest and Recuperation) center for the troops. When Bob told Nancy that there was no way he could get out of the duty, she went nuclear. She went straight to the Orderly Room looking for Lt. Graham. She came in and at the top of her formidable voice demanded of the poor Specialist who was serving as Charge of Quarters,

"I want to see that little bastard right now!"
"Uh, who do you mean, Ma'am?"
"Lt. Graham, of course! Who the hell do you think I mean?"
"Oh...well, he's pretty busy right now...."
"Busy! I'll give him busy! You tell that little shit that I want to talk to him, and I mean RIGHT NOW!"
"Uh...yes Ma'am. If you'll just wait here a minute?"

He went over and knocked on the Lieutenant's door. Not getting a response, he asked,

> "Uh...Lt. Graham? Mrs. Johnson is here to see you...Lt. Graham?...Lt. Graham?"

Overcoming his timidity, he opened the door. Graham was nowhere to be seen,

> "Huh?...I'm sure he was here...I **know** he was here...."

The window was wide open. Totally puzzled, he walked over to the window to close it. About a block away he could see Lt. Graham, hatless, and walking very quickly toward the Officers' Club....

Not only was his scheduled duty canceled, but I don't recall Bob ever having to pull duty after that.

BRIDGE

Most evenings you could find at least one group at the Club playing Bridge. Often there would be three or four tables going. I played quite a lot. Usually my partner was Evan Lowrey. Goren would have been aghast at the way we played, but we won a lot. We must have had the same idiosyncrasies—it sometimes seemed like we were reading each other's minds.

One night we were teamed up against two other guys, and had just started bidding a hand. Just as Evan bid, I got a tremendous cramp in my right thigh. I don't know what I had been doing earlier in the day—perhaps it was shortly after I arrived, and my body was still adjusting to the altitude. I had had cramps occasionally before, so I reacted instantly. In addition to the loud moan of pain (first reaction), I snapped my right foot up, trying to straighten my leg so the cramp wouldn't tie me up in knots. Unfortunately, my foot caught the front of Evan's chair. I grabbed my thigh to begin trying to massage the cramp out. As my eyes were coming back into focus, I noticed everyone else's startled expression, and the fact that Evan was falling over backward—a look of surprise on his face.

I was too busy trying to make the pain going away to say anything. Then, Evan's face appeared over the other edge of the table. He asked,

"Was that the wrong bid?"

It was hard to laugh while I was in that much pain, but I managed. From that evening, every time we sat down to play, he would make a big deal about checking to see where my feet were. I guess he deserved his kicks, after taking one of mine.

R & R

Not much more than two weeks after I arrived in Ethiopia, Charlie Riggs came up to me at the site to tell me he was volunteering for transfer to Vietnam. He had discovered that Ethiopian society was even more bigoted than back in the States. The society was rigidly stratified. Ethiopians, of course, were in the top tier which they shared with Europeans/Caucasians. Indians came next, followed by Asians. At the very bottom of the social totem pole were the Negroid peoples. They were shunned by everyone except the prostitutes. Charlie's dream of the African Motherland had been cruelly shattered. He couldn't face dark-skinned people who treated him like a pariah. I tried to dissuade him, but it was easy to see that he had lost heart. We promised to keep in touch, but I never heard from him again.

On a more pleasant note, there were two places in Ethiopia where the Army had established Rest and Recuperation centers for the troops stationed in country. Keren was a little town about halfway down the side of the mountain. The Army maintained a little hotel there for the troops. The other was in the city of Masawa, Ethiopia's port on the Red Sea.

As Protestant Chapel Organist, it was hard for me to get a weekend off to take advantage of them, but finally in October I had a free weekend. Ron was going down to Keren for the weekend, and asked if I would like to ride down with him. It sounded like a great idea. I was a bit burned out, and curious to see more of Ethiopia.

We left early Saturday morning—because of the Shifteh, the Eritrean Liberation Front guerillas, you didn't want to be on the roads at night. The sun was shining, as usual, and it was a beautiful day. It didn't take long to reach the edge of the plateau, and then it was all downhill from there. And do I mean **downhill**. In places, the road looked more like a ski jump. As Ron eased the little car down the mountain, I was astounded by the engineering marvel we were on. When the road twisted around so that my side was on the outside, the sheer drop outside my windows was enough to take my breath away. For long stretches there were no shoulders—just space. The road was a major commercial route, maybe the only one. Even though it was Saturday, trucks occasionally rushed past us. I was happy that Ron didn't seem to want to race anyone.

Finally we came to the town. It was tucked around a wide spot in the road. Clinging to the mountain, it was indeed a picturesque spot. We drove to the hotel and pulled around the drive to the front door. We were about to get out when Ron said,

"Hey, it's almost lunch time. What say we go down to the *suq*[3] and look around. We don't have to check in right away."

"Yeah. That sounds good."

"They've got some great jewelers here. And I know a terrific little restaurant—we could get there before the lunch rush."

"Why're you still talking—let's go!"

Ron's dad was stationed in Turkey and had a good friend who was a jeweler there. Soli Bencuya had pretty much adopted Ron, and Ron had learned a lot about the jewelry business from Soli. So if Ron said the jewelers were great, it would be worth investigating. In that part of the world in those days (and probably still today) you bought jewelry pretty much by weight. Jewelry there was almost always 14-karat, but you paid what the piece was worth by weight as if it were a lump of pure (24-karat) gold. So a bit less than half of the price you paid went for labor. Still, it was generally a great deal—jewelry cost a fraction of what it would in the United States. Many of the jewelers were very good. The artistry often matched anything you could find back home, and they would usually design to your specifications. The goldsmiths there used a different mix of alloys, and the gold had more of an orange tint than the yellow we see here.

Ron had also learned how to barter from Soli. He relished the challenge, and would do his best to beat them at their own game. I have watched him barter for a half hour for a sweater—and finally get it for a fraction of what I would have paid for it. I'm sure he was more interested in the haggling to come than in lunch. Ron seemed to know his way around Keren. The little car was perfect for the crowded, narrow streets. Finally we turned one last corner and were in the town square. Where we stopped in astonishment...and horror. Bodies were hanging from lamp posts around the square. The open space was nearly empty save for the Ethiopian soldiers stationed around the square. They were tense—constantly scanning the windows and doors around the square, and watching everyone intently. They kept their carbines at the ready, held across their chests. Their fingers were on the triggers.

We crept around the square, trying not to stare. The hangings must have been recent. We would have heard about this incident back in Asmara if it had happened even a day before. We finally came around to the road we had come in on and slowly headed back toward the hotel. With the gruesome sight behind us, we both breathed easier. We hadn't gone halfway back to the hotel, however, before Ron said,

"Let's get the fuck out of here."
"I'm with you, man."

In silence we drove past the hotel, and headed back up the mountain.

Later we learned that the Shifteh had ambushed an Ethiopian Army patrol earlier in the week. In retaliation, the Ethiopians hung the men we had seen as collaborators and terrorists. Their bodies were left there for a week as a lesson. I never went back to Keren.

* * * * *

Months later I had another weekend off. I decided to go to Masawa, but this time I would fly. I had thought about riding the Littorina— this was the passenger train that ran down the mountain from Asmara to Masawa. But I didn't think I wanted to be packed in a train for several hours with too many people and their livestock. The train's passengers regularly traveled with chickens, goats, and other animals all packed together in the same cars with their owners. I had learned that Ethiopian Air Lines had a Saturday morning flight, and decided to go. The ticket was pretty inexpensive, and I thought it would be interesting to see the country from the air.

When the flight was called, I joined the others heading out onto the runway. Then I saw what we were heading for: it was a DC3. You know, the two-propeller plane that was the U.S. Air Force's principle transport during the Second World War. I hadn't given a thought to the 707 I had flown in from Athens when I first came to Asmara. But now I had been in country for a year, and had first-hand knowledge of how unimportant preventive maintenance was to most Ethiopians. And here I was getting into an airplane that had been built before I was.

It looked to be in pretty good shape, and it was clean. I probably had nothing to worry about. I climbed up the aisle, and settled into the window seat in the first row. An Ethiopian woman sat next to me. As the engines started, she grabbed the arms of the seat, trying to leave her fingerprints for posterity. She spoke a little English, and a little Arabic, and I had learned a tiny bit of Amharic, so we talked at each other—shouted at each other is more accurate. It was her first flight, and she was terrified. I told her I thought she might be more comfortable if she could see out the window. She understood, and we switched seats.

The plane roared down the runway, and she tried to add another set of fingerprints—this time, however, she was clutching my arm. Then we were aloft. The country slipped past close beneath us. I wondered why the pilot didn't climb, but after a few minutes, I had my answer: we flew over the edge of the plateau and the ground was instantly 7,800 feet farther below. The pilot put the plane into a lazy spiral, and we coasted down toward the Red Sea.

As I looked over her shoulder, I could occasionally catch a glimpse of the road I had traveled on my last, ill-fated, attempt at rest and recuperation in Ethiopia. It didn't look nearly as impressive from this new vantage point. And of course, there was no evidence of the Shifteh from up here. This, I decided, was the right way to travel in Ethiopia—or at least the safer way.

Soon I could see the Red Sea, and then, there was Masawa. The buildings were startlingly white. They seemed to gleam like teeth in an improbable sandy mouth. As we touched down my new friend created one final set of fingerprints. Then we were rolling toward the terminal. I was in no hurry to get out. I was in the first row, after all, the door was in the rear, and I knew I would have to wait for all the folks behind me. I heard the stewardess open the door, and then it hit me. A blast of hot air rushed up the aisle. I turned around to see if we were on fire. No one looked panicky—they were descending into the heat. I couldn't understand it: it had been about 70—when we left Asmara. And the humidity, as always, had been low. And then my memory kicked in. The only reason it was so temperate in Asmara was the elevation. The Red Sea was, of course, at sea level. It was quickly becoming apparent that only five degrees north of the Equator could be very hot indeed—specially at noon in what was summer in Ethiopia.

I am not a person who handles extreme heat well. My shirt was soaked before I got off the plane. I was sweating as though I had just run a marathon...in Miami...in August. I retrieved my bag and made my way into the terminal. I found a garry cart to take me to the Transportation Terminal Unit. The TTU was a little hotel that the Army maintained for use by soldiers in Masawa.

When I entered the tiny lobby, I shivered. The place was air conditioned, and the employees might have been Eskimos. It felt like it was 50—inside—maybe even colder. I registered, took my key, and walked back out into the stifling heat. Like a motel, you had to go outside to get to your room. When I opened that door, the cold hit me again. My internal thermostat was going crazy.

I put on some dry clothes, and reentered the furnace. The desk clerk had given me a little map and visitors' guide. I headed to the port area. Everything looked like it had been built in the last century. The incessant heat and humidity had taken their toll. From the air, everything had sparkled. From the ground, it all looked tired. The people were listless. I wondered how they managed to do the heavy manual labor associated with loading and unloading ships.

After an hour or two of touring, I found myself back at the hotel. Just breathing the soupy air was an effort. Once again, I was drenched in sweat. The hotel was right on the Red Sea, however, and it looked very inviting. I opened the door, and went into the refrigerator that was my room to put on my swimming suit and sandals. Goose bumps popped out all over me. My skin instantly had the texture of a football.

I changed as quickly as I could, grabbed a towel, opened the door, and stepped back into the furnace outside. The goose bumps promptly melted into buckets of sweat. I walked down to the water, kicked off my sandals, and dropped my towel. Summoning what little strength remained, I ran into the water, intending to dive in when it got deep enough. I ran and ran, splashing in the shallow water. Then I stopped, turned around and looked back. I must have been 100 yards from the shore. The water was just about up to my calves. Not only didn't it get deep enough, but it was so warm it felt like bath water. As far as I could see, the water remained the same blue-green color. It didn't look like I was on a sand bar. It looked like the Red Sea never got much deeper than a foot or two.

Disappointed, I started back to the hotel. An Ethiopian rowed up to me in a shallow boat and asked,

"You want go Green Island? Five dollars. I row you."

Now Green Island was about a half mile offshore. There were some ruins there that I had been told about.

"Round trip?"
"Sure, my friend. Round trip."
"Five dollars—Ethiopian."
"Wah! What? You **crazy**? Five dollars **American!**"

An Ethiopian dollar was worth about 40 cents. But this was a common point to begin haggling. We finally settled on three American dollars—to be paid when I was back from my trip. I didn't want him to leave me stranded on the island. I had a few dollars in the pocket of my swimming suit, so I crawled aboard the little craft.

He offered to show me around the island for another five dollars. This time we settled on two American dollars for this additional service. The heat had drained me. I felt like someone with a grudge was focusing the sun's heat and light on me with some enormous, invisible magnifying glass in the sky. You could see the bottom of the shallow sea all the way across. It couldn't have been more than 50 feet deep at the deepest point.

"Are those sharks?"
"Sure. Sharks. Plenty sharks here. You want fish?"
"No. I'm not a fisherman."
"You want swim?"
"Here?"
"Sure. Here."
"What about the sharks?"
"Sharks—no worry! You no worry sharks."

"I'm sure I don't worry the sharks. But they sure as hell worry me."

"No. Sharks no problem."

I dipped my hand in the water. It didn't feel any cooler than it was right off the shore.

"No, thanks. I'll pass on swimming."

"OK, GI."

He continued to row, with little enthusiasm, but with considerably more energy than I could muster. My two dollar tour consisted of a short walk up to the old compound. The buildings were slowly decomposing in the heat and humidity. My guide was content to rest under a tree while I walked the beach. Even the little crabs I found seemed listless. But, then, maybe it was just me.

We got back into the little skiff, and my guide rowed us back. The return trip took longer, it seemed. At least the sea was calm.

"Do you ever get waves?"

"Sure. Look. Waves."

"No. I mean big waves."

"How big?"

"You know—big. A couple of feet or more."

"Wah! No, man. No big waves."

Even the sea was listless. I rode the rest of the way in silence, hoping the rest of my life essence wouldn't leak out my pores before we got back. I paid off my guide, and trudged back to the hotel.

By now it was about 5:00. I went back to my room, changed into another set of dry clothing, and headed back to the front desk. I asked the desk clerk where I could get something light to eat. He referred me to a nearby restaurant. By the time I had walked the short distance, I realized that I was neither rested nor relaxed. The food was not bad, but certainly nothing to write home about. I found I wasn't very hungry. There was no air conditioning in the restaurant, and I was just too hot to eat.

When I got back to the hotel, I used the desk phone to call the airport. The next flight back to Asmara was at 9:00 A.M. the next day. I was on it.

NOW THAT'S ITALIAN

Eritrea had been an Italian colony off and on for much of the first part of the Twentieth Century. There was still a large Italian population, especially in Asmara. Many of the businesses were owned by Italians, including some wonderful restaurants. My favorite was Menghetti's. At least once a month, Evan Lowrey, Ron Hartwell and I would go down there for dinner. Playing bridge one night shortly after I had arrived, Ron said,

"Do you like Italian food, John?"
"Sure."
"Evan and I are going to Menghetti's tomorrow for dinner. Want to come along?"
"Menghetti's?"
"It's an Italian restaurant downtown. If you like Italian food, you'll love it."
"Sure. What time?"
"We'll leave about 6:00. I'll drive."

We piled into the little Topolino the next evening and headed for the restaurant.

"The owner's an old timer. But he likes Americans."
"How do you know him, Ron?"
"Are you kidding? Ron knows everybody in Asmara."
"Not everybody, Evan. Signor Menghetti and my dad have some mutual friends. He's quite a cook."

The place didn't look too impressive from the outside. But once inside,

> "Ron! Buon giorno my friend! And Signor Lowrey, good evening!"
> "Buon giorno, Signor Menghetti."
> "How's your Papa, Ron?"
> "He's fine. I had a letter from him Saturday. Signor Menghetti, this is our friend, John Leeger. He just got here."
> "Welcome! Welcome, Signor Leeger. You enjoy yourselves. If you need anything, send for me."

Mr. Menghetti was a rotund, ebullient Italian man in his forties or early fifties. I never saw him without a smile on his face. He had a little accent, but his English was excellent. The staff treated us like long-lost family. Mr. Menghetti had known Ron's dad. I guess Ron had more adoptive parents than any other guy I had ever known. We were ushered into one of the little rooms that surrounded the main dining room. For the next nearly three hours we dined like the ancient Romans must have. Each course had a separate bottle of wine, and as there were several courses, we put away a lot of wine. Dinners at Menghetti's usually consisted of at least antipasto, a pasta dish, some sort of fish or chicken, a red meat dish, and a dessert. After each course, menus would be presented so you could choose the next course and wine. Mr. Menghetti preferred that you not order everything at once. This gave you more time to savor the last course and to anticipate the ones yet to come.

The cuisine was a blend of Italian, Mediterranean, and anything else that Mr. Menghetti took a fancy to. One of my favorites was curried prawns. It was so spicy that when they set the dish down in front of you, the skin under your eyes would start to sweat. By some culinary magic, however, the spiciness didn't overwhelm the prawns. It was wonderful! They also made a dish called beef in a box. This was a phenomenally tender filet cooked in a little metal box with the most delicious brown sauce, or gravy, that you could imagine. When it was served, the waiter removed the top of the box and finished cooking the beef flambé at the table.

By nine or nine thirty we were stuffed, and feeling so mellow that we had to take a long time finishing the last bottle of wine before we could consider getting up to leave. To top off the evening, the check would only amount to about $10.00 each, including tip. That's $10.00 Ethiopian, or all of $4.00 in U.S. currency!

There were other great places to eat including the restaurant in the Imperial Hotel, as well as lesser-known places on almost every block downtown. Only a few, however, had been approved by the U.S. Army. Those that wanted that approval had to allow weekly inspections of their establishments. These were time-consuming and very thorough. They had to be. Ethiopia was home to some interesting parasites that were almost never seen in the United States. The approved restaurants were checked diligently for a wide variety of microbial monsters, and could be put off limits in a very short period of time.

One Saturday, Ron and I had stopped in a little Italian café to have some pasta for lunch. The dining room was just off the street. With a brownish-red tile floor, white furniture, and checked table cloths, it looked picture perfect. Cheeses hung in little nets from the ceiling, and the bar was well-stocked.

While we were sitting there waiting for our lunch to arrive, a fellow came in the front door. He was an older Ethiopian man, and was dressed in pants and shirt that were mostly white, but were stained rusty brown in numerous places. He had on a similarly-colored and stained apron and cap. Flies encircled him, but he paid them no mind. He talked with the proprietor for a minute or two and then they disappeared back into the kitchen area. After a few minutes he walked back through the dining room and out the front door. Soon he reentered the front door pulling a little red wagon—it looked like a child's American Flyer wagon. Draped across the wagon was half a side of beef. The hind leg dragged across the floor leaving a streak of blood from the entry door into the kitchen. The Ethiopian, his wagon and its grisly cargo were accompanied by a cloud of flies. At each jolt of the wheels as the little wagon crossed a line of tiles, some of the flies would leave their feast, only to be quickly replaced. The delivery man pulled the wagon into the kitchen, and in a minute he re-crossed the floor—this time the wagon was empty, but many of the flies hadn't given up on it. He came back through the restaurant with a mop and cleaned his way from the street back into the kitchen. Well, 'cleaned' is perhaps a bit too strong a word. The water he carried with him couldn't be too clean after even one usage. Working from the sidewalk back to the kitchen, he was probably pushing germs into the very place he should have been keeping them out of. At any rate, after a few minutes the trail he had left looked much like the rest of the tile in the dining room.

Although we had a great deal to say about the operation of the café, the pasta was great, and even though it was not on the approved list, I never heard of anyone getting sick from eating there. Ron said,

"Have you been to Signor Firenza's shop?"
"Not yet. Who's he?"
"He runs a leather shop. If you don't mind, I'd like to stop by there on the way back. He's making a jacket for me."

Signor Firenza was about five feet four inches tall and stocky. He had white wispy hair. His brown eyes were never still. He never seemed to look directly at you, but glanced here and there, occasionally focusing on your face. He spoke English well enough, but always appreciated hearing whatever Italian we could produce. Ron had a better command of the language than I, and they slipped from one language to another as the need arose. I looked around his shop and saw all sorts of things artfully crafted from various leathers. Signor Firenza was checking the fit of the jacket he was making for Ron. It was light brown with a covering of short, thick hair. The hair was not silky fine, but straight and smooth.

"What is that, Ron?"

"Oh. It's unborn calf."

"What?"

"Yeah. When they slaughter cattle here, occasionally the cow will be pregnant. The unborn baby dies too, of course, but nothing is wasted."

"Well, yeah, I knew that....but the skin? I didn't know they used the skins for anything."

"I don't know what they do with them in the States, but here they often make things like this leaving the hair on. How does it look?"

"Well...I guess it looks nice. Yeah. Why not? It sure is different, isn't it?"

"Yeah."

"Do you mind telling me how much it cost?"

"It's $30.00 American."

"Is that all? Signor Firenza, would you make me a coat like that?"

"Certainly, Signor Leeger."

"Could I get it in black?"

"Oh...all black? Well it would take a while to find enough skins that matched. But, certainly, in black."

"The same price?"

"Yes, certainly."

Well, it took about a month, but it was the most unusual jacket I ever had. I had it for about five years, until the hair wore off the elbows. It was warm, waterproof, and a great conversation starter.

Probably the finest contribution the Italians in Ethiopia made to the world, however, were the caffolattis. I have no idea how the word should be spelled in English, but it was an Anglicized, or maybe Italianized, version of the French term *café au lait*. Caffolattis were the children of Italian-Ethiopian marriages, and they are some of the most beautiful people I have ever seen. Invariably they were tall and lithe with a blend of the Ethiopian and northern Italian features. Their skin color and texture, however, set them apart from mere mortals. Coffee with milk was the proper description of the color, but the texture was pure silk. They were aloof, and untouchable. Although Ron knew a couple of the girls, they were never allowed to be alone with American servicemen—or with any men, I suppose. The few that I eventually met took my breath away, but I had no better luck than Ron in getting close to them. Indeed, although as chapel organist I played at several weddings during my stay in Ethiopia, I never heard of any GI marrying a Caffolatti.

A HORSE IS A HORSE

One night a guy named Billy got really drunk at the Oasis Club. When the club manager refused to serve him any more alcohol, he decided to go downtown. Now Billy was a big fellow—about six feet two and 240 pounds—and there wasn't much about him that wasn't muscle. He headed out the front gate with one of his friends who was somewhat more sober than Billy. Sober enough, at any rate, to be able to provide me with the details of this story afterwards. They hadn't gone 50 feet before an ambitious garry cart driver approached them.

"You want ride, GI?"
"No."

The garry cart driver angled his horse a little close to the curb,

"C'mon, GI, I give you ride downtown. Just fi' dolla'."
"I said no. Beat it!"
"Hey! Whatsa matta you, GI? I give you ride. Good price. Fi' dolla'. You get in."

He angled the horse so it was just at the curb.

"Hey! You get in, GI. I give you ride. Fi' dolla'. You get in, now!"
"Get that smelly critter away from me, shithead!"
"Hey! You no talk to me like that, GI! You cheap sonbitch! You get in! I give ride! Fi' dolla'!"

Now, this guy had obviously never had the benefit of any sales training. Maybe he was having a bad night. At any rate, he crossed whatever line Billy had set for himself. He drove the horse right onto the sidewalk, blocking Billy's path.

"You take ride, now, GI! I charge fi' dolla'!"
"You dumb shit!"

Billy grabbed the horse's bridle, pushing it away, but the driver kept trying to force it back. Then, Billy cocked back his fist and hit the horse right in the temple. The animal dropped to the ground, dead.

The garry cart driver got very quiet. Billy and his friend continued down the street. When the driver realized that his means of livelihood had just shuffled off to a better land, he went nuts. He started to run after Billy, screaming,

"You shit, GI! You kill my horse! You pay my horse! Two hundred dolla'! You pay! You shit, GI!"

Billy turned around and took a half step toward the driver. Cocking back his hand again, he said,

"You come right up here, asshole. I'll give you what I gave your horse!"

The garry cart driver stopped in his tracks. But he kept yelling at Billy until he was out of sight. Eventually, Billy had to leave the country. The Ethiopian law was very similar to the old eye for an eye requirement in the Bible. I don't know what compensation the garry cart driver got for his horse, but whatever it was, it was probably too much.

Those poor animals were generally harnessed when they were just old enough to pull a cart, and stayed in harness until they dropped dead. That usually wasn't more than a couple of years. In a country (a continent, for that matter) which valued human life so little, the life of a garry cart horse wasn't worth much at all.

I watched a driver one day whose horse had slipped and fallen in the rain. He stood up in his cart and beat the poor beast to death. No, I had no sympathy for Billy's garry cart driver. I think the horse probably was happy to go.

HELP

One morning, the bus stopped on the way out to Tract C. Paul, who lived with his wife off post, was standing by his car and had flagged the bus down. Lying on the ground, next to his car, were a bicycle and an Ethiopian man who seemed to be in some pain. The bus driver opened the door.

"That guy swerved into the side of my car."
"Is he alright?"
"I think so. Does anyone on the bus speak Tigrinie or Amharic?"
"Yes. I'll talk to him."

Tom Haslip was one of the few Americans who were fluent in both languages. The driver said,

"When I get to the Site, I'll call the hospital, and have them send an ambulance."
"You know they won't do that for an Ethiopian."
"Well, I'll have someone send help."
"OK. And let people at the Site know Tom and I may be out here for a while."

By treaty, the base hospital was not allowed to treat anyone who was not an American. If that weren't the case, I suppose we would have had Ethiopians purposely running into buses just for the medical care. It was just before lunch when Paul and Tom finally got to Tract C. We all gathered around to hear what had happened.

"The guy seemed to be OK, right up until the time the Ethiopian police came."

"Yes. He told me where he lived, and talked about his family. He was conscious and cogent all the time I was talking to him."

"He didn't seem to be too badly injured. I thought he might have had a couple of broken ribs. His right arm hurt a great deal, too. It may have been cracked—you know, not a clean break."

"How long did it take before the police came?"

"Just a few minutes ago."

"Didn't you wait for the ambulance?"

"What ambulance? This is Ethiopia, remember. These two Ethiopian policemen arrived in one of their Volkswagens...."

"No ambulance?"

"I'm coming to that....They sauntered over and talked to the man. Then they took my name and Tom's. One of them flipped the passenger seat forward. Then, each of them took an arm and a leg, lifted the guy like he was a sack of wheat, and threw him in the back seat."

"Of the Volkswagen?!"

"The guy screamed when they picked him up. He must have passed out when he hit the seat. Then the two cops got into the car, did a U-turn, and drove off."

....

"That's incredible...."

"Do you think the guy will be OK?"

"Who knows?..."

"Tom has his name. We'll try to find out what happened to him after work."

Well, the guy wasn't OK. One of his broken ribs must have punctured a lung. He died that afternoon. Paul and his wife had to leave the country. Even though the U.S. paid a settlement to the man's family, you never could tell whether a relative might get it into his mind to enforce the *eye for an eye* rule.

Tom managed to contact the man's family, and did his best to console them. We in America don't often think about how little a human life is worth in other parts of our world.

JOHN AND SALLY THROW A PARTY

John Chase had also brought his wife to Ethiopia. He and Sally lived off post in a little house that they rented from an Italian landlord. Houses in Ethiopia were considerably different from what I was used to. To begin with, most of them were surrounded by six- to eight-foot high walls. The walls were made of masonry or stone and were topped with broken glass or some other sharp material embedded in concrete to keep the casual thief out. Then, there were bars on all the windows. The places were regular fortresses—but colorful. The Ethiopians seemed to feel that the more colors graced the outside of your house, the wealthier you appeared to be. Accordingly most houses were painted at least five or six different colors. John and Sally's house was light blue with pink shutters and window trim. The tile roof was light green. The masonry wall was tan with a dark brown stripe at the top providing a little camouflage for the mandatory broken glass. The door was a dark, almost royal blue as was the gate in the wall. And the sidewalk was made of blood-red tile. In Ethiopia, labor was so cheap that throughout the city, tile was used instead of concrete for sidewalks.

One Saturday night, John and Sally had a party—actually more of an open house. About fifty people had been invited, and by the time I got there, the party was in full swing. Now, John and Sally both liked to drink, and the bar was well stocked. The party had been roaring along for several hours, and most of the guests were pretty well sloshed. At 7,800 feet altitude, it didn't take too long to get that way. Suddenly, over the din of the hi fi and the babble of conversation somebody yelled,

> "I'm gonna throw up!"
> "First door on the right—down the hall! Don't you puke in my living room, asshole!"

I heard the door slam over the noise. After a couple of minutes I heard a scream and the sound of the door slamming open. And then,

> "Jesus, Chase! Your fucking toilet blew up!"

He came into the room with vomit in his hair and eyebrows, and all over his face.

> "What the hell happened to you, Tony?"
> "Your fucking toilet blew up all over me!"
> "What the hell are you talking about! Show me!"

About 15 people crammed into the bathroom. Tony was barely able to stand up. He stood there reeling. He pointed and said,

> "Look, that fucking toilet on the left blew up all over me!"

It got really quiet for a split second, then a couple of people started snickering. Then, more and more people joined in. Soon everyone was laughing. John said,

> "Tony, you moron! You threw up in the bidet!"
> "Huh? What the fuck is a bidet?"
> "You dumb shit! **That's** a bidet! The one on the right is the toilet! You're supposed to use the bidet to wash your ass!"

By now, it was hard to hear over the laughter.

"Wash my ass?"

"Yeah, you ignorant son of a bitch! You squat over the bidet and the water cleans your ass!"

"Get the fuck out of here!"

You can probably imagine how much flack Tony took about this incident over the coming months. Of all the people in this book whose names have been changed to protect their identities, Tony may be the one who would be most embarrassed to be correctly identified.

CHRISTMAS CONCERT

Since before I started accompanying them, the Kagnew Singers had been working on a Christmas Concert. To his credit, Neil Billingsley had put together a nice mixture of songs—none too difficult for the singers—and by the end of November, it looked like we would really have something pretty nice. We gave two performances the second week in December. They went very well, and we were quite pleased.

At our next rehearsal, Neil announced that there would be no more rehearsals until after Christmas. Neil also told us that some of the members of the Royal Family had come to the second concert, and had obviously said some nice things to the Emperor. We had been invited to sing in the palace for Haile Selassie. It seems that every year, choirs across Ethiopia were invited to perform for the Emperor. We were to sing two numbers.

On the appointed afternoon, we were driven to the palace in one of Kagnew Station's buses. Everyone was nervous. On our way in, we looked for the lions that roamed the palace grounds[4], but no one saw any. Although the palace had looked impressive as we drove up, inside things looked a little tatty.

We were led into a large room. There were four other choirs. Our group was positioned to the left of all the Ethiopian choirs (the Emperor's left). All the accompanists were grouped around the piano which was still farther off to the left. From where we stood, we could see down the long hallway as the Emperor entered. He was surrounded by six or seven courtiers. Two of them looked like body guards. As he approached the room, the Ethiopian National Anthem was played through a sound system. He was dressed in one of the uniforms he was always pictured in.

He had two little dogs—Chihuahuas, I think—that raced around frenetically. First ahead of the entourage, then behind, they yapped incessantly. As the Emperor was entering the room, one of the dogs lifted his leg on the wall in the hall. All of the courtiers studiously looked in other directions. But the minute the dog resumed his running around, one of the courtiers ordered another to clean the wall. He hurried down the hall and returned with a maid who furiously scrubbed the wall and carpet. Oblivious to it all, the first choir was already preparing to sing. The other accompanists and I tried our best not to snicker.

The Emperor had taken his seat on the throne, and the concert began. As soon as the first choir started to sing, the little dogs raced to a spot halfway between Haile Selassie and the choirs and started barking ferociously. Again, all the courtiers looked away. The little dogs yipped and yapped for most of the time the first choir was singing. Then the Emperor leaned over and said something to one of the courtiers. That courtier relayed the order to another, and eventually the little dogs were picked up and carried, still barking enthusiastically to the music, out of the room.

When all the choirs had sung, the Emperor stood and thanked us in Amharic. Then he left. We were ushered back to the bus in short order. Everyone thought that was the end of it, but the next day we were invited to the palace to meet the Emperor. Back on the bus we went. We were taken to the same room and, one at a time, we were presented to the Emperor. He shook everyone's hand, very formally. We were told that he didn't speak much English, but I think he just didn't feel comfortable speaking English where he might be recorded, because several of us had short conversations with him.

When we were led away from the Emperor, each of us was presented with a little red leather box with the Lion of Judah symbol stamped on the cover in gold. Inside was a presentation coin about the size of a half dollar. On one side was the Lion of Judah symbol and some Amharic writing. On the other side was an image of Haile Selassie. I found out later that the little coins were 24-karat gold!⁵ I noticed that none of the other choirs was there. I hope they came at another time, but I suspect that the little ceremony was just a political gesture.

CHORAL MUSIC RETREAT

Before the worship service the Sunday after Christmas Colonel Vaughn, the Protestant Chaplain, asked me,

"John, how would you like to go to the Choral Music Retreat the Army has every year. It's in Berchtesgaden, Germany the first week in February."

"That sounds terrific, Colonel Vaughn! Uh...but I don't think I have enough leave."

"You don't need any leave. The Army gives you Permissive TDY for things like this. In fact, you would have 20 days to include time for travel."

"Well, in that case, you can count me in!"

"I've also invited Neil Billingsley. And Ron Hartwell is going."

"Did you say Berchtesgaden? Isn't that near Austria?"

"Yes. It's right on the Austrian border, very near Salzburg. You'll be staying in the General Walker Hotel. It was the headquarters building for the SS in that area during the Second World War."

"Oh, I've heard of that. It's way at the top of a mountain, isn't it?"

"In fact it's on a promontory of the Übersalzburg Alp—the General Walker Hotel is about three fourths of the way up the mountain."

"Wait a minute. Germany in February—won't it be next to impossible to get around?"

"Not at all. The Germans are very efficient people. The snow hardly slows them at all. But take plenty of warm clothes!"

I was really excited. But when I told Sergeant Thornton, he said,

"I don't think that will be possible."
"Why not, Sergeant Thornton?"
"Well, you've only been here for a short time. I don't think it's fair for you to go on something like this so early."
"What does that have to do with it? How many of the other guys work for the chapel every Sunday?"
"That's not the point. You're just too new."

Well, I didn't see his point at all. It seemed to me that he was just jealous. That Thursday night when I went to choir practice, I saw Colonel Vaughn as he was leaving. I told him all about Sergeant Thornton's response.

"Well, John, that doesn't make any sense to me, either. Why don't you step into my office with me for a minute. Let me make some phone calls....Hello, Don? It's Tim Vaughn....Fine, thanks and how's everyone there?....I have a little problem, Don. I've selected my organist to make the Choral Music Retreat, and his boss, uh, what was his name, John?"
"Sergeant Thornton."
"Oh yes, Sergeant Thornton says that he hasn't been there long enough to go....That's just the way I felt....Well why don't you just tell him that **Colonel** Vaughn wants him to go?....I think so, too. Well, thanks, Don....I'll see you Sunday?...OK....Goodbye. Well, John, I think you should hear a more positive response when you show up for work tomorrow. And if anyone gives you any guff about this, just call me."

"Thanks, Colonel Vaughn."

"Not at all. Thank you for showing up every Sunday morning."

Needless to say, Sergeant Thornton was less than thrilled the next day. The *Don* Colonel Vaughn had called was the Site Commander, Colonel Mosley. Thornton was, however, most contrite.

I didn't really have any winter clothes, but surprisingly the PX had some things that would help. I bought the only winter coat they had there, a Mao Tse Dung sort of quilted black nylon coat that turned out to be very warm, and a very heavy Fisherman's knit sweater that was touted to have been hand-knit in Ireland. As a matter of fact, as I write this it's twenty-five years later, and I still have the sweater—and it's still warm.

I packed the only suitcase I had, and at the appointed time, we went to the Asmara airport to catch a ride on a MAC[6] C-141 cargo jet. The C-141 is a four-engine jet about the size of a Boeing 707, but with the wings mounted at the top of the fuselage. It was the Air Force's main cargo lifter then, and still is today.

Remembering the flight from Athens on an Ethiopian Air Lines 707, I thought we were in for a fairly short flight. Boy, was I mistaken! In 1969 the Middle East was far hotter politically than it is today, and due to treaty obligations, the Air Force couldn't fly from Europe to Ethiopia in a straight line. In fact, we had to fly east, land in Saudi Arabia to take on fuel, then fly northeast, skirt Israel and finally fly across Iraq's northern border into Turkey. It took us eight hours to get from Asmara, Ethiopia to Adana, Turkey!

And they were eight of the more uncomfortable hours I had ever spent in an airplane! The military jets were long on cargo space, and short on passenger comfort. They had virtually no insulation, which made them cold and incredibly noisy. The seats were nylon webbing over aluminum tubing. No matter which seat I chose, my tail bone seemed to be centered over one of the hateful aluminum tubes that connected the front tube with the back one. I remained seated as little as possible. You took whatever you wanted

ONE IN A HUNDRED

to eat on board with you. There were only a couple of tiny windows, and since Ethiopia was the last stop on the cargo route, the remainder of the aircraft was one big, empty, reverberant room.

On the other hand, it was absolutely free. This made up for a lot. I was still only a Specialist Fourth Class (just above a Private First Class, but with little command authority), and didn't make a whole lot of money. If I had to pay for a ticket, I certainly wouldn't have been able to go. When we got to Adana, we spent the night at a temporary billet there, and the next day waited *stand by* for spots on the flight to Frankfurt. This was called the Turkish Courier, or the Diplomatic Shuttle. It was an Air Force DC6 passenger plane. This was a four-engine, propeller-driven plane, but unlike its civilian counterparts, the military version had all the seats facing backwards. Although this is safer, I didn't like it as much. In fact, I was borderline airsick every time I was on one of these planes.

We did get a nominal snack on the Turkish Courier, however, and with it came one of those little packages containing a moist towelette to wipe your hands. Now the Army has a system for describing things, and like many things in the Army, it requires that you revise your idea of how things should be done. This little package, for instance, just barely managed to contain the following label on its face:

TOWEL, PAPER, CLEANSING, WET
(PACKET), ANTISEPTIC

Stock No. 8540-782-3554

I had always enjoyed seeing how the Army described various items, but the label on this little towlette was so silly that I put one in my pocket to show the other guys when I got back to Ethiopia. I still have it, and it still tickles me.

After another full day of travel that included touching down in Athens and Rome, we arrived in Frankfurt. Actually the plane arrived at the Rhein-Main Air Force Base which is co-located outside Frankfurt with the Frankfurt-am-Main airport. We were bused to a barracks in Darmstadt. When we went out for breakfast the next morning, I immediately fell in love with Darmstadt. It is now the capital of the German state of Hesse, but it was once the home of Grand Duke Ludwig. Two beautiful and unusual buildings from his reign stand next to each other in a pretty park. When Ludwig married a Russian princess, her father, the Tsar, had a Russian Orthodox church built so that she would remember her homeland. There it stands today with the gold of its distinctive Russian domes and crosses glinting in the sun. And next to it is the Wedding Tower that Ludwig had built to show his friendship for Russia. It is about 50 feet tall and suggests a hand raised palm-outward, fingers together in a sign of peace. Nearby is a cemetery dating well back into the Middle Ages. The German on many of the tombstones is indecipherable to most German citizens today.

At breakfast we met still another friend of Ron's. With a name like Heinrich Koenig, there could be no doubt that he was a German. But he spoke English without a trace of accent. We learned that he also spoke French, Russian, and Italian, as well as a little Polish and Czech. Heinrich was about our age and worked for Radio Lindt, an electronics repair shop, as a technician. But he was also a member of the chapel on post, and sang in the choir. He had arranged for us to drive to Berchtesgaden with a couple of other singers from his choir. We would leave the next morning.

That night we took the Strassenbahn (streetcar) to one of Heinrich's favorite restaurants for dinner. It was an amazing place. The large room was filled with three rows of heavy wooden tables placed virtually end-to-end. They reminded me of the picnic tables that you can find in many parks in America. Chairs, stools, and benches were placed on the long sides of the tables. At one of the short ends of the room there was a Bavarian *Oom-pah-pah* band, and at the other short end was the waiters' station and kitchen. And the rest of the room was full of Germans out having a good time. We had bratwurst with sauerkraut and rolls and lots of beer. I had never liked the taste of beer before, but the unpasteurized brew of Germany changed my mind. As the evening wore on, the band's playing got louder and louder. The patrons sang along at the tops of their lungs. People from little toddlers to septuagenarians linked arms and rocked from side to side in time with the music. I hollered over the din,

> "Heinrich, is it always like this?"
> "Oh, yes, John. This is a very popular family place. And, of course, it's Friday night. It's not quite so crowded on work days."

It was late when we got to bed, and early when we got up the next morning. The Kagnew contingent dressed, packed our things, and went out into the parking lot to meet the rest of our entourage. Bill Zimmerman and Bob Harmon were stationed at Darmstadt. They had nearly identical BMW four-door sedans that would carry us to Berchtesgaden. Sarah Thompson and Karen Smith also went with us, along with Bill Marriott and his wife Pam. Yes, Bill Marriott. He told us he had no connection with the hotel/restaurant chain that shared his name. He was, indeed, a dentist stationed with the Army at Darmstadt.

Now, if you have been doing a little counting, you have found that there were 10 of us to share two cars. Although this was well before minivans, the BMWs swallowed us all, along with our luggage. What's more, we were pretty comfortable during the four-hour trip. But first, we went to breakfast in a place in a little shopping center nearby. Now I knew it was cold in Germany in February, but I was unprepared for the sight of penguins frolicking in a large open area in the center of the outdoor mall. Although there was a fence, you could go through a gate and socialize with them, as many people were doing.

I was delighted to finally ride on the autobahn. It didn't take Bill and Bob long to push the big BMWs to 130 kilometers per hour. We were really making time, by my reckoning. But every so often someone would come flying up behind us and whoosh past in a big hurry. We were passed often by Porsches, Mercedes, and even a Ferrari or two.

> "Look at the sign,"

Bob said. As it flashed by, I read the letters on the arrow pointing to an off ramp,

> "*Ausfahrt?*"
> "That's the German word for exit. It literally means *go out*. I thought you would get a kick out of that."

Ron, Sarah, Heinrich, and I were passengers in Bob's car. I was the only one who hadn't seen it before. I laughed enough for everyone, though. I was so tickled that I got my camera out and took a picture of one of the signs through the windshield.

A bit later, Heinrich said,

> "Look up ahead, John. On that bridge coming up. See the couple standing there?"
> "Yeah.... What are they doing? They look like they're watching the cars go by."
> "That's exactly what they are doing. We Germans like to take walks. And on weekends the walks are often several hours long. Many older people are still fascinated by the numbers of cars that go past on the autobahn, so they stop on bridges and watch the cars go by. Sometimes there will be 10 or 12 people just watching."
> "That's like when I used to watch the trains go by with my Grandfather."
> "Yeah. Just like that."

After that, I noticed lots of people standing on bridges, watching. Whenever I sat in the front seat, I would wave at them.

"Why don't they wave back, Heinrich?"
"I don't know. They're probably too shocked at the idea of someone noticing them to react in time."

I continued to wave, anyway.

"Remember last night when I told you to save your Strassenbahn ticket, John?"
"Yeah. I've got it right here."

A Strassenbahn ticket stub was about three inches square.

"Give it to me, and I'll teach you a little about German frugality. Germans always save their Strassenbahn tickets."
"What good are they?"
"When we go on particularly long walks, we use them as toilet paper, if we have to go in the woods."
"Get out of here, Heinrich."
"See, when we need to use one, we fold the ticket twice, like this, so it makes a little square. Then we tear off this corner where all the folds are. Don't lose this little corner: it's necessary later. Next we unfold the ticket. See, it has a little hole in the middle."
"Yeah, I see."
"Well, you stick your finger through that little hole, and then use that finger to clean up your butt."
"That's gross, Heinrich."
"Yeah, but if you're in the woods, you don't have much choice. Then when you're done, you use the piece of paper to wipe your finger with. See, it just kind of slides everything off like this."
"Yuch!"
"Then you just throw one little piece of paper away."

"OK, OK....But Heinrich, why do you save the little triangle of folded paper?"

"Well, you take it with the other hand, like this, and use it to clean out from under your fingernail!"

"Oh, man, that's really gross!"

"Yuch!"

"Perhaps. But it's quite effective."

To this day, I don't know if anyone other than Heinrich actually does that, or for that matter, if Heinrich actually does.

* * * * *

Berchtesgaden was the quintessential Bavarian town. Bill and Bob had attended the retreat the year before, and they acted as tour guides. Unfortunately, the majority of the spots of interest to them had something or another to do with beer. It was hard to miss the cable cars, though.

"Hey, look at the cable cars!"

"Yeah. Lots of the people who live up the mountain commute on the cable cars."

"Is that right? Wouldn't that be cool?"

"Well, they get pretty crowded in the afternoons when people are going home."

"Yeah, I guess that would hold true for any kind of public transportation, though. Will we get a chance to ride them?"

"Sure. There's plenty of free time. Actually, there's as much free time as you want."

"What do you mean by that?"

"Oh, they didn't really take attendance at any of the workshops that I went to."

"Oh....So you skipped some, huh?"

"Well...you could say that."

Actually, I was to find that he had skipped most all of them.
You could see the General Walker Hotel clinging to the side of the mountain. There was a lot of oohing and ahing on the way up. But the view from the terrace of the hotel was probably the best of all. Later in the week, when we met before breakfast, we would find ourselves looking down on the top of a cloud. The entire village would have disappeared in fog. From the terrace, all you could see was white—you couldn't tell where the fog left off and the mountain across the valley began. That first day, after we had registered and dropped our luggage in our rooms, we met on the terrace before going in to dinner.

> "Wow! The view is spectacular!.....Where's the Eagle's Nest?"
>
> "Oh, it's up there. You can't really see it from here. I should have pointed it out to you while we were down in the valley."
>
> "What's over the mountains?"
>
> "Well, down that valley is Salzburg, Austria. It's only a short drive. Around to the right is the Königsee—it's a glacier-fed lake. And if you follow the valley that way you'll come to Munich."
>
> "That's where they have the Oktoberfest, right?"
>
> "Well, yes and no. Oktoberfest is celebrated all over Germany. But that's where the breweries set up their tents, and the big festivities take place."
>
> "I'll bet that's a good time."
>
> "Yeah. Too bad you won't be here in October."

Heinrich added,

> "Way across the Königsee, John, is the St. Bartholomew Pilgrimage Church. You can only get there by walking, or in summer by taking a boat."
>
> "How do they get supplies in the winter?"

"They carry them in. Actually, they lay in what they think they are going to need for the winter before the weather gets bad."

"What if someone gets sick, or something?"

"Then, they are in trouble."

"Nice place to visit, but I wouldn't want to live there. Hey, can we tour the Eagle's Nest?"

"Not now. It's closed from late fall until spring."

"Shoot! That's too bad."

"Well, maybe on your next trip."

"If there is one...."

The dining room was immense, and crowded with guys (and a few women) from all over Europe and the Mediterranean theater of operations. That night we closed the Rathskeller. It seemed like half the conference attendees were in there!

There was a chapel service Sunday morning, then an introductory meeting where badges and schedules were passed out. You could sign up for a wide variety of lectures and activities. You were encouraged to leave blocks of time for sightseeing and other activities. We all tried to leave the same blocks open.

I attended all the Monday classes I had signed up for. But Tuesday at lunch, Bill said,

"Why don't you guys go rodelling with us this afternoon?"

"What's rodelling?"

"Well, a rodel is a little sled, about two feet long and a foot wide."

"I don't think I can get my butt on something that tiny!"

"Most people have some overhang! Anyhow, you sit on this little sled and slide down the mountain."

"Where? Is there a place, like ski trails or something?"

"Yeah. The Germans call it a Rodelbahn, right Heinrich?"

"Yes. Here they take some little backwoods roads that are basically impassable in the winter and set them aside just for rodelling. There are banked turns and everything."

"Like bobsleds?"

"Yeah. Like bobsleds. Only these little things don't go much faster than 40 or 50 miles per hour."

"Holy cow! When your butt is close to the ground as you're describing, 40 or 50 miles per hour must seem like 100!"

"That's about the way it feels to me. How about you, Heinrich?"

"Just about right."

"Well, sure. Let's give it a whirl."

We rented eight rodels from the hotel and drove to the Rodelbahn. It was just as they had described. The surface was hard-packed snow, about 10 feet wide in most places with excess snow pushed to the outside of the track as a barrier to keep you from going over the side. It turned out that in some of the places on the way down, the drops were 40 or 50 feet—eventually we fell down most of them anyway, at one time or another.

We drew straws to see who would drive the two cars down to meet the rest at the bottom. Later we set up a rotation, so that everyone got the same amount of rodel time.

"You sit on it like this, with your feet tucked behind the curve of the runner in front, see?"

"How do you steer?"

"If you want to turn right, you put your right heel down in front of you and the drag turns you to the right. Use your left foot to turn left."

"What about stopping?"

"To stop, you put both feet in front of you."

"And pray a lot."

"Yeah, and pray a lot. These things go like spit, but stopping is another thing entirely."

"That's for sure!"

Those of us in the first eight sat down and pushed off. I knew in seconds that I had found a new love! It was totally quiet on the Rodelbahn, except for the hissing of the runners on the snow—oh and the occasional scream as someone went off the path into the trees. We crashed a lot, at first, but later the crashes came less often—except for one particular turn. It was a sweeping left turn that wasn't banked correctly. You really had to work your speed down and stay on the inside to avoid going off the trail. And when you went off, you really went off. There was a large snow field running down the mountain, and you could end up 100 feet below the trail, if you went off too fast. There were also some large rocks in the snow field. I nearly found one the hard way the first time I went off there,

"EEEEYYYYAAAAHH!"
SPLAT!

I landed spread-eagled and face-down. When I rolled to my left to get up, I found that just under the smooth-looking snow was a boulder. It had been completely invisible as I sailed through the air. If I had landed two feet further to the left, I would have been in real trouble! We were all more careful around Dead Man's Curve from then on.

We laughed and screamed and carried on like a bunch of 10-year-olds all the way down. It was a great time! Then we piled into the two BMWs and headed back up to do it over again. And again and again and again. None of us could get enough. There were a couple of classes that I attended regularly that week, but much of the rest of the time was spent sitting on little sleds.

Once I had a great crash at Dead Man's Curve. While I was picking myself up I saw Pam Marriott fall, too. She didn't go over the bank, but her rodel continued on down the Rodelbahn without her. She was standing in the track watching the rodel going on without her, and we were joking about it as I climbed up the bank. Then out of the corner of my eye, I saw another rodel coming behind her,

"Look out behind you, Pam!"
"Where?"

She turned around to look, and a split second later, her husband ran right into her. He hit her right on the shins and she did a perfect flip, landing right on her rear end. Bill came flying through the air in my direction, just missing me. We climbed back up to the track. Pam was still sitting there, dazed.

"Geez, Pam! Are you all right?"
"I don't know. What happened?"
"I ran right into you, honey. Can you stand up?"
"I think so. Ow! My legs hurt!"
"They should! He hit you right in the shins—flipped you right over!"

Fortunately, nothing was broken. She had some neat bruises that evening, however. She and Bill managed to fit themselves on Bill's sled and they went down the Rodelbahn looking for Pam's rodel. They had to go all the way to the bottom! The rodel had been going slow enough that it managed to stay on the path all the way down! Usually they would only go a few hundred feet at most before stopping.

That same day, Neil Billingsley and Karen tried to make it all the way down on one rodel. They must have fallen off 10 or 12 times. I think they enjoyed the falling off more than the riding!

We even rodelled on Saturday. By the time Saturday night

came along, we were pretty exhausted! We all got together for the nightly *Closing of the Rat*. No one was up before 10:00 a.m.

After the closing ceremony on Sunday we piled back into the BMWs for the long ride back to Darmstadt. We couldn't catch a flight back to Turkey until Thursday, so Neil decided to take a train to Frankfurt and visit some people he knew there. Ron and I stayed in Darmstadt and did all the tourist things. Heinrich took us under his wing, drawing up a list of attractions that we just had to see. He also invited us to his home a couple of times where we met his parents as well as his lovely sister Marlena (about 17 years old) and his brother Ludwig (about 12).

One evening we were sitting in his living room talking with the family when he said,

> "Oh! I almost forgot! Come on up to my room. There's something you should see."

We hurried after him. He turned on his television set, and there on the screen was that champion of law and order, the Lone Ranger, speaking fluent German. As did Tonto and everyone else in the cast. Heinrich explained to us that American films and television shows were very popular throughout Europe. Some actors made their living lip-synching American shows in their native languages. Many, in fact, were celebrities in their own rights with their own fan clubs, newsletters, and the like. It was funny, later, to see Hoss Cartwright who seemed to have some trouble with English in the U.S. saying,

> "Guten morgen Papa. Was ist los?"

or the like. But now it was Clayton Moore's and Jay Silverheels's time to become bilingual. The show was almost over, and Heinrich said,

> "Now listen to this...."

Just then, the masked man's great white stallion, Silver, reared back on his hind legs, and with a flourish the Lone Ranger exclaimed,

"Hi yo Silber! Fart! Fart!"

Well, it took Ron and me a good while to pick ourselves up off the floor and stop laughing. We watched some other American favorites while we were there, but nothing caught us so off guard as that scene.

Before Neil went to Frankfurt, Heinrich organized a dinner for everyone at another one of his favorite restaurants. It was quite a long way out of town in a place called Nieder Bierbaum. The restaurant was a family operation. At least three generations were represented—mama served, children cleared tables, grandma cooked, and papa ran the cash register. The little road house was packed when we got there, but everyone seemed to know Heinrich.

They seated us at a large table and started bringing food. Although the main course was served individually, everything else was family style. Large bowls of salad, French fries, and bread never seemed to need filling, no matter how much we ate. At Heinrich's urging, most of us had Wiener Schnitzel. It was incredible! Rather than the pounded thin cutlets that I was used to, these were nearly an inch thick, and so tender that you didn't need a knife. As we were finishing up, our waitress (who must have been the mother) came up and asked us in broken English how we liked dinner. Everyone praised the food—except for Ron. She came next to him and said,

"Was Gut, yah?"
"Well...it was OK."
"OK? Was ist los, *OK*?"
"Well...there could have been more...."
"More?..."

Well you could have fooled me. I had eaten the same thing he ate, and could hardly move. Well, she looked at him, and slowly a smile came to her face,

"More! You good boy! You wait ein moment!"

She rushed back into the kitchen, and in a few minutes she returned with another schnitzel. Ron devoured it, in turn. Once again she appeared at his shoulder,

"Gut?"
"Well...."
"Hah hah hah!"

Smiling broadly, she almost tripped over herself getting Ron still another schnitzel. When he managed to finish that one off, she was there again,

"So?..."
"Wunderbar!"
"Ach, so! Gut boy! You eat gut!"

She gave him a big, motherly hug and went back into the kitchen praising him to the rest of the family. There was no extra charge for Ron's gluttony—except, perhaps, to his waistline!

The trip back to Ethiopia was dreadfully long—it seemed to take twice as long as the trip up—and terribly boring. And after the crisp, cold, clean air of Germany, the Ethiopian air took a lot of getting used to.

I was telling the story about the Lone Ranger shouting "Fahrt, Fahrt" when Evan Lowrey asked,

"Have you ever been to a movie in Asmara?"
"No."
"Well, if you think the German lip synching is something, you should go see one here. In fact, *The King and I* is playing downtown now. Why don't we go see it?"
"Well, OK."

Boy, was he right! *The King and I* was shown in English with subtitles in French and Arabic. On top of that, at each end of the stage was a little box with an Ethiopian holding cards with subtitles in two additional languages—Amharic and Tigrinie. Every now and then, one of the card holders would nod off, or get the wrong card, and the people who were depending on him would shout at him and, when necessary, throw things at him to wake him up. In addition, the subtitles I could read were hilarious. One line, in particular, nearly had me on the floor. The King assumes one of his notable poses and says something like, *I have magnificent visions in my mind about the future of my beloved country*. The French wasn't too bad, but the Arabic translation was *I have OK ideas in my head on my country*. Whatever poetry was in the original, never made it to the Arabic-speaking viewers. With translations like that, it's no wonder people have trouble understanding one another.

MARK WILKINS

It was about this time that I got to know Mark Wilkins. He worked mids, so we only met in passing, but he turned out to be my best friend. Mark is about five feet eight. He spent all the time he could outdoors, often driving to Masawa over weekends. As a result, he was in good shape and always darkly tanned. He wore thick, round glasses and a mustache that kept him in trouble. The Army allowed mustaches only if they did not extend past the edges of the mouth or past the top line of the lips. Mark's constantly extended past everything. Working on mids, he got away with a lot, but at least once a month or so someone would give him a hard time about his mustache or the fact that his hair was growing over his collar. The hassles never seemed to affect him, though. He nodded his head as though he were actually listening to what his current inquisitor was saying.

> "You're right, Sergeant Farnsworth. I guess my hair is getting long. I hadn't noticed. I'll get it trimmed right away."

Of course, *right away* might mean most anything to Wally. Wally had been his name at Monterey when he was taking Arabic. We picked up on the name because it reminded us of *Leave It to Beaver*—as in the Beaver's older brother. From then on he was Wally to us.

Wally was and is the most deliberate person I've ever known. Nothing he did was without ritual. He smoked a lot—always Camels—and when he had finished one, he flicked off the ash and carefully tore the paper, spilling the unused tobacco on the ground. The rolled-up paper went in his left front pants pocket for later disposal. This particular ritual he adopted from Army training (Field-stripping your butts, remember?), but others were uniquely his own.

Everything he did seemed to be in slow motion, as though he were continuously performing some elaborate, lifelong Tai Chi ritual. To watch Wally prepare and then drink a cup of coffee requires a considerable amount of patience as well as restraint. It never did any good to try to hurry him along. Anything worth doing was worth doing well—if not to say meticulously.

Like many guys in Ethiopia, Wally decided to buy a motorcycle. Cars were expensive to keep running and parking on post was scarce. If you didn't want to have to depend on garry carts or other public transportation, a motorcycle was a good choice. Wally thoroughly researched the field, and decided to buy the best. The best available in Ethiopia in 1969 was a BMW. And not just any BMW, of course, but the biggest BMW motorcycle. This was a monstrous machine. It must have weighed three hundred pounds. A masterpiece of Teutonic engineering, it made lovely mechanical noises when it was moving. Even standing still, it had a glowering, brutish aspect that engendered respect, or downright awe. But the minute Wally mounted up, it took on a new aspect. Looking like a pimple on the back of a rhinoceros, Wally imbued this rortling, snortling machine with a comic grandeur worthy of Ringling Brothers, Barnum and Baily. He shepherded the beast with the care and diligence one might bestow on an old, favorite horse—one that might collapse if not treated just right. And of course, if this particular beast ever did lie down, there wasn't much hope of Wally standing it up again. It would have taken two people, I think, to pick up that big BMW.

Mark was one of the organizers of the more-or-less unorganized softball games that happened occasionally on post. With no rhyme or reason, we would find ourselves on the dusty playing field engaged in something that somewhat resembled baseball—and the resemblance deteriorated as the innings progressed. The principle reason for that deterioration was, you might have guessed it, beer. It was an unwritten and unspoken rule that all the players should consume as much beer as humanly possible during the course of a game. If someone managed to get on base, one of his teammates would hustle out to him, and bring him his beer. Did it hamper base running? Well I suppose it did, but not nearly as much as it impeded whatever fielding work was happening. It's definitely difficult to catch a ball with one hand, and throw it with another while you're holding a beer in still another hand. The soberest people on the field were the pitchers and catchers. And that wasn't for lack of trying. It was a good thing that we played with those soccer-sized softballs, or no one would ever have had a hit. I'm sure there were winners and losers, but I can't for the life of me remember which I was, or for that matter, how many games I played in. But as someone wiser than I once said, "It matters not who won or lost but how (or maybe in our case, *if*) you played the game."

TALENT CONTEST

Paul Sealey was one of the Special Services people on post. When I found out there was a Service Club on post, I was surprised. For some reason I had thought it was for the dependents only. When I finally walked in to see what was there, Paul introduced himself. He was a heavyset guy with straight black hair that he was constantly pushing up out of his eyes, and a round face that would have been cherubic, if it hadn't been for his eyes. He always looked somewhat somber, as though he were privy to some deep, dark secrets that he was on the verge of sharing. He had a deep, rich baritone voice and used it as though he had been trained. And trained he had been. He had studied theater in college and acted in community projects as well as some professional jobs. He had just been in Ethiopia for a couple of days, and was excited about all the things he wanted to do. There hadn't been much in the way of theater at Kagnew Station, and he wanted to get something going on post as quickly as possible.

It didn't take much to recruit me. We talked about the resources available and discussed possibilities. We decided to try to perform *You Know I Can't Hear You When the Water's Running* in December. I volunteered to help with lights and sets, as well as doing two of the parts. The play consists of four one-act playlets. I would be in two of them. While we were talking, he said,

"Hey, do you want to go to Athens? There's a talent contest there next month. I've got a couple of other people who are interested."

"Sure! I may have some trouble getting permission,

though. I've had a permissive TDY trip already, since I've been here. It might be kind of tough."

"No problem. Once you've passed the audition, my boss will push it through. Do you know anyone else who might be interested?"

"Who've you got so far?"

I was surprised to find that the only person I knew in his list was Mark Wilkins.

"Accordion?! I didn't know Wally played the accordion?"

"Wally?"

We talked some more, and I auditioned *a capella* for his boss, who declared I would be going along. On the way back to the barracks I ran into Terry Dolan and told him about the upcoming trip.

"I'm going, too!"

"Great! What are you going to do?"

"I don't know....Let me think....I know! I'll do a tumbling routine. No! Better! I'll do a trampoline routine!"

"Uh...I don't know if there is a trampoline on post."

"Exactly!"

"Huh?"

"That way, I won't have to do an audition. They'll have to take my word for it!"

"Well....Yeah....I guess they will."

And they did! Terry was accepted on the strength of his promise that he would do a socko routine on the trampoline. And Paul's boss was true to her word. My boss agreed to let me go. I couldn't believe my luck. This would be my second trip out of country in as many months. And I would finally get to see more of Athens. I kept trying not to remember the long rides in the MAC C-141s that went along with the trip.

Three guys from the Navy Security Group were going along with Paul, Wally, Terry Dolan, Ian McDowell, and me. Travel plans were somewhat tentative due to the fact that the contest date had been rescheduled twice already. But at last, the day arrived. We trundled aboard the C-141 and strapped ourselves into the nylon webbing seats. As usual, I managed to get one that had an aluminum support right underneath my tail bone. These supports ran fore and aft connecting the front and rear longitudinal supports. Every air pocket reminded me that it was there. It's too bad they didn't hand out Purple Hearts for bruised tail bones.

We arrived in Adana, Turkey, and Terry Dolan, nominally in charge, was told to check in with the Base Services Club. He came back a half hour later, fuming.

"I can't believe it! They told me that the talent contest has been called off, and we have to go back."

"What?!"

"No!"

"What'd you say, Terry?"

"I demanded that they connect me with the Services Club in Athens where the thing was supposed to be held. After a lot of farting around, I finally talked to some Airman there. He told me that the guy here was wrong—the talent contest was held last month!"

"Huh?"

"Last month?!"

"What the hell's going on?"

"Well **I** told **him** that we're coming there anyway!"

"All right!"

"Yeah. I'm going to see if we can't compete there for the next level of competition. It's supposed to happen in Frankfurt next month. Isn't that what you heard, Paul?"

"Yeah. But then, the scheduling for this thing has been so messed up, I don't know what to think any more."

"Whatever. All I know is we're getting on the 1:45 flight to Athens."

The Turkish Courier brought us to Athens in considerably more comfort than we had experienced coming to Adana. By the time we arrived, it was too late to do anything other than check in to the hotel and have dinner.

The next day we all trooped down to the Services Club. Terry and Paul and the Club director went into her office to determine our fate. A half hour later they rejoined us.

"Well, guys, we've got some good news and some bad news."

"Bad news first, Terry."

"Well, there won't be any competition for us."

"Oh, great."

"What's the good news?"

"We've got seven days in Athens with nothing to do but enjoy ourselves."

"Yeah! Great!"

"You mean, we don't have to go right back?"

"Nope. The next Turkish Courier to Adana is not until next week, and I don't want to drive there, do you?"

The answer to that was unanimous. So we started planning our week. The three squids (Navy guys) wanted nothing more than to find all the bars in Athens. Paul and I left immediately for the Acropolis. We wanted to do all the tourist things first, just in case the Army changed its mind and found a way to get us out of Athens sooner. Wally and Terry went in a different direction, but the four of us promised to meet that evening to discuss the adventures of the day.

It took Paul and me three days to see the remains of ancient Athens. Between the crystal blue of the Aegean Sea, the pearlescent blue of the sky, and the vistas of cool, pale marble, Athens is a visual intoxication. Wally and Terry, meanwhile, were busy discovering modern Greece. While Paul and I had walked practically everywhere we went, Terry and Wally had rented mopeds to get around. We thought that would be a great plan for an excursion up the coast. It turned out that though the little mopeds were sufficient in the city, they were easily winded on some of the hills we encountered. Nonetheless, we spent a wonderful day following whatever hugged the coast north of Athens. Unlike Germany where at least half of the people you met knew some English, hardly anyone outside of Athens spoke any English. We managed just fine with pantomime and what few Greek words we had picked up. It was a marvelous adventure. I was going through film so fast that I'm certain Kodak stock must have skyrocketed.

At that night's get together with Wally and Terry I said,

"You were right. The mopeds were just the ticket. We only had two problems. They aren't much good on the steep hills, and the crazy local drivers don't seem to see you when you're on one. We've both been nearly killed several times today."

"Yeah. The hills are tough, but Terry and I have discovered a cure for the invisibility problem."

"Share."

"Well, whenever we see someone who's about to merge into us, we scream at the top of our lungs as though we're being tortured."

"Like this,"

And with that, Terry let out a truly terrifying scream.

"You didn't have to demonstrate. It'll be a wonder if we don't have the cops in here."

"Maybe. But it really works on the road."

"Yeah. The cars part in front of you like the Red Sea for Moses."

"We'll have to try that tomorrow."

And they were right. Whenever our doom looked imminent, we hollered like the world was coming to an end. And sure enough, the drivers moved away from us like we were lepers. Of course, by the end of the week we were so hoarse we could hardly talk.

On Tuesday night the three squids came to Terry and told him that, since there was a flight the next day, they were going to Adana then in hopes of getting an earlier flight back to Asmara.

"What's the matter, fellows, don't you like Athens?"

"Yeah. It's OK. But it's our duty to get back as soon as we can."

"Duty, shmooty. I've got news for you guys. There won't be a flight back to Asmara until Saturday."

"How do you know?"

"I've been through Adana twice already, and I can guarantee you they only fly to Asmara on Tuesdays and Saturdays. You've already missed today's flight."

"Wouldn't you sooner spend those days in Athens."

"I say we should get back."

"And I'm in charge here, remember? I say we go back to Adana Friday and catch the Saturday flight."

"Well, we're going tomorrow. And we're going to report you."

"For what? Having brains?"

"You'll see, Dolan. You're going to be in big trouble."

"You can go back whenever you want. But if you want to talk trouble, I'll tell you this: if you don't get the hell out of my room, I'm going to move your mouth around to the back of your head."

"Oh, yeah?"

Well, a closer look at Terry's face convinced them that it would probably be a good idea to pack their bags. Sure enough, they got on the Wednesday morning puddle jumper to Adana. The rest of us enjoyed two more days in beautiful Athens. When we arrived in Adana, we found them in the Enlisted Men's Club. They wore surly expressions that were a mixture of the effects of alcohol and boredom. They had gone downtown both nights to sample the local prostitutes. They had spent most of their money there, and to add insult to injury, we learned later all three of them had picked up the clap. We felt they had deserved it.

The flight back to Asmara took an unexpected turn when, due to a problem at the Asmara airport, we were forced to land in Addis Ababa and spend the night there. Things suddenly got very interesting. Most of us had planned to come back to Asmara essentially penniless. So we didn't know what to do in Addis. I had about two dollars, and I had more money than anyone except Wally. He had fifty dollars left, and was kind enough to give Paul, Dolan and me a couple of dollars each. He and Terry went downtown. After asking the airline representatives for permission, the rest of us determined to sleep in the airport. This promised some security, although not a lot of comfort.

Paul and I went to the airport restaurant to see if we could get something to eat for the little money we had. We just had enough to buy a plate of pasta and something to drink. The waiter first brought a basket of bread.

> "Hey, I'm going to stash some of these rolls away for breakfast tomorrow."
>
> "That's a great idea, Paul! Let's eat one each, and stash one each. Then we can ask the waiter for more."

We ended up with four rolls each hidden away in our luggage when we left. I felt like a criminal. By the time we left, the restaurant was closing for the night. So was the airport.

Because it was a strategic resource, the airport was guarded by a number of Ethiopian soldiers with carbines at the ready. They were somewhat bemused, I think, to see a bunch of Americans trying to get comfortable on airport furniture. Ian McDowell was a terrific guitarist. He played for a while. The guards relaxed and became more friendly. Between them they knew some English and some Arabic, so with the little Amharic we had, we conversed after a fashion. This was considered pretty easy duty for them, and they enjoyed talking with us and listening to the music. Eventually, we managed to get some sleep.

In the morning, Paul and I shared our meager ration of rolls. By now, they were pretty stale, but everyone was hungry—and broke!

About an hour before the plane was due to leave for Asmara, Wally and Terry showed up. They had made some friends downtown who took them home, fed them, and entertained them, and set them up in the guest bedroom. The rest of us felt even more uncomfortable from the effects of the Addis Ababa Airport accommodations.

When we finally got back to Asmara, everyone went directly to the barracks to get whatever money we had left. Then we headed to the club to eat. After dinner everyone agreed it had been a terrific trip, whether or not we actually got to compete!

RE-QUALIFYING

"Hey, John! Wait up!"

"Where've you been, Dick? I thought you had already gone to breakfast."

"No. I was over at the Orderly Room. Have you seen the notice?"

"Uh oh...what is it this time?"

"We have to re-qualify Saturday."

"Saturday? Oh, come on. Can't they give us a week day to shoot their precious guns?"

"Rifles, John, rifles. Remember? And they can't spare us from our super-important security work. After all, you know that the fate of the Western world lies in our hands."

"Yeah...yeah, I know. But I didn't know we had any quantity of rifles here."

"Have you forgotten the parachuting rumor?"

During the last flare up of hostilities in the Arab-Israeli war a rumor had circulated that all of us linguists would be issued rifles and radios and parachuted into the various Arabic countries to provide intelligence for the Army.

"I never bought into that, Dick. You know they couldn't afford for us to be picked up and interrogated. After all, we have all this vital, secret intelligence information between our ears. If they're so afraid of us being interrogated that they won't let us visit Arabic countries as tourists, you can bet that they won't try to use us as spies. And besides, how long do you think that any of us could pass for Arabs?"

"You know I agree with you. But there are, nonetheless, scads of M14s in a warehouse in case we ever have to defend the post. At any rate, we have to form up at 07:30 Saturday."

"Well, at least we'll get it out of the way early."

Saturday morning we were bused out to the firing range where a truck full of weapons and ammunition awaited us. Out in front of us were foxholes, and way out beyond them there was a ridge about three feet high. Above the ridge we could see the targets on wooden frames. The white paper bull's eyes shone in the morning sun. There must have been 50 of them, standing all in a row.

After the usual briefing (Why do they call them *brief*ings? In the Army it would be more appropriate to call them *long*ings.), we were divided into two groups. The other group was marched out behind the ridge to move the targets.

We fired standing, kneeling, prone, and from the foxholes. By the time we were finished, it was 10:00 or so, and the Army stopped for a smoke break. Then it was our turn to man the targets.

When we reached the target area, we found that there was a trough cut out behind the ridge, affording a place where you could walk upright and still be a foot or so beneath the top of the ridge. It was cut out a little into the ridge so that there was a slight ridge of earth above your head. The targets were on ancient metal and wood frames set about six feet behind this earthen sanctuary. When the other troops were just about ready to begin firing, the sergeant, down at the end of the trough, told us to kneel down facing the dirt. As soon as the firing started, the wisdom of his counsel became immediately apparent. It seemed like half of the bullets must have missed the paper targets, because we could hear splinters and shrapnel flying around behind us. I tried to crawl into my helmet, but just couldn't quite make it.

Incredibly, Sergeant Abrams called out,

> "Positions three through nine and 14 through 32, clear your targets!"

I say "incredibly" because the other positions were still firing. I was in position nine, and I didn't budge.

> "Position nine, clear your target!"
> "As soon as the firing stops, Sergeant!"

I hollered back.

> "Didn't you hear me, Specialist? I said to clear your target!"
> "If you want it cleared this minute, Sergeant, you'll have to do it yourself!"

I noticed that he waited until everyone had stopped firing before he came storming down to chew me out.

> "Who the hell do you think you are, Specialist? I told you to clear that target!"
> "I'll be glad to, now, Sergeant."
> "Why didn't you do it when you were told?"
> "I didn't see you standing in the middle of all the shit that was flying around, Sergeant."
> "You didn't answer my question, Specialist!"
> "I don't think your question is worthy of an answer, Sergeant."
> "I'm putting you on report!"
> "You do that!"

As soon as we got back to the buses, Sergeant Abrams went over to Lt. Graham and started ranting and raving. Eventually, Graham called me over,

"Did you refuse a direct order, Leeger?"

"Not at all, Lieutenant, I just thought it wise to wait until I was certain I wouldn't lose an eye...or my life."

"Damn it, Leeger, that's disobeying a direct order!"

"Sir, have you been out there when people are firing?"

"No...."

"Well, Sir, I'm sure you wouldn't want to have to write a casualty report because of a Sergeant's excessive zeal during some Mickey Mouse training exercise. If our task at the Sites is really as important as everyone constantly tells us, this is not only a waste of time, but it also poses an unnecessary risk to valuable personnel. If you really want to throw the book at me, I guess you can, but I think you'll be making a mistake."

You could see the wheels turning in his head, but having watched Nancy Johnson face him down, I didn't think Graham had much of a stomach for direct confrontation. Fortunately, I was right about him. Less than happy, Sergeant Abrams went back to his MP unit, and I never saw him again. I still had my Expert Marksman badge—and both my eyes.

PROMOTION

Shortly after I returned, Sergeant Farnsworth, Thornton's boss, took me aside,

"Thornton is rotating back Stateside. How'd you like to run the Saudi section?"

"Oh. Well, sure. That'd be great!"

"Good. We'll cut your orders today."

"I need orders for this?"

"Well, we have to make you a Spec 5, if you're going to run a section."

"Well, that's even better yet!"

"Yeah, I thought you'd like that part."

The extra money was nice, but with it came the inevitable responsibility. And as Thornton had not kept up with the reporting, I was actually faced with a tough decision. I could either leave things screwed up and hope that nothing big happened in the Middle East for the next year or so, or I could work my tail off getting things straightened out.

I chose the latter course, and set myself up for a lot of extra work. For the next several weeks I submitted report after report putting things right. I think Mr. Smith, the Warrant Officer in charge, and Sergeant Farnsworth, probably had second thoughts about me before it was all done. Even Colonel Monroe, the officer in charge of the site, was involved in some of the work. We had weekly, if not daily, communications with DIA, CIA, NSA, ASA, and several of the other mysterious collections of letters that make up our nation's security apparatus. Some of the reports my section had been using were so far out of date that they had to be scrapped, and others had to be modified to accurately reflect the situation in Saudi Arabia. But eventually, it was all right, and I felt I could take it a good bit easier, while still keeping on top of things.

One morning, some months later, I was sitting at my desk scanning the morning radio traffic. My technique was probably not Army-approved. I would pull out the little shelf at the top left of my desk, put my feet up there, stack the multi-fold sheets on my lap, and lean back while filling out the forms on my desk. I was engrossed in my work this particular morning when suddenly an arm was thrust in front of me. It ended in a finger that began thumping on the report I was filling in.

"That data doesn't go there, Specialist. It goes here!"

I looked to my left. There stood a brand new Second Lieutenant who turned out to be a recent graduate of that epitome of oxymorons, Military Intelligence School.

"Uh...What did you say, Lieutenant?"

"I said that data doesn't go there, it goes here!"

"Oh...Ordinarily you would be right, Lieutenant, but for this project only, the report has been modified, and the data goes here."

"Don't argue with me, Specialist, I'm telling you that data goes there!"

"Look, Lieutenant, I've had this report modified for Saudi Arabian reporting. You can ask Mr. Smith, the Warrant Officer over there. I've had this cleared with NSA, ASA, CIA, and DIA, and for this project, the data goes there."

"Don't argue with me, Specialist. I'm a Lieutenant!"

Well, the logic behind that just took my breath away. So I replied,

"Well screw, Lieutenant."
"WHAT DID YOU SAY?"
"I said, *Screw, Lieutenant!*"

He was stunned. He stood stock still for a minute. Then he read my name tag carefully, turned on his heel, and stormed over to where Mr. Smith and Sergeant Farnsworth were sitting.

"Mr. Smith! Mr. Smith! Specialist Leeger just told me to screw!"

Now there were about 25 people working in that big room, but at that instant, all you could hear was the cover music outside. Everyone had stopped typing, talking, or doing anything else. Eventually Mr. Smith broke the silence,

"Leeger?"
"Yeah, Mr. Smith?"
"Did you tell this Lieutenant to screw?"

I leaned further back in my chair and looked around the partition to make certain we were talking about the same lieutenant.

"Uh, yeah. I sure did Mr. Smith."

There was another of those nerveless silences. Then Mr. Smith quietly said,

"Well...then...screw, Lieutenant."

Pandemonium erupted. The enlisted personnel all applauded, whistled, and yelled. And the lieutenant—well he looked like a thermometer that had just been rapidly overheated—you could literally see the color go all the way up from his collar to the top of his head. I half expected to see smoke come out of his ears like a cartoon character. He stammered and stuttered, and finally stormed out of the room.

Eventually the room quieted down, and people went back to work. A few minutes later a Private came up to me and said,

> "Uh...Specialist Leeger?"
> "Yeah?"
> "The Colonel wants to see you."

Well, I certainly wasn't surprised. I walked down to his office, and just as I arrived there, Mr. Smith came out the door.

> "You, too?"
> "Yeah. Go right in, he's expecting you."
> "I'm sure...."

Now a soldier is supposed to knock first, wait for an invitation to enter, step smartly to in front of the officer's desk, snap to attention, salute, and say something like,

> "Specialist Leeger reporting, **SIR!**"

Then you're supposed to freeze until the officer returns your salute. In the Army Security Agency, things were a bit more lax. I opened the door, walked up to his desk, and said,

> "Did you want to see me, Colonel?"

He looked kind of tired when he turned his eyes up to me,

> "Yeah. Leeger? Did you tell that Lieutenant to screw?"
> "I sure did, Sir!"

He looked a little pained, now,

> "Why did you do that, Leeger?"
>
> "Well, he was telling me how to do my business, Sir. And I already know how to do my business....And you know I know how to do my business."

He sighed,

> "Yes, I know it, and you know it...And now the Lieutenant knows it, too, and he won't bother you any more. But in the future, please don't tell my lieutenants to screw."
>
> "OK, Colonel. Anything else?"
>
> "No. Get back to work."
>
> "Thanks, Colonel."

I want you to know, that Lieutenant never even looked at me for the rest of time he was in Ethiopia. But he didn't just make a fool out of himself once, that day. In fact, he came straight from the Colonel's office to the little room where the duty officers worked. As he was walking in, a couple of enlisted men were setting up his desk. Now this wasn't the biggest office in the world, and there were already desks for the Captain and First Lieutenant on the two available walls. The other two walls had doors in them. So the enlisted men were putting the new desk in front of the square pillar that stood in the middle of the office.

> "Here's your desk, Lieutenant."
>
> "What?...No! I am not going to spend the next year and a half staring at the side of a stupid pillar, goddamn it! I'm going on break! And when I get back, I do not want my desk facing this side of this stupid pillar! DO YOU UNDERSTAND?!"
>
> "Uh...yes, Sir."

He stormed out of the room. The enlisted men looked at each other. Then they looked around the room. There was just no other place for a desk in the room. The other officers were already on break, so they got no help from them. Then, in a moment of sheer inspiration, they rotated the desk around so it was facing a different side of the pillar. From then on, whenever that lieutenant was out of the office, the desk was rotated another ninety degrees. The Lieutenant fumed, but never said another word about his desk.

He only lasted about two weeks. Then he transferred to Vietnam. I understand some officers who endangered their own troops over there were fragged (killed by their own men). I wouldn't be surprised if he made the list.

JOHANNESUE

Back then, Ethiopians enjoyed (?) one of the poorest standards of living on the planet. For many families, prostitution was the only way to rise above the multitude. Brothels were abundant. We had heard about one of them back in Language School. The proprietress was called Mama K. All the garry cart drivers knew her establishment by her name. She must have been pretty well off by Ethiopian standards.

One of the guys really made an impression on her. His name was L.T. Hartman, and he was quite a character. Whatever his charms may have been, they were sufficient to cause her to fall in love with him. No one called her anything but Mama, or Mama K. Whenever he went down there, however, instead of banging on the iron gate, he would call out softly,

"Katerina...Katerina...Your L.T. is here."

She must have waited for him by the window, because she would come at a run, squealing,

"L.T.! L.T.! Your Katerina is so happy to see you!"

He must have promised her the moon. When he finally left for the States, those of us who had gone down to the airport to see him off were surprised to see Mama K and several of her girls sitting in the waiting room. As he walked across the tarmac to the waiting 707, she called,

"L.T.! L.T.! See you after several monthes!"

The girls ululated[7] and waved for all they were worth. Although you will hear about him later in this book, I never found out exactly what promises he had made to her.

The Oasis Club (for enlisted men) held dances every Saturday night. They would send a bus down town to pick up some young ahtees[8] for the dance. The girls liked being in a place that for them was very sophisticated, and of course, it did wonders for their business. The bus was called the cattle truck, and sometimes it had to make two or three trips down town to find enough girls to go around. The American wives were not too pleased to find themselves in such company, and most of them, and of course their husbands, avoided the dances.

There was an ongoing competition to see who could *get jumped* (have sex) for the least expense. Mark Wilkins won this one by getting one of the girls to take him for the night for 10 cents in chits at the Oasis Club and a burned out light bulb. I couldn't imagine anything cheaper than that. She might have thought that the light bulb was good, but she should have known that only enlisted men were allowed to redeem chits at the club.

One night, a bunch of us talked Winston Cassidy into losing his virginity. Now everybody liked Winston. He was quiet, studious, and very shy. He had a high forehead and wore the original Coke bottle lens glasses. He always looked slightly surprised.

"Hey, Winston, do you want to go get jumped tonight?"

"Oh...I don't know...."

"C'mon, Winston. What's a tour in Ethiopia if you don't get jumped at least once?"

"Well...I don't know...."

"You've already said that. C'mon. Go with us and see if you see something you like."

"Well..."

"Don't say you don't know again, Winston."

"Well...OK...."

So we were off. We went to a bar that one of the guys recommended. There were half a dozen girls there. We bought them drinks and made idiotic small talk while deciding who wanted whom. Everyone waited until Winston had been talking with the same girl for a while. He was actually beginning to tell her about his father's dentistry practice when George Carpenter said,

"OK, girls, let's do a little boom boom!"

We started out but Winston was lingering.

"C'mon, Winston!"

The girl he was with timidly grabbed his hand and led him, like a lamb to the slaughter, out the door. The girl I was with was called Johannesue. She and Winston's girl worked out of the same place. They led us around the corner to the gateway at a large courtyard. There we haggled for price. Eventually we settled on amounts and went to the gate to enter.

It was locked. Neither of the girls had keys, but the houseboy was supposed to come when they called. Well, they called and called. They rattled the gate. They fairly shrieked. But no houseboy. Finally Winston, the gallant, volunteered to climb the gate and open it from the inside. Up and over he went, but as he jumped down, his sleeve snagged on one of the points at the top of the gate. His jacket was torn, but he was unscathed. His girl cooed and made a great deal of him. Winston fell in love.

He mooned about her and went to see her for weeks—as often as he could afford her. In the end, his passion for her cooled, and we could stop worrying about him.

I found my single experience degrading and completely unsatisfying. Most of the population in Ethiopia was Coptic Christian and practiced female circumcision. In this ritual the sensitive parts of a girl's genitals are removed, forever denying them any pleasure in the sexual act. Johannesue had definitely been mutilated according to this practice. She may as well have been having a manicure, for as much as she showed any reaction to what I was doing. Every once in a while after the first few minutes she would say,

"Finito, GI? Finito?"

I kept at it as long as I could, determined to get some reaction from her. But it was in vain.

Probably all prostitutes share the same boredom, but I was certain her response was caused by the rite. At any rate, between that and the ignominy of haggling for price, I was so put off that I was never again tempted to engage the services of any prostitute.

* * * * *

In my capacity as Protestant Chapel Organist I played at several weddings. All were young American men marrying Ethiopian women, most of whom I suspect were prostitutes. These girls were invariably pretty, but I shuddered to think of the reception the couples got when they returned Stateside. Though a couple of the guys were black, several were white. In the sixties, acceptance of mixed-race marriage was considerably poorer than it is today, and a couple of these young men were from the deep South. I had visions of these fellows from Alabama and Mississippi taking their new wives home to meet Mom and Dad.

At any rate, the girls had fulfilled their dreams. Most of them had been supporting families in the countryside. Now they would be able to continue to do so, while moving into a life style they could barely imagine. I added my prayers for them to the Chaplain's.

BEGGARS

Some Ethiopians resorted to begging to eat. We were told never to give beggars anything—that it would just encourage the practice. Some of the children, however, were so irresistible it was very difficult not to give in. Occasionally they would come up with something really original. Most asked for some small change, but one little imp stopped me in my tracks,

> "Hey, GI! You give me fi' dolla'!"
> "Five dollars?"
> "Yeah! You give me fi' dolla', GI—American!"
> "What makes you so special, ahtah[9]?"
> "I **good** ahtah. You right, GI! I need fi' dolla'. You give me. OK?"

Well, that was so outrageous I gave him five dollars—Ethiopian! We were routinely offered various types of boom boom,

> "You want jump my sister? She virgin!"
> "Hey, GI! Look there, inna door! You want boom boom? All night, only ten dollar!"
> "You want little ahtee, GI? I know good one. You come with me."

But best of all was,

> "Hey, you want boom boom my mama? She virgin!"

And there were always things to sell. All kinds of street boys, as the vendors were called, had souvenirs of one kind or another. Miniature shields and swords were big items, as were monkey skins, and all sorts of unidentifiable items. I believe you could have bought relics from King Solomon, if you had been dumb enough to ask.

Sadly, people were driven to such extremes that some women broke the limbs of newborn or little children and let them set improperly to improve their begging value. You could find people who were horribly malformed on many streets. I don't know how they survived—everyone I knew steadfastly refused to give those people anything for fear of encouraging that practice.

One day, Ron Hartwell, George Carpenter, and I took a table on the sidewalk at a café and ordered cappuccino. We intended to spend some time carefully ogling the caffolattis who passed by there regularly. A peddler approached us bearing the usual miniature shields and swords. As he passed the other tables offering his wares, he was ignored. Then he came to us.

"Hey, GI. You want buy shield, sword?"

"No."

"No."

"How much?"

"Carpenter! Don't encourage him! He'll never leave us alone!"

"Hey. For you, GI, shield $40.00, sword $20.00. I give you both—only $50.00."

"That seems a bit high to me."

"For crying out loud, George, shut up!"

"No, wait. I tell you what. I'll give you $5.00."

"Wahna Allah abu[10]! You crazy, GI! This good stuff! $50.00! Good price!"

"No. I think $5.00 is fair."

Well, I want you to know, despite our entreaties, George kept talking to this street boy. Actually boy was a relative term. This guy was familiar to nearly everyone. In fact, he was called the oldest street boy in Asmara, with some little affection. He was diligent, and seemed to be everywhere. But today he had met his match. George would not budge from his five dollar price. The Ethiopian gradually lowered his price, becoming more and more belligerent. The other patrons of the café started to stare at us in bewilderment, and eventually, all the tables near us were deserted.

Still, George kept goading the poor fellow. At last, having lost any control in the desire to make a sale, he fairly shrieked at George,

>"OK! OK! I give you for five dollars!!"
>
>"Five dollars for everything you have."
>
>"What?!?! You CRAZY, GI! No! NO! Everything, one hundred dollars!"
>
>"Five dollars for everything. That's my offer."

I thought the poor guy was going to have a stroke. Little drops of spit flew about while he raged, brandishing a shield and two swords in George's face. The bargaining continued apace. George was the image of serenity as he carefully drove the street boy to the brink. After another long session with George refusing to budge from his position, the street boy lost it again,

> "OK! OK! I GIVE YOU EVERYTHING!
> # FIVE DOLLARS!"

There was total silence. Even the street boy stood, frozen, knowing that he was making the most ridiculous deal ever, but determined to sell **something** to this crazy American. It seemed that even the traffic had paused to see what would happen. Then, into the unbearable silence, George quietly said,

> "Yes. Everything for five dollars…Ethiopian."

That did it. The street boy's eyes nearly achieved orbit. The veins standing out on his forehead would have made Clint Eastwood proud. At last he found his voice,

"YOU CRAZY, GI! YOU CRAZY, AMERICAN! FIVE DOLLARS?!?! NO! NO! WAHNA ALLAH ABU!!! AAAAAAIIIIIEEEEE!!!"

He ran screaming down the street, dropping some of his treasures as he went. Every few steps he would turn and scream some curse at us. He made all sorts of evil signs in our direction. We laughed until we ached. Every time any of us saw him after that, he would cross to the other side of the street and scream curses at us. But he continued to peddle his wares.

L.T. HARTMAN

L.T. worked the midnight shift when things were pretty strange at the site. If discipline was a bit lax during normal working hours, there wasn't much discipline at all for the skeleton crew that worked after midnight. No analysis was done at night, unless some sort of crisis was on, but people still talked on radios, and we still eavesdropped. As messages were intercepted by the ditty boppers, the resultant traffic was delivered to the long room called the bowling alley. There it was stripped of its carbons. Then the original and four copies were distributed for the analysts to work on during the day. By the time the days shift arrived, there was usually a considerable stack of stuff to be digested.

There was a lot of slack time for the middies, and they put it to good use. One of the favorite pastimes was swivel chair racing. We had these big, gray, metal arm chairs with rollers that were just made for competition. The middies made it a bit more interesting by having two-man teams. One of the guys, generally the shorter, would tilt the chair back, and lie down across it. His team mate would grab his legs and push this teetering contraption head first around the obstacle course that had been laid out for the evening. The horizontal member of the team was not completely inactive—his hands were kept busy fending off things that might cause cranial trauma and other undesirable side effects.

Paper airplanes were another big attraction. Many a forest was leveled to provide material for the budding aeronautical geniuses who worked the odd hours. Sometimes the trash cans were so full first thing in the morning that we had to improvise additional storage space from boxes or empty desk drawers. Although I don't know it for a fact, I would bet that the hang gliding industry employs some of the old Tract C air foil innovators.

But when it came to weird midnight pursuits, L.T. outdid everyone one fateful night. When I arrived early in the morning, he pounced on me,

"Hey, John! You'll never guess what I've been doing."

"You're probably right, L.T., what was it last night?"

"I've been compiling statistics about Asmara."

"Statistics?"

"Yeah. Consider this—Americans have been here since 1952, right?"

"I think that's right...."

"And during that time, the number of single GIs in Asmara has averaged 1,200 each year."

"If you say so, L.T."

"Now, assuming that of those 1,200 guys, an average of a bit less than half, say 500, get jumped once a week. That means that GIs got screwed about 26,000 times each year."

"Do I want to hear more of this, L.T.?"

"Now if we figure that each of these acts requires an average of 300 strokes, and that the average erect penis is six inches in length, and that the average stroke is five inches in each direction—we don't want any fallout now, do we?"

"No. Of course not."

"Then, each time a GI has gotten screwed in Asmara, he has moved his penis back and forth about 3,000 inches, or 250 feet."

"Oh, brother...."

"This means that, since we opened this station, 6,500,000 feet of cock has moved through ahtees each year. This comes, if you'll pardon the expression, to precisely 1,231.06 miles per year. For the 17-year period of 1952 until now, that makes 20,928.02 miles total—almost the circumference of the globe!"

"I guess that's amazing, isn't it, L.T.?"
"Yeah! Now let me tell you about rim jobs...."

Well, he proceeded to tell me not only about rim jobs, but about many other questionable conclusions, including how much energy had been expended in these pursuits. I think he figured that the entire city of Asmara could be provided with electricity for a number of weeks just on the calories that we had consumed in these pastimes. Lest you think that this was idle work, remember that in 1969 there were no portable calculators—L.T. had compiled page after page after page of calculations (to many decimal places accuracy) in this evening's peculiar work. I'm sure that his math teachers would have been proud of his effort, if not of his motivation. I am also certain that Mama K took pride in her establishment's contribution to these amazing statistics.

SMOKE SIGNALS

At work one day, Sam Sampson from the Yemeni section said,

    "Got a minute?"
    "Sure. What's up?"
    "There's something back in voice intercept that you have to see."
    "Yemeni?"
    "Yeah. This will crack you up."
    "OK. Let's go."

We walked back to the voice intercept room. There guys in headsets translated directly from audio tape whatever the antennas had captured in the previous hour or so. I'm going to try to recreate the transcript that Sam wanted me to read, but first, you have to remember that in the Yemen a lot of hemp is grown. They export a lot of it as rope, but most of the rest goes up in smoke. The other thing you need to know is that in the late 60's the Arabs still used simple substitution codes—one letter for another. For what they considered as highly secure messages, the code might consist of as many as five characters to one in the plain-text message. A phrase such as *Attack now.* might look like this in a high-security encoding:

ABABC CDLMN CDLMN ABABC QRFZY MNLKN XXLXL
XLZTN UZCUM RQIML ZBDBZ

    The two extra characters, as you might have guessed, are the space between the two words and the period at the end of the sentence. Ditty boppers would have to receive each of the characters as Morse Code, while voice intercept operators only had to hear the character and write or type it. After all this introduction, here is what the English transcript looked like:

(COMMENTS)   MUHAMMAD   AHMAD

(MUHAMMAD AT xxx GROUP CALLS AHMAD AT yyy GROUP.)
        HEY, AHMAD, THIS IS MUHAMMAD. HEY, AHMAD, THIS IS MUHAMMAD. DO YOU READ ME?
(AHMAD REPLIES.)
        HEY, MUHAMMAD, THIS IS AHMAD. I READ YOU LOUD AND CLEAR.
        HEY, AHMAD, HOW HAVE YOU BEEN?
        HEY, MUHAMMAD, I HAVE BEEN GOOD. HOW ABOUT YOU?
(MUHAMMAD AND AHMAD CHAT.)
        I HAVE BEEN GOOD, TOO. HEY, AHMAD, I HAVE A 1500-WORD TOP-SECRET MESSAGE FOR YOU. ARE YOU READY?
(LONG PAUSE.)
        HEY, MUHAMMAD, THIS FREQUENCY IS NOT GOOD. GO TO ALTERNATE FREQUENCY THREE.
        HEY, AHMAD, I AM MOVING TO ALTERNATE FREQUENCY THREE.
(WE MOVE TO ALTERNATE FREQUENCY THREE, ALSO.)
        HEY, AHMAD, THIS IS MUHAMMAD. HEY, AHMAD, THIS IS MUHAMMAD. DO YOU READ ME?
(LONG PAUSE.)
        HEY AHMAD, THIS IS MUHAMMAD. HEY, AHMAD, THIS IS MUHAMMAD. DO YOU READ ME?
(ANOTHER LONG PAUSE.)
        HEY, AHMAD, THIS IS MUHAMMAD. HEY, AHMAD, THIS IS MUHAMMAD. DO YOU READ ME?
(LONG PAUSE.)
        HEY AHMAD, THIS IS MUHAMMAD. IF YOU READ ME, GO BACK TO FIRST FREQUENCY.
(WE MOVE BACK TO FIRST FREQUENCY.)
        HEY, AHMAD, THIS IS MUHAMMAD. HEY, AHMAD, THIS IS MUHAMMAD. DO YOU READ ME?
(LONG PAUSE.)

> HEY, AHMAD, THIS IS MUHAMMAD. HEY, AHMAD, THIS IS MUHAMMAD. DO YOU READ ME?
> (MUHAMMAD CALLS FOR A LONG TIME, THEN GIVES UP.)

Poor Muhammad! He should never have told Ahmad what was coming. We laughed at the thought of Ahmad sitting back and letting the guy on the next shift handle that 1,500-word message.

CHICKENSHIT

Unlike all the other barracks I had lived in, we didn't have to keep this one spotless. Oh, it still had to *be* spotless, it's just that *we* didn't have to keep it that way. We had two Ethiopians who did the work. We each chipped in a little bit every month, and for that, these two houseboys kept the floors spotless, shined our boots, took care of our laundry, and even made our beds. Actually, house*men* was more like it. One of them was probably about 30, and the other was about 45 or 50. For an Ethiopian, 45 was very old—this one looked like a 60- or 65-year-old American.

The younger fellow's name was Tesfai. He spoke English pretty well, and was obviously in charge. The older man hardly spoke at all, and in fact, was rarely seen. He seemed to avoid us, generally, and whenever I heard any of the other guys address him, they called him *Hey You*, or just by his first name, *Hey*. Occasionally someone would call him other things that weren't quit that nice.

So everyone made their wishes known through Tesfai. He was the one who collected their wages, as well as the extra charges for laundry and other services rendered from time to time. If you wanted to have something made, he knew the best jewelers, leather workers, tailors, and other craftsmen in town—at least the ones who paid him the best commissions for his recommendations. All in all, it made life a lot easier for us, and provided them with what was a very decent living.

One day, for some reason, I was in the squad room while the older man was working. I must have been sick, or something, because we were almost never there when they were cleaning. I was curious about this man, who must have lived through the war and Haile Selassie's takeover in Eritrea.

> "Hey! What's your name?"
> "Huh?"
> "What's your name?"

He looked behind him to see whom I was addressing.

> "Huh....Me?"
> "Yes, you. What's your name?"
> "Chickenshit."
> "What?"
> "Chickenshit. My name Chickenshit."

Come to think of it, I had heard some of the other guys call him that.

> "No. What's your real name? You know, your name in Tigrinie, or Amharic. What's your real name?"
> "Oh...Uh...Chickenshit."

Just then, Tesfai came in.

> "What you want, Mr. John?"
> "Tesfai, what's his name?"
> "Chickenshit."
> "No. No. His name can't be Chickenshit. What's his real name? In Tigrinie or Amharic, or whatever. What name was he given when he was born?"
> "Oh."

He conferred with the other man in Tigrinie for a minute, then said,

"He says his name is Chickenshit."

"No. That must be a transliteration."

"A what?"

"Uh...The way a Tigrinie name sounds in English. What name is Chickenshit in Tigrinie?"

"Oh! I see...Uh...There is no name that sounds like Chickenshit in Tigrinie."

"Well, in Amharic then? Or Arabic?"

"Uh...No. There is no name like that."

"You mean his name is really Chickenshit?"

"Yes! Chickenshit!"

"Yes. He says, Chickenshit."

"Well...I don't want to call him that. What can I call you? I don't want to call you Chickenshit."

"Oh...."

"What can I call you?"

"...Chickenshit."

He had been working at the site since it was first built, and somewhere along the line, Americans started calling him Chickenshit. By this time, he had forgotten what his name had been before. He didn't know what his new name meant. I don't know whether or not he knew it was a derogatory term. It was simply his name. I wasn't very proud of my countrymen, or of myself. They spoke some more Tigrinie.

"Mr. John, you want have lunch with us? Chickenshit says you come with us—have lunch."

"Uh..."

I had been warned about eating in places that weren't approved. I was all set to say no when I looked at Chickenshit. I had made a friend.

"Well...sure...OK."

"It's lunch time now. You come with us, OK?"

"OK."

We walked off post, and just outside the back gate there were four or five Ethiopians squatting around a little fire. A pot was simmering over the fire. We squatted with them. I listened, mostly. Tesfai told them I spoke Arabic. Though none of them knew Arabic very well, they included me by using it and whatever English they knew whenever they could.

One of the most common dishes was zignie. This was a spicy stew with lots of vegetables, and a little bit of meat. We GIs had joked about not knowing exactly what kind of zignie you might get—beef zignie, chicken zignie, dog, cat, rat....Well, you get the picture. They handed me a piece of anjara, the local sourdough bread. This stuff looked like the foam rubber stuffing that you used to find in pillows. It had the same texture, but if you liked the taste of sourdough, it was OK. Taking my cue from the other men, I dipped a piece of bread into the stew and tentatively tasted it.

"This is good."
"Yes. Good zignie. Ibrahim is good cook."

In Arabic, I told Ibrahim he was a good cook. He smiled shyly. Then he offered me some homemade beer. It was called muhss, and other than the fact that it was warm and had lumps in it, it tasted pretty good, too.

It was a typically beautiful day in Asmara. The sky was a fragile blue with hardly a cloud to be seen. It was warm, but with very little humidity and just enough breeze to remain comfortable. We squatted there for a while, eating and drinking. They talked, and I listened. Chickenshit was very quiet, but the other men seemed to treat him with respect. And, yes, they called him Chickenshit.

After a little while, it was time to go back. The other men stood up, but when I tried to, I found that my legs wouldn't work. When I said that we were squatting around the fire, you must understand exactly what that entailed. We squatted with our feet flat on the ground. This was a normal position for Ethiopians, but not for me. I had been determined to be as polite a guest as I could, and to mimic the behavior of my hosts to the best of my ability. Between the warm temperature, the spicy zignie, and the beer, I hadn't even noticed that I had lost feeling in my legs.

Tesfai and Chickenshit helped me to my feet, to much general amusement. I massaged my legs back into working order while the other men laughed and joked at my expense. And I laughed with them.

BLOODY SHAME

Ron Hartwell got transferred out of Tract C just after we came back from the Protestant Men of Chapel Retreat.

"You're going to be a **what**?"

"A meat inspector. You know, the Army inspects all the meat that is used on post, as well as what is sold to the approved restaurants in Asmara."

"Yeah, but why do **you** want to do that? Don't you need some training, or experience, or something?"

"They train you on the job. And I'll be able to do this when I get out of the Army."

"You want to do this when you get out?"

"You never know…I'm just getting bored out at the Site."

Ron threw himself into his new job, and within a week he was promoted to Specialist Sixth Class.

"Oh, that's great, Ron, now you have to go to the NCO Club. You can't come to the Oasis any more."

"Yeah, that kind of sucks. The food isn't any better. The company stinks. They don't bring Ahtees from downtown on weekends. But at least I'm getting paid more. That helps take away the sting."

"But what the hell do you do there?"

"Ah, that's the beauty, John. I go there for lunch every day."

"Yeah, so what?"

"Well, you know I have to wear an apron at my new job."

"Yeah, you've told me all about it. I can't believe you **want** to work in all that blood and gore."

"Yeah. Well, anyway, the apron just comes down to my knees, and after spending the mornings in the slaughterhouses, my pants are covered with blood from the knees down. So I take a table near the entrance and sit there with my knees crossed, swinging my foot up and down, like this."

"Oh..."

"You're getting the picture. Nearly everyone who walks in glances down at my leg as they walk by. I figure I've grossed out pretty nearly every NCO on base, as well as their wives."

"That's disgusting, Ron!"

"Yeah. I'd bet that food consumption at lunch time has dropped at the NCO Club since I've started eating there."

"I'm sure it has! Let's go to Menghetti's tonight. Dinner's on me! Just don't wear those pants!"

TOM AND MONROE

Two guys in our barracks were really interested in the Ethiopian people. Tom Haslip was one of the 18 guys in my room. He looked a lot like the Walrus from Disney's movie *Alice in Wonderland*, but with the addition of very thick glasses. He sounded like Richard Nixon when he spoke. He spent nearly every weekend living in mud-hut villages far away from Asmara. You could learn a good deal from him about the Ethiopian people, if you had the patience to pull the data from him. Tom was reticent to a fault. But he must have had a cast-iron stomach. Although we had been warned since we first arrived not to eat anywhere in Ethiopia that had not been approved by the Army, Tom never seemed to get sick.

He had a heart of gold—couldn't stand to see anyone or anything hurting. One day he rescued a hawk that must have run into the barracks. Its wing was broken. Tom set it, and put the thing in his locker. He fed it and nursed it. When its wing seemed to be well, he'd let it fly around inside our room. Unfortunately, it used the whole room for its bathroom. We complained, and Tom promised it wouldn't happen again.

"Why don't you just let the poor thing go, Tom?"
"I don't think it's quite healthy enough just yet."
"Well, it can't be doing the bird any good to keep it locked in the dark most of the time."
"That's true....But it won't be for much longer. I'll let it go soon."

That was Thursday evening. Friday, Tom left for another weekend in the country. We thought he had released the bird, but by the time he came back from his three-day weekend, his corner of the room was starting to smell.

"Tom! Boy, are we glad you're back! Something stinks in your locker."
"What!"

He rushed to his locker, unlocked it, and threw the door open. The bird fell out, dead, at his feet.

"Oh....It seems to have died."
"**Seems**?...Tom, that thing stinks! And look! You can see little bugs crawling all over it! Yuch!"
"Hmmmm...Wonder what I should do?"
"Put the damn thing in the trash and send everything in your locker out to be fumigated, that's what!"
"Oh, crap! I hope I didn't get any of those things in my locker!"
"Open all the windows, guys!"

Well, everyone in his area had to have all their stuff de-loused. And the room smelled for a couple of days. Eventually, we forgave him—it's hard to dislike someone as gentle and naive as Tom.

One Sunday evening, Tom came back from a special occasion.

"Hey, Tom! How was the wedding?"
"Oh, it was very...interesting...."
"Come on, Tom. Tell us about it. Was it Coptic?"
"Well, yes, the families were Coptic Christian...."
"Well, what was the wedding like? I don't know much about Coptic Christians."
"Well...it was much like a typical Christian wedding back home...."
"C'mon, Tom, give us some details. Did they have a reception, afterward?"

"Yes...it was similar to an Irish reception...."

"Did everyone get drunk?"

"Was there a wedding cake?"

"What did they eat?"

"And drink?"

"Well, they had zignie, of course, and anjara, and muhs. And for this rite, they also had cow...."

"What do you mean, cow?"

"Yeah, did they roast a whole cow?"

....

"Tom?"

....

"Well...no...the cow...wasn't...uh...cooked...."

"Uh...Tom...Was the cow...uh...dead?"

"Well...not at first...uh...it wasn't."

....

"Uh...what do you mean, *not at first?*"

"Well, the cow was...tied to a tree....The Coptics believe, you know, that the life essence of a beast can be transferred..."

"Wait a minute! Do you mean they ate the cow...alive?"

"Well...yes."

....

"Uh...Tom...Did you...uh...eat any of the...cow?"

"Well...yes....It would have been inhospitable...not to...you know...."

"How...how...was it?"

"Yeah. What did it...taste like?"

"Well, it tasted like...uh...cow....I guess."

Yes, Tom was the perfect guest. Even raw—make that *still alive*—cow couldn't make Tom sick.

* * * * *

Monroe Heckman worked mids and lived at the other end of the barracks I was in. I didn't know him as well as I knew Tom, but he, too, was interested in Africa. He ate things that were nearly as disgusting as Tom's raw cow, but he dreamed them up himself. Whenever you ordered French fries in the club, you could only count on getting two or three before everyone else at your table polished off the rest. But not Monroe. He had a remedy for the disappearing French fries problem. As soon as his French fries arrived, Monroe would smother them in chocolate syrup. Or mustard. Or whatever unusual thing he happened to find on the table. No one else would touch the things. But Monroe seemed to enjoy them covered in almost anything imaginable.

Monroe had planned to get out of the Army in Ethiopia, and then tour Africa for as long as a year before going home. About a month before he got out, however, he fell out of the back of a jeep and landed on his head. He had to spend a week in the hospital to determine how bad his concussion was. Evidently, the doctors thought he was OK, because they sent him back to work for the last three weeks he was in the Army.

He got out of the Army about six months before I went back to the States, and sure enough, he set out from Asmara to tour the continent. Three or four months later, however, a letter from Monroe's parents appeared on the company bulletin board. It seems that Monroe never showed up at one of the places he was expected, and his parents were trying to find him. I never did find out what happened to him.

RE-UP

When you got to within two years of your ETS[11], you had to have a reenlistment interview. The Army had these nice books full of lovely pictures and lush, descriptive prose that showed what a good deal a 20-year hitch could be. One illustration pictured an old geezer wearing glasses, long pants, shirt, shoes and socks sitting in a lawn chair propped up at one end of a pool. There are five young women sitting around and a couple more in the pool all dressed in revealing bathing suits. All the girls are looking at him. The caption says, "The joys of retirement can be further enhanced when Social Security benefits are added to military retired pay." Isn't that an image to make **you** want to spend 20 years in the Army?

You sat down in a little room with a Sergeant whose job it was to sell you on the idea. Unfortunately for him, the majority of the ASA enlisted troops were college drop-outs who had no intention of making the Army a lifetime vocation. Consequently, his was an unrewarding task. It wasn't uncommon for people to interrupt him with vile comments, or to call him various and sundry unwholesome names.

When Ralph went in for his interview, however, things were different.

"Sit down, Specialist Boswell."

"Thanks, Sergeant Zimmerman..."

"Let me start by..."

"Before you get started, Sergeant Zimmerman, I have a gift for you."

"....A...gift?...."

"Yes. This is for you....Here, take it."

Sergeant Zimmerman looked at the long, slim box wrapped in pretty paper with a matching bow as if he knew it held a poisonous snake. Gingerly, he accepted it from Ralph. He stared at it for a minute, mouth slack, uncomprehending. Then he carefully put it to one side of his desk.

"No. Open it now, Sergeant Zimmerman."
"Now?..."
"Yeah. Open it now."

Sliding the package to the center of the desk, he began, timidly, to open it. When nothing popped out or exploded, he became a bit more confident. At the end, he got into the spirit, and tore it open, revealing a kit. Yes, a kit to build...a kite.

"A kite?..."

Ralph nodded. Sergeant Zimmerman looked at the kite. Then he looked back to Ralph. Slowly, comprehension settled in.

"Oh....I get it....You can go, Boswell."
"Thanks, Sergeant."

Thus ended what well may be the shortest reenlistment interview in Army history.

RAINY SEASON

Rainy Season. That doesn't look bad in print, does it? It was, though. I think they used the word rain simply because there isn't a word that really does justice to the phenomenon. It might be more accurate to say it waterfalled. Walking out into the stuff was like walking into a wall of water. Fortunately, however, it didn't rain all day. The rain in Asmara kept to a schedule. From about 7:00 until 9:00 in the mornings and from about 4:00 until 6:00 in the afternoon the rain came down. The rest of the time it was beautiful.

Now you may notice that the times that it rained closely paralleled the times that we had to get from the barracks to the site. We were drenched by the time we got to work, and just when we were beginning to dry out, it was time to get soaked again.

Ralph Boswell, one of the guys in my barracks squad room, just couldn't wake up in the mornings. Everyone routinely shook or poked him or tried talking to him to get him up. He was often late. He would pull the pillow over his head and do his best to ignore us all. One day as I was coming back from the shower one of the other guys said,

"Hey, John, see if you can wake Ralph today—I've been trying, but I have to take a shower."

"Hey, Ralph! Wake up! C'mon, man, you're going to be late again!"

He just rolled over. I pulled his blanket and sheet off, but he just curled up in the fetal position facing away from me. I had an inspiration. Ralph was only wearing those thin boxer shorts that we had been issued in Basic Training. I took my can of spray deodorant, pointed it at his backside and let fly. That can packed a lot more punch than I had ever imagined—it launched Ralph right out of that bed. He screamed and jumped around, trying to figure out what had hit him. He recovered his good nature and what was left of his dignity pretty quickly. He wasn't late for work that morning.

But one day during the Rainy Season we couldn't get him up again. After the first deodorant episode, he always kept himself securely wrapped up, so that wasn't an option. Everyone had tried to wake him that morning, but to no avail. Finally, four of the guys picked him up, bed and all, and marched the whole lot out into the downpour. They came running back inside, and we all expected Ralph to be close on their heels. It took nearly a minute, however, for him to wake up, figure out what had happened, pick up his mattress and bedding, and get back inside. He went back out, brought in the bed frame, and without saying a word headed for the shower. His mattress was sort of dried out when we got back from work that evening.

It rained like that for a month or so. After going through that, none of us could believe the bulletin that came down from the Post Commander in March. Lt. Graham called a rare formation to read the bad news:

> "Pay attention! The Post Commander has just issued an order which I am supposed to read to you. It states:
> Since the recent Rainy Season did not produce sufficient levels in the country's reservoirs, water must be rationed at Kagnew Station. To that end, water will only be available in the barracks four times daily—from 0530 until 0830, from 1130 until 1300, from 1730 until 2000, and from 2300 until 0100 only. Shower time will be limited to two minutes per soldier per day. Shower monitors will be stationed in each latrine to assure compliance. Thank you for your cooperation.

A roster has been posted on the bulletin board. This order is to take place immediately. Are there any questions?"

"Hey, Lieutenant, what does that mean, *shower monitors?*"

"It means that troops will be stationed to clock the amount of time you run the water when you shower."

"How can we take a shower in two minutes?"

"Get wet, turn off the water, soap up, turn on the water, and rinse off. It can be done."

"You've got to be kidding."

"I'm not kidding, soldier. Failure to comply can result in an Article 15."

Now, an Article 15 is a disciplinary action that is written up in your permanent file—serious stuff.

"Uh, Lieutenant?"

"Yes, Meyers?"

"Does this mean that the toilets can only be flushed during the times you mentioned?"

"That's right."

"Oh...Won't it get pretty smelly? I mean, what about germs and all?"

"I think they've taken that into consideration, Meyers. If you have to use a toilet and it's not when the water's running, you'll just have to not flush."

"How'll we wash up afterwards?"

"....You won't, I guess. Are there any other questions?"

What could we say? If there wasn't enough water, there wasn't enough water. But by mornings, things were pretty odorous in the bathrooms.

This went on until the next Rainy Season. But while we were still rationing, the post swimming pool remained open. One day in February, I asked the life guard, Terry Dolan, how he kept the pool open.

"The miracle of chemicals."

"You mean you're just adding more chlorine?"

"That's the ticket! Haven't you noticed how red your eyes get, or how murky the water is at the deep end?"

"Yeah, come to think of it, it does seem worse lately."

"It's about to get worse still, my friend. Didn't you tell me you swam in high school?"

"That's right—breast stroke and butterfly."

"How'd you like to get out of here for a couple more weeks."

"What do you have in mind?"

"There's a swim meet the end of next month, and it comes with 20 days permissive TDY. Are you interested?"

"Sure! That sounds great! Where?"

"Adana, Turkey."

"Well...now it doesn't sound *so* great."

"Hey, didn't you say that any place out of Ethiopia was worth the ride?"

"I guess so. But from the layovers I had in Turkey, I don't see that it's much better than being here."

"Maybe not. But at least it's a change."

"That's true...well, OK. Do you have enough guys?"

"With you along, there'll be seven of us. I'll handle the diving. I'll want you to swim breast and fly."

"I don't think I can handle 200 meter fly."

"Your lucky day, my friend. There is no 200 meter fly event. But I will want you to do the 100 and 200 meter breast, the 100 meter fly, and swim breast in the medley relay."

"Who's going to do the fly in the relay?"

"I can handle the short distances."

"OK, man, I'm in."

"I want to start practicing tomorrow from 5:00 until 6:30. Can you make it?"

"Sure, but won't it be too late to shower after we're done?"

"I have special dispensation to allow the team to shower here at the pool."

And so, while the rest of the guys were limited to two-minute showers, some of us were swimming in the heavily-chlorinated pool and showering there five days a week. While we didn't have shower monitors, none of us abused what we perceived as a privilege. And we actually worked hard, assuming that all the other teams would do the same. It was a struggle at that altitude, but we figured if we could get into shape in Ethiopia at 7,800 feet, we should have a little edge in Adana, nearly at sea level. We knew there would be teams from seven or eight U.S. military bases around the eastern end of the Mediterranean Sea, and we wanted to win. Several of the guys got ear infections from the pool water, but with enough medication, we all survived.

Eventually, it was time to go. We had been training for a couple of months, and felt like we were in pretty good shape. Everyone was excited to be leaving the country, although my excitement was tinged with the dread of spending hours on a C-141. When we finally staggered into the sunlight and heat in Adana, still vibrating and cold from the plane, we were tired and hungry. An airman gave us a quick bus tour of the base, and then showed us to the barracks where we would stay for the week. (That's right, the week. Our 20-day TDY had shrunk to ten.) It was a one-story cinder-block building pretty well removed from everything. It looked clean, and actually had running water. However,

"Hey, Airman, isn't that a dead mouse under this bunk?"
"Uh...yeah, it sure is."
"Do you think he has relatives?"
"I don't know. I'll call someone about that."
"Why don't you take him with you?"
"I'll leave that to maintenance. Have a good stay."
"...."

"Hey, Terry, do you think this is some kind of conspiracy?"

"What do you mean, Bob?"

"Well, you know, maybe they are putting all the other teams up in dumps like this to, you know, demoralize us, so their team will win."

"Could be…Could be…."

"Oh, what the hell! We're only going to sleep here, guys. We'll spend the rest of the time at the pool and the club. Mice or none, we're going to win!"

The pool was beautiful. Eight seven-foot wide lanes of sparkling, clean water. It was an outdoor pool, and we had just about bought out the suntan lotion section at the PX before we went to swim. It was hot, and the air felt heavy after training in the thin air of Ethiopia. But all that oxygen! We had two days before the meet, and we spent most of it resting. We had decided not to sample the local culture until after the competition.

But there wasn't much competition. It turned out that the other teams hadn't bothered to prepare much for the meet: they treated it like a mini vacation. As a result, we slaughtered them. We only took one second place—everything else was at least a first, and sometimes first and second. I'm sorry to say that our one second place was the 100-meter butterfly—my race. But I did win the 100-meter and 200-meter breast stroke races and was part of the winning medley relay team. That made three firsts and a second. We weren't terribly popular in Turkey. And when we got back to Asmara, no one was terribly impressed there either. We did get a bit of a write up in the post newspaper, but no ticker tape parade. On the other had, we had the best tans on post!

APOLLO

On Saturday, July 20, Neil Armstrong set foot on the moon. Armed Forces Radio and Television Services couldn't provide live television coverage—at least not in faraway Africa. But we did have radio coverage. Everyone who had a radio had a group of people around him listening to what was happening a quarter-million miles away. For someone like me who had read science fiction since he was ten, it was a dream come true. We sat in our little far-away slice of America listening to voices of our countrymen who were walking on the moon, surrounded by people who still relied on the wind to separate chaff from grain. It was an interesting juxtaposition.

Later, when we began to pick up reactions from the countries we monitored, we were even more perplexed. Many people in the Mid-East believed that the American government hadn't really landed men on the moon, that it was all some sort of propaganda trick. At the same time, many of the un-educated people blamed their poor harvests on us, because they believed that Allah lives on the moon and our landing there must have angered him. We were vilified whether people believed us or not.

CONGRESSIONAL

"Have you seen the officers watering their lawns?"

"Are you nuts, Ron? There's a water shortage! The officers can't be watering their lawns."

"Well, you need to open your eyes, boy. Haven't you noticed that the lawns are still green?"

"Well...yes. But I thought..."

"You didn't think, you just assumed."

"Well, you're right about that. But have **you** seen the officers watering their lawns?"

"Yup. You just have to go by there about 9:00 P.M. They're not stupid enough to do it during broad daylight."

"Well, that really pisses me off!"

It wasn't the only thing that pissed me or Ron off. We sat stewing at the Club. A few other malcontents drifted over and joined us in our grousing. After a while, someone started writing things down. Soon we had a whole list things that redefined the old Army acronym SNAFU[12].

"I think it's high time we did something about all this."

"Like what, Ron?"

"Well...I think we should put together a letter and send it to our Congressmen."

"Yeah! And Senators!"

"Well, of course!"

"And a copy to Tricky Dicky!"

"And one to the ASA Inspector General!"

…

The seeds of rebellion had been sown. We all looked at one another. It suddenly got very quiet around the table. The call to action had been sounded, but the next step was a big one. People who sent Congressional Letters while serving in the Armed Forces never seemed to fare well. There were five of us—would we **all** keep the faith? Or would one or more knuckle under and tell the powers that be what they wanted to hear—that our complaints were groundless. One backslider could make it very hard on the others.

The silence deepened—the normal sounds of the bustling Club seemed to fade away as each took the measure of the others.

"Well...I'm for it. Anyone want to drop out?"
....
"I'm in."
"Me, too."
"Yeah."
"Yeah. I'm with you guys."
"Just remember, that if there's something you're not completely in agreement with, let's get it out of the letter right away. The slightest weakness will kill us."

With our commitment, enthusiasm crept back into our voices. We walked over to the barracks to start putting the thing together. I had a typewriter and typed faster than the other guys, so I was elected to do the drudge work. Much later, we had an eighteen page double-spaced draft. I promised within three days to produce enough copies so that each of us could have one to review separately. Then we would meet again three days after that to sort out the various revisions.

Using one of the mimeograph machines on Post was out of the question, so I sat down and typed the whole thing twice making two carbon copies each time. It took me two long nights.

When we met to revise the original, it took all weekend. First, we had to settle on the tone of the letter. Were we to be belligerent and confrontational as a couple of guys wanted, or should we appear to be altruistic patriots who just wanted to make a basically good system better? We settled on the second course, and in fact proposed one or two practicable and inexpensive solutions for each of the problems we outlined.

Ron had looked up the names of Senators and Representatives whose constituents in far away Africa didn't know them, so we had all the information we needed on that front. We had lined up witnesses for some of the problems that we hadn't ourselves witnessed. We were ready.

Well, almost. We hailed from five different states, so that meant that with two Senators and one Representative apiece we had 15 Congressmen to write. Adding a copy for President Nixon, one for the Inspector General of the Army Security Agency, and one for each of us, we needed a total of 22 copies of a document that promised to be 10 pages in length! I spent the next week typing.

When all the letters had been typed, we met to sign and mail them. Then we sat back to watch the system work.

It didn't take too long. In less than two weeks, we had letters from Senators, Representatives and other *Powerful People* pouring into Kagnew Station. The initial letters we received indicated that the officials we had contacted were investigating our claims and that we would be apprised of their findings later.

From the officials at Kagnew Station, however, we heard nothing. Their silence was ominous. There were a lot of rumors going around, but no one in charge appeared to be doing or saying anything out of the ordinary.

Things quieted down after about a week, and we were beginning to think that nothing else would happen. On Friday we were told to report to base headquarters Saturday for interviews concerning our letter. We met that night to compare notes.

"According to these orders, we are each going to spend an hour with some representative from the IG[13] office."

"*Some representative*? I heard it was a full bird colonel—maybe even the ASA IG himself!"

"What does this sound like to you guys?"

"I think we're being set up."

"What do you mean, Ron?"

"I think they're going to try to catch us in a lie so they can throw dirt on the whole letter. We aren't going to be interviewed, we're going to be interrogated!"

"You're overreacting, Ron."

"I don't think so. I agree with Ron. After they had to bust that Sergeant Major for all that embezzlement in Vietnam, the Army doesn't want to have any more bad publicity. I think we're in for a bad time."

"I think you're right, John. We may have opened a can of worms."

"Yeah, well that was the point, wasn't it? Now what are we going to do?"

"I think we should go through the letter point by point, so that when this Colonel tries to pick it apart, we'll be ready for him."

"What can they do to us, Ron?"

"They can't do anything to us. We haven't done anything but tell the truth about some nasty little goings on here. As long as we're careful and none of us says anything stupid, we'll be OK."

"All right. Let's go through this thing, then."

We studied our letter far into the night. It was the officer in charge of the Army Security Agency Inspector General's Office who interrogated us—and it **was** an interrogation. He had a captain there taking notes. I was the last one to go through the ordeal. He spent the whole time pulling phrases out of context to try to get me to make an unsubstantiated claim. It went something like this,

> Well, Specialist Leeger, on page three of your letter you state, *Post Administration wants soldiers to be unhealthy.* Now, just what did you mean by that?"

"Colonel, if you will look at that complete sentence, I believe it reads, *Since the pool filter has been reported broken for so many weeks, one can only assume that Post Administration wants soldiers to be unhealthy*, which I'm sure you will agree means something completely different from the fragment you quoted. Furthermore, if you'll read the next sentence or two, you'll find that we offer a solution for the problem. I think it says, *It shouldn't be prohibitively expensive to ship a new filter system here. There are people at Kagnew who can install it without outside help.*"

"Oh...Yes...Well...Um...On page five you state that...."

After having typed the whole letter so many times, I had no problem seeing what he was up to, and turning the thrust of the questioning back toward him. I had to hand it to him, though, he didn't quit early. He kept trying to get me to agree that what we had written was actually a meaningless slandering of the Army. Eventually, however, he must have realized that he wasn't going to get anywhere with me, so he dismissed me. Before I left, though, I wanted to get my two cents in.

"May I say something, Colonel?"

"Certainly."

"You've just spent several hours talking with all of us, and from what the other fellows said, your questions haven't had anything to do with trying to find out what is wrong here, and everything to do with trying to frame us."

"Now, just a minute, Specialist..."

"Didn't you say I could say something, Colonel? I wasn't finished."

"...Go ahead."

"Sir, all of us are conscientious about our jobs and our duty to our country. None of us are draft dodgers, or people who are looking for any preferential treatment. We just think that there are a number of situations at this post that are unfair and in some cases wasteful. Now, throughout our letter, for each complaint that we made, we made one or more suggestions how the problem could be rectified, usually at a savings to the government. I understand that this can cause some discomfort to the military, but I really hope that you are as diligent in your questioning of those in charge of this post who have allowed these situations to exist as you have been in trying to catch one of us in a lie."

It was silent in that room for what seemed like a very long time.

> "You really believe this stuff, don't you Specialist?"
> "Absolutely, Colonel."
> "...Well, thank you for your candor."
> "Will that be all, Colonel?"
> "You may go."

And go I did. I found that I was sweating when I got out into the sunshine. We adjourned to the Club to discuss what had happened. Each of us felt that the Colonel hadn't been able to get us to say anything that could be construed as incriminating.

> "So, what happens next?"
> "I guess we just sit and wait to see what the Army will do."
> "Well, from today's performance, I can guarantee that nothing constructive will happen."
> "Yeah. I'm pretty disgusted with the whole situation."
> "Me, too."
> "At least, things can't get much worse."
> "I wouldn't bet on that."
> "What do you mean by that, Ron?"
> "Yeah. You're starting to sound like the voice of doom."
> "That may be, but I'll bet a dollar to a doughnut that those bastards have tagged our 201 files."

Now, for those of you who have never had one, a 201 file is your personnel record. It follows you everywhere you go in the Army and records everything you ever did—well, everything you ever did while in the Army, anyway. It is consulted when you are up for promotion or assignment. It contains your medical records and records of any disciplinary actions that you have been involved in. In short, it's your Army career.

"What do you mean, *tagged* it?"

"Next time you see your 201 file, look for little colored tags on the side..."

"Yeah, I've noticed that on mine."

"Well, those little tags are codes to those in the know."

"What do they mean?"

"Yeah, and how do you know all this stuff?"

"Well, remember my Dad is a Sergeant Major. I've overheard him talking about the things. It never meant much to me before, so I don't know what any of the colors mean, but I don't think you'll find them written in any book."

"Oh, man!"

"Do you mean we're going to be picked on for the rest of the time we're in the Army?"

"Probably...But how long do you plan to be in the Army?"

"Not a damned day longer than I have to be!"

"Yeah!"

"That's for sure!"

We didn't hear another official word from the Army, but we did, eventually, get letters from our elected officials. They all said the same thing. We were just whining about insignificant matters. Why, the few things that had turned out to actually be verifiable had already been cleared up. For example:

The swimming pool filter that had been defective for so long that everyone was getting ear infections—The Army fixed that by closing the swimming pool.

The $34,000.00 that was found in the desk of the Sergeant who had requested transfer right after Sergeant Major Woodruff was cashiered for embezzling funds—The Army said that was just the result of unusual accounting practices. Why, when they had balanced the books, adding the cash in the desk, the books actually showed a surplus!

And on...and on...and on....

And yes, though we were never openly criticized for writing the letter, each of us reported that a black piece of tape had found its way to the edge of our 201 files.

MEN OF CHAPEL RETREAT

"I hear you're getting some heat, John."

"Uh...yeah...some, I guess, Colonel Vaughn."

"It sounds like you need a break. There's a Protestant Men of Chapel Retreat next month—want to go?"

"What? You mean, like the Choral Music Retreat? Well, sure. Uh, where is it?"

"Same place, Berchtesgaden."

"Yeah, I'd love to go. Who else is going?"

"Well, dependents aren't allowed on this one, so Neil won't be going—he doesn't want to leave his wife. I've asked Paul Sealey. He's getting some heat, too, huh?"

"Uh, yeah. But are you sure you can get us off? I mean, with the, uh, *heat* and all?"

"Didn't I get you out in February?"

"Well, that's certainly a fact."

"It runs the last two weeks in September. In fact, it's over just in time for you to stop by Munich for Oktoberfest on your way back to Frankfurt."

"Oh, wow. Thanks, Colonel Vaughn...You're really a life saver."

He folded his hands together, looked up, and with just the hint of a smirk said,

"Well...that's my job."

The Chaplain was true to his word. We had our orders by the end of the week. The thought of returning to Germany made putting up with the usual baloney a whole lot easier for the next couple of weeks. I wrote to see if Heinrich was going. He replied that he would be happy to share his car (and driving expenses) with Paul and me from Frankfurt to Berchtesgaden and back.

Once again we flew courtesy of the Military Airlift Command. This time when our C-141 landed in Saudi Arabia we were told we could get out to stretch our legs. There was one ominous caveat, however. We weren't to wander farther than 20 feet from the fuselage. It was blazing hot—like Masawa. The elevation couldn't have been more than a hundred feet or so above sea level, but the air field was well inland and thus parchingly dry. Heavily-armed Saudi military forces were patrolling in the area, and I could see machine-gun and antiaircraft emplacements dotted down the runways. As eager as I was to use my Arabic with natives, I didn't think it would be wise to advertise the fact that trained linguists were stationed just across the Red Sea. I stayed near the plane.

Germany looked different without the uninterrupted blanket of snow it had sported in February. Heinrich was just as entertaining a host as he had been earlier in the year. We were up well into the night rehashing the intervening months. Heinrich was particularly interested in the talent show fiasco. The local base in Darmstadt had sent a contingent to the event that we missed— seems the communications were better in Europe than down in Africa.

Berchtesgaden was lovely. I had written Heinrich and asked if he would help me plan some sightseeing trips. He was more than willing. The first morning we set off from Berchtesgaden for Salzburg and did all the tourist things. We saw Mozart's birthplace, the great fortress of Hohensalzburg, the Residenzplatz, all the cathedrals, and even the salt mines that the town was named for. The next time I saw the movie *The Sound of Music*, I recognized many of the places we had visited on that day.

The next day Heinrich took us to the Königsee. This glacier-fed lake is nestled among the Alps just outside Berchtesgaden. The waters were crystal clear. A good many people had rented rowboats, and Heinrich suggested we do the same.

"We can row out to see the abbey."

"What abbey, Heinrich?"

"At the other end of the lake is St. Barholomew's Church. During the winter months the only way out there is across the ice. This time of year there's a road that's passable, but most people get there across the lake."

"Is that where the tourist boats go?"

"They go by there, but they don't stop. The monks don't want a lot of visitors."

"When you say, *at the other end of the lake*, Heinrich, just how far do you think it is to the other end?"

"Well, it's been a while since I was last there, but I don't think it's too far. Just around the bend, I think."

So we rented a rowboat. It was a beautiful fall day. We rowed around a couple of bends, shouting hellos at the rowboats we passed. Two or three of the tourist boats also went by. Their wakes made our task a little more interesting.

"Just how many more bends are there before we get to this alleged monastery, Heinrich?"

"Yeah. This is the twistiest lake I've ever been on."

"Really, guys, I thought we'd be there by now."

"Well, I'm starting to get blisters. Remember, we still have to row back, and I haven't noticed many rowboats coming toward us lately."

"Well, just one more turn, then...."

And there it was. You could see the roof of the place from the water. We came ashore at a little beach, and got out to stretch our legs. All we could hear were the songs of the birds and the light slap of wavelets on the side of our boat. Heinrich had told us that we shouldn't stray far from the beach, so we didn't tarry too long before starting the long row back.

> "I had forgotten you could see that from here. Look, fellows, it's the Kehlstein Haus—Hitler's Eagle's Nest. See it way up there?"
>
> "Oh, yeah. Way at the end of that promontory. That's amazing!"
>
> "I thought we might go up tomorrow and see if it's still open."
>
> "What do you mean?"
>
> "They close it when the snows start. It's only open to tourists about five months a year."
>
> "I hope it's still open. I'd like to see it."
>
> "That's assuming we can row back before the conference is over...."

We did get back late in the afternoon. All of us had blisters, but we were proud of our accomplishment. I had taken a couple rolls of film. That night we found we had terrific appetites for dinner. The lake, it turns out, is about five miles long. At its widest, it's about a mile across. But in some places, it shrinks to about 500 yards. The mountains on either side rise quickly to about 8,000 feet! It's no wonder we were starved. The other conference attendees at our table must have thought we were gluttons.

Eagle's Nest was an impressive building. And the view was awe-inspiring. There were scattered clouds that day, and the sunlight was visible as it streamed through the openings and down into the valleys. We felt like gods must feel, looking down on the poor mortals below.

Most of the serpentine Königsee was visible, but we couldn't quite see all the way to St. Bartholomew's. Nearly straight down the escarpment on one side was a tiny farm. The buildings stood out from the intense green of the fields. Berchtesgaden sparkled in the clear air. I couldn't get enough of it. I went through film like a kid goes through candy.

On the last day of the conference we left as early as we could, and made the short drive to Munich. It was the last weekend of Oktoberfest, and we wanted to drink in as much as we could (pun intended). It was amazing—an entire carnival devoted to drinking beer! We settled in the Höffbrauhaus tent. Only one of many, it must have been 75 feet wide and at least 200 feet long. We went up to a balcony that stretched the width of the entrance end of the tent—the regular seating was all taken. What looked like long picnic tables were arranged lengthwise down the tent with stools full of thirsty Germans pushed up to them. In the middle of the tent was a band stand with a Bavarian band in full swing. There was plenty of room for the six or eight musicians there, and they seemed to be having a ball. We ordered beers and some barbecued chicken and joined the festivities. Everyone was singing. People at many of the tables linked arms and swayed back and forth to the music. The beer was great, and the price was right. A liter of the best beer I had ever had cost one German mark—25 cents, at that time!

We were there for quite some time. About an hour before we left, Heinrich joined in conversation with some Germans who sat at the other end of our table. In the car, driving back to Darmstadt he said,

> "That was a funny thing that happened back there."
> "What was, Heinrich?"
> "You know those people I was talking to?"
> "Yeah. That seemed to be quite a spirited conversation. What were you talking about?"
> "Well, you know there is an election coming up?"
> "I had read something about it."
> "It's very important, I think. And those folks had it all wrong. I was trying to convince them to support my party.

Well, anyway, when we were leaving, they said to me, It has been nice talking to you. You have really shown us something we didn't expect. *Most of you Americans don't even take the trouble to learn German, but you are even conversant about our politics.*"

"They thought you were an American! That's great! Did you tell them?"

"No. I didn't want to break their bubble."

"So, it takes a good German to put the ugly American syndrome to rest?"

"Well, maybe just for those people. You guys still have to work harder!"

....

"Hey, how about taking a drive up to Bad Frankenstein tomorrow?"

"You mean Frankenstein's castle? The one that inspired the book? Sure! Where is it?"

"Well, you'll be happy to learn it's pretty near Nieder Bierbaum."

"Well, all right!"

We left early the next morning. Bad Frankenstein was an eerie place. The day was very foggy, which added an aura of malevolence to the sinister feeling that embodied the place. Home of a family of robber barons in the Middle Ages, it was fairly well preserved. The walls and towers were intact, and we spent the day climbing over and around them. Standing by the stele that commemorates Mary Shelly's book, I said,

"I can see why they were inspired to write stories after visiting a place like this. Is it as spooky when there isn't any fog, Heinrich?"

"It seems spooky to me whenever I come up here."

"In all the castle plans I have ever seen a chapel is a

major feature inside the curtain wall. Did you notice that the chapel is located outside the wall here?"

"That's right. I'd never thought about it, but that is unusual."

"This is not a wholesome place."

"That's an understatement, John."

Heinrich's sister Marlena went with us. She had grown up a lot since our visit eight months earlier. Seventeen, blonde, attractive—and most of all, approachable—we spent the day getting closer. We got separated from the others in the fog several times, but never from each other. Dinner at Nieder Bierbaum was terrific. The woman who had made such a fuss over Ron the last time we were there remembered him and fussed over him again. I tried not to show that I was becoming more than interested in Marlena, at the same time trying to get her more interested in me. By the time we got back to Darmstadt, I thought that something was definitely developing between us. No sooner had Heinrich dropped us off at the base than Paul said,

"Boy, have you got the hots for Heinrich's sister!"

"Oh...you noticed?"

"Noticed? Heinrich was kidding me about it all day."

"Heinrich?"

"Of course, Heinrich. You'd have to be blind not to notice the way you two were acting."

"Oh....Do you think he's mad?"

"No. He told me that you're the kind of guy he'd like his sister to date—trustworthy."

"Trustworthy? He didn't say that."

"Yeah...trustworthy."

Well, after that, how could I be anything but. Although we had some time together, nothing much really happened. I don't know whether to be proud of myself, or disappointed.

Paul and I had planned to buy an unlimited mileage rail pass and see more of Germany as well as some spots in France and Spain, but we found we couldn't really afford it. So we spent an extra week in the Darmstadt area doing day trips. Although not what we had planned, it was a great week. I was surprised to find so many Germans, particularly the younger people, spoke some English. They all seemed happy to have a chance to practice, so we had little trouble getting around. One of the trips involved spending the night out of town. We went into a little hotel, and what little German I had ran out on me. I attempted to ask the clerk for a double room with two beds, but I found I couldn't remember the German word for bed. The Arabic word came right to my tongue, but I knew that probably wouldn't do me much good. The conversation went something like this.

"Guten abend."

"Guten abend. Ein dopfel zimmer, bitte, mit zwei...uh...mit zwei....Oh, crap, Paul, how do you say bed in German?"

"You want a double room with two beds, sir?"

I complemented the clerk on his excellent English, and we booked the room....

Eventually it was time to head back to Ethiopia. We got on the Turkish Courier for the flight to Turkey. The modified DC6s that the Air Force used for passenger duty had seats facing the rear of the plane. This was supposed to provide better protection in case of a crash. We strapped ourselves in and settled back for the first step of our long journey. The plane taxied out to the end of the runway and paused, quivering with readiness. The engines roared, and the plane started moving. Faster and faster we sped down the runway. It was a different experience to be pushing myself back in the seat to stay upright. Then, suddenly, we were slammed back into our seats. The engine sound dropped then pitched up again as the pilot tried to abort the takeoff. The tires clawed at the tarmac, and, eventually, we stopped. We sat for a minute as everyone's heartbeat cycled down. Then the pilot turned the plane around—the end of the runway was just under the wing tip as we turned. We taxied back off the runway.

> "Uh...ladies and gentlemen, this is your pilot speaking. It seems that our number four engine isn't working quite right. I think the spark plugs might just be fouled with carbon, so I'm going to sit over here on the pad and rev it for a while to see if it clears."
>
> "The spark plugs might be fouled?"
>
> "That's what he said, Paul. Boy, wasn't that something?"
>
> "Let me check my pants...yup, that was something, all right."

We sat there for a good five minutes while he revved one engine—all the way up, then all the way down. The plane shuddered while the brakes fought to keep the thing from pinwheeling around on the runway. Finally, everything settled down.

> "Well, ladies and gentlemen, this is your pilot, again. I think everything is in order. We're going to give it another try."
>
> "Try? **Try**? What the hell does he mean, try?"
>
> "What does he mean, he **thinks** everything is in order?"
>
> "Well, this was a *Men of Chapel* retreat, wasn't it? We **are** men of chapel, aren't we? It's not too late to pray, I think."

Maybe our prayers helped, but we did get airborne this time. The flight was pretty uneventful, other than an unplanned stop in Rome, and by the time we landed in Izmir, Turkey, we had all but forgotten the extra take off at Frankfurt. Everyone had to get off the plane while the fuel tanks were topped off. After a half hour or so, we were looking out the window to what the status of our plane was. The tanker truck pulled out from under the wing. We figured it must be about time to get back on. Then we saw the weirdest thing. The tanker truck pulled away from the plane and slammed on its brakes. Then it backed up and slammed on the brakes again. It repeated this a few times, then pulled back under the wing. The guy got out of the truck and they pulled the hose back up to the wing. A couple of minutes later, they disconnected and the truck pulled away again. This time it moved away from the plane and started going around in circles real fast. Every once in a while it would slam to a stop, then start again.

I found a guy who looked like a ground crew member, and asked him,

> "What's he doing out there, Airman?"
> "The truck?"
> "Yeah. Why's he going around in circles? I thought we'd be out of here by now."
> "You'll be a while yet. They've got vapor lock in the truck, and can't get gas to flow out."
> "What? That can't be—uh—can it? I mean, isn't that thing a bit large to have vapor lock?"
> "It happens every once in a while here. Vapor lock is what it is."

The truck driver looked like some guy doing a road test for a car magazine for the next half hour. Finally they must have been successful. We were told to get back on board for the last lap of our trip.

About 20 minutes after we got airborne, the number four engine started smoking and bucking. Occasionally flames shone through the smoke. Then the pilot shut the engine down.

> "Ladies and gentlemen, this is your pilot speaking. We've lost the number four engine—I've had to shut it down. This aircraft is very stable with three engines, however, so there is nothing to worry about."

He was probably the only one on board who felt there was nothing to worry about. The cabin was very quiet for the rest of the trip. When we finally landed in Adana, everyone seemed to breathe a sigh of relief.

We had to wait three days in Adana for the C141 to Ethiopia. The second morning, I awoke feeling that something was in my eye. I rinsed it out as well as I could, but the pain got worse and worse. By noon, I decided to go to the base clinic for treatment. The doctor there gave me a salve for it, and told me if it wasn't well by the time I got back to Ethiopia to see the ophthalmologist there. When we finally got to Asmara, it was worse. I immediately went to the base hospital. The doctor I saw examined me thoroughly. While he was looking through the ophthalmoloscope, he called to his assistant,

> "Hey, Bill. Come take a look at this. I've never seen uveitis before. Have you?"
>
> "No. Do you think that's what he has? Let me take a look."

Well, needless to say, I got a very bad feeling about the whole thing right then and there.

> "I'm sorry, Specialist Leeger, I'm just an optometrist, and you really should see an ophthalmologist. I'll have to send you to the nearest hospital where you can be treated properly."
>
> "Where's that, Sir?"
>
> "Frankfurt."
>
> "Frankfurt? I just came from there."
>
> "Well, you need to go back."

And that's just what I did. With just about enough time to have my laundry done and repack my bag, I was back on another C141 heading back to Germany. The doctor there verified that I did indeed have uveitis. It's an inflammation of the iris, and must be treated to avoid blindness—it's sort of like arthritis of the eye. The treatment consists of dilating the pupil and then dropping prednisone right on the eye. Since that's pretty much a direct shot to the brain, it really affects the metabolism. The disease goes into remission, but never goes completely away. I've had it ever since then, at first two to four times a year. Lately it's only happened every couple of years or so. The treatment requires one to four or more weeks, and then your body must be gradually weaned from the prednisone for another couple of weeks. It made for some interesting times. Originally I had it in my right eye, and with that pupil dilated, it made sight-reading music very difficult. Normally you read several measures ahead of where you're playing, and with the lead eye out of focus, things were considerably harder. The disease doesn't run in my family, and none of the doctors I have consulted since have been able to tell me where or how I got it. I chalk it up as just one more little thing I received from my time in the U.S. Army.

SERGEANT KRUGER

Sergeant Kruger was one of the noncoms at the site who was Regular Army through and through. He didn't approve of us college boys who were only in for the short haul. And he made his disapproval well-known.

"Dammit, Leeger, I thought I told you to trim those sideburns!"

"Oh...that's right, sergeant, you did. But I just spent two weeks in Germany on medical leave, and I forgot all about it."

"Yeah, I know all about your *medical leave*, and that don't hold no water with me. You're in the Army, Mister, and you should know by now that those sideburns can't go any lower than the middle of your ear."

"I'll trim them tonight, Sergeant."

"You damn well bet your ass you will, Leeger!"

Sergeant Kruger looked a lot like the cartoon Neanderthal, Alley Oop. Beady little eyes glared from beneath his prognathous eyebrows. But the minute you stared back, his eyes slipped away, as though he were afraid they might reveal something of his inner mind. I don't think there was a whole lot to reveal. The best thing about Sergeant Kruger was that his memory was not so hot. Usually it would be a week or so before he'd remember that he told you to do something neat like trim your sideburns or get a haircut. But someone must have tipped him off while I was in Germany about making notes, because early the next morning he was after me again.

"Leeger, I told you to trim those sideburns! What the hell's the matter with you?"

"Well, Sergeant, I have uveitis. It's an inflammation of the iris, and..."

"I don't care about your eye, dammit!"

"Well, the medicine I have to take kind of makes me forgetful, Sergeant."

"...Well...I don't care about your medicine either. Write yourself a note, if you gotta. Just get those sideburns trimmed!"

"Right."

Fortunately, this was a Friday, so I wouldn't see him again until Monday. Now that much time should have guaranteed that he wouldn't remember my sideburns. After all, he had a lot of hair to check up on out at Tract C. But, sure enough, first thing Monday morning he was screaming at me again. Now, I hadn't had much sleep over the weekend. We had play practice twice, and construction sessions for the sets and lighting. Of course, I was still playing the organ for the Protestant Chapel services, so that accounted for Sunday morning. Then we had stayed up much of Sunday night playing bridge and drinking. Add in the uncomfortable situation with my eye, and I wasn't in much of a mood for Army discipline. (Well, OK, I was never in much of a mood for Army discipline.)

"Leeger, you still haven't trimmed those goddamn sideburns!"

"You're right, Sergeant Kruger. I was pretty busy this weekend."

"You smartass college shit, you're in the Army, now, boy! Your business is the Army business! Now get those sideburns trimmed, you stupid son of a bitch!"

Well, that was getting a bit too personal, even for Sergeant Kruger. It was very quiet for a minute. My head was throbbing. My eye hurt. I was a little hung over. And Sergeant Kruger had bad breath. We were the only two people in the bowling alley at the time. I rubbed my forehead, and as I put my hand down, it dropped onto a Scotch tape dispenser on the table next to me. You know, one of those little things with about a pound and a half of lead in the bottom. I glanced down at it, and picked it up. It made a surprisingly comfortable weight in my hand. In the stillness, I heard myself quietly say,

"If you ever talk to me like that again, I'll break your face."

The tension now was palpable. Sergeant Kruger looked at me. I glared back at him. He looked down at the Scotch tape dispenser. At the edge of my consciousness, I could hear the cover music outside. An eon or two passed. Then, without a sound, Sergeant Kruger turned and walked away.

I stood, shell-shocked, for a minute. I couldn't believe that I had actually said something like that. I guess Sergeant Kruger couldn't believe it either. I waited for the inevitable disciplinary action, but it never came. Sergeant Kruger never gave me a hard time about my sideburns again, but then, I trimmed them that night.

CRITICS

Things started getting very interesting at work. We had known for some time that a group of young officers had been conspiring to overthrow King Faisal in Saudi Arabia. The King, however, didn't seem to know anything about it. Never had we heard a murmur about the conspiracy in the Saudi Royal family traffic. These officers were scattered all over the globe in special training programs, colleges, and universities, mostly in the U.S., but in other countries as well. Because of that, most of their communications with one another was outside the reach of Saudi security. We had been apprised of what was going on by other branches of the security services, and told to be on the alert. They seemed to be all talk and no action, however.

Then all the officers studying abroad were suddenly ordered to return home. The messages that accompanied the first class tickets read something like this:

> "The fatherland requires your presence immediately. Return with all haste so that the will of Allah can be implemented."

Even allowing for the ritual formality of written Arabic, the message was urgent and hinted at upcoming action. The young officers were certain that their desire to avenge the Arabs' previous defeats at the hands of the Israelis was finally going to be acted upon by the old King. The communications we intercepted between the young officers at home and abroad indicated that they were excited about the upcoming war, and couldn't wait for their opportunity to crown themselves with glory.

At the site, a different sort of message activity accompanied theirs. Our regular reporting volume increased to reflect the increase in activity. We also sent several CRITICs concerning the matter. Now a CRITIC was a message that was guaranteed to appear on the President's desk within 24 hours of its origination, so sending one was not an everyday occurrence. In fact, not a single CRITIC had been sent from Asmara since I had arrived. I was glad that I had decided to update the Saudi section more than a year before, when Sergeant Thornton had returned to the States. It would have been impossible to provide the level of detail that was suddenly required, if I had had to rely on the inaccuracies that he had piled up.

For several days we pulled a lot of extra hours checking and rechecking our reports. Officers were being shuffled around within the country as well as those who were being recalled from overseas. Then things took a sudden turn toward the bizarre. As the officers returned home, they were met at the various airports and rushed away—to prison! It seems the wily old King had been aware of the plot for a long time. He had the officers in the conspiracy arrested as they arrived and simultaneously had those who were in country imprisoned. When he was sure he had them all, he had a couple of the ring leaders executed, and required all the others to swear a bond of personal loyalty to him before they could be released from prison.

The tension level at the site dropped back to the nonexistent level. But I had an increased respect for King Faisal. Years later, when he was assassinated by one of his nephews, I felt like I had lost a favorite uncle.

ZAP!

The only room at Tract C that was off limits was the Comm Center. (Well, I guess the Colonel's office was generally off limits, too, but you know what I mean.) From this room we could communicate with any ASA site around the world, as well as with a lot of other super secret places. In 1969, we were in the middle of the Cold War, and security was paramount. People had to be highly screened and trained before they were allowed near the government's super-secret encoding/decoding equipment. I was very curious about this little enclave of secrecy in the middle of our secure building, but I had never been able to talk myself into trying to get in there to see what was what.

When the first of the CRITICs was to be sent, however, I found a way to get through the door. The security clearance that each of us at the site had was called Top Secret—Crypto. One of the things that this clearance granted us was the need to see anything for which we had a *need to know*. There was my wedge. I approached the Dutch door to the Comm Center. The bottom half was closed and locked, as usual. I knocked.

"Excuse me, Specialist, I have a CRITIC that needs immediate transmission."

"Do you have all the proper authentication?"

"As you can see, everyone who is anyone has signed off on this one."

"OK. I'll get right on it."

"I want to watch you transmit it."

"You don't need to do that, Specialist. I'll take care of your baby."

"You don't understand, Specialist. That message is extremely important to the reporting in my section. I have a *need to know* that it was transmitted and received."

Yes, I spoke the three magic words in what must have sounded like italics. The Comm Center technician looked at me intently.

"You have a *need to know*?"

There were those italics again.

"Yes."
....
"C'mon, Specialist, you're really just curious, aren't you?"
"Uh...I don't know what you mean. I need to know that the message was received."
"Sure....Well, c'mon. You can watch."
"Thanks."

We co-conspirators grinned at each other as he opened the bottom part of the door. We went around a corner, and there it was! Whatever it was....It looked like Mr. Wizard's home radio set. Lots of dials, gauges, lights, and switches. He explained as he worked.

"First, I have to re-enter your message into this machine. Then it prints it back out, so I can verify that it has it right."

It took him a while to re-enter it.

"This is, uh, 5,328 words—sound about right?"
"Uh...yeah. I guess."

"OK....Now it prints out....Looks the same to me. Does it look OK to you?"

"Looks good."
"Now we call DC."

He used the radio to call headquarters.

"….OK, DC. I've got a 5,328 word CRITIC for you. Are you ready to receive?"
"Not yet, Asmara. Let's try another frequency. This one's a little noisy. How about four?"
"Roger. Moving to frequency four….How does that sound?"
"Much better. I'm ready to receive on your count."
"OK, DC. Counting from five…four…three…two…one…."

ZAP

The machine didn't actually say **ZAP**. The noise it made sounded more like a strangled blender. It only lasted for about two seconds.

"OK, Asmara, I've got it."
"Thanks. This is USASAFS Asmara signing off."
….
"Wait a minute! That was it?"
"Yeah. Your message was transmitted and received."
"But….You couldn't possibly have sent 5,328 words that quickly….I mean…could you?"

Of course he could. He spent the next few minutes giving me a very brief overview of sideband transmission and modulation before he sent me on my way. I had finally looked into the unknown. And it was still unknown.

Isn't that the way it always is?

YOU KNOW I CAN'T HEAR YOU

Paul had decided to expose our little drama club to the harsh world of criticism. In mid-October, about the time I returned from Oktoberfest, he announced that we would perform *You Know I Can't Hear You When the Water's Running* in early December. This set of four one-act plays seemed perfect for our little fledgling company.

We set to work learning lines, building what little scenery was required, acquiring costumes, scrounging together lighting, and organizing the myriad of other details that had to be seen to. I was to appear in three of the playlets, and was also responsible for the scenery and for help with the lighting.

Of course, the choir was also putting together its Christmas concert, so I had a lot of music to accompany. And the CRITIC situation at the Site added another layer of complexity to my life. It would have been a bit less hectic without the strain of the uveitis that struck a second time in November. What with the extra rehearsals for the play, the extra hours at the Site, and the extra rehearsals for the Christmas concert, I was beginning to get a little run down.

Then, the Friday after Thanksgiving I had an evening with nothing to do. Before anyone could come up with something that just couldn't wait, I went down town. I was just wandering around, relaxing. I did a little Christmas shopping, had dinner, and watched the caffolattis. It was a refreshing interlude.

About three o'clock Saturday morning I woke up with the trots. It seemed like another case of Eritrearrhea. But then I started vomiting. By ten o'clock I wasn't getting any better—in fact, I felt like I was getting worse. Then I started having muscle cramps. First my stomach muscles cramped up badly. I attributed that to the vomiting. But when my leg muscles started to cramp, I began to be worried.

I kept thinking that the cramps would go away, but then my arms and hands started to cramp. That was too much. I guess I've had a sort of hand fetish for a long time. I've been aware of my hands since I started playing the piano as a five-year-old. When my hands started to cramp, I panicked. I called for help, but it seemed like no one was in the barracks. It was Saturday morning, after all, and most people were out doing something. I laid in my bunk with the cold sweats and cramps. Finally I managed to get up and shuffled around trying to find someone who could call an ambulance. It seemed like everything hurt. Just walking down the hallway was a tremendous effort. I staggered into Wally's room and sure enough, he was there, sound asleep.

"Wally! Help me! I can't move my hands!"

He snored on.

"Wally! Help! I can't move my hands!"

I pleaded. I couldn't move enough to shake him—for that matter, I couldn't even reach him to touch him. I nudged the bunk with my leg, trying to jostle him into consciousness.

"Wally! Wake up! Help me! I can't move my hands! Call an ambulance!"

I don't know how long I tried to wake him up, but nothing seemed to work. Finally someone from down the hall must have heard me screaming. He called the hospital, and an ambulance came in a few minutes. By then, I was pretty hysterical. They took me to the base hospital, and put me on an examination table. By this time I could hardly move anything but my mouth. Mostly, I was pretty incoherent, but I kept trying to tell them that I couldn't move my hands, and asking for help. I heard voices outside of my field of vision:

"...This one's a malingerer—wrote a Congressional."
"What? Do you think he's just trying to get out of work?"
"Could be? "

Well, that turned **my** volume level up!

"I don't care what that says! You've gotta help me!
I can't move my hands! Please help me!"

Then I started swearing at them. I called them every name I could think of, and I could think of quite a few. Eventually, they put an IV drip in my hand and started doing some tests. No one had much patience with me, however, until the test results started coming in.

It turned out that the combination of my run-down condition and the severe case of Eritrearrhea had wreaked havoc with me. I had contracted something called shigellosis. In addition, my blood sugar and potassium levels were extremely low. Basically, I was a mess. They put me in a room and started dripping lots of stuff into me. I was told that I would be in for a week.

"No. I can't be here for a week. The play is next weekend."
"You won't be in any condition to be in a play next weekend, soldier. Do you have someone else who can do it?"
"We barely have enough cast members to cover all the parts. I **have** to be in that play."
"I don't think that's wise."

I got a message to Paul, and he came over.

"The doctor said you shouldn't do the play."
"What are we going to do?"
"Well, if I juggle things a lot, we can just about cover all the roles."
"Surely, I could do **one** of the plays, don't you think?"
"Hey, I'm not the doctor."
"Well, I'll see if he'll let me do one. Who's going to run the lights?"
"I can get Suzanne to do them. All she was going to do was hand out programs. Someone else can do that."

When I explained to the doctor that they were just short one-act plays, he said it might be all right for me to do one of them,

"The shortest one. Understand?"
"Not more than one?"
"I really don't think you should even do that. And, by the way, have you ever been tested for diabetes?"
"Diabetes? No! Why? Do you think I have diabetes now?"
"Not necessarily. Some of your symptoms suggest it, but I can't be sure until we run some tests. You'll have to have the tests run after you get back to the States. You need at least a month after we get you straightened out to make sure the results are reliable."
"Oh. Well, then, I'll have the tests done when I get back home."

I was due to return to the U.S. at the end of December, but had requested an earlier departure so that I could be home for Christmas. I had had no reply to my request, and was going on the premise that I would miss Christmas at home one more year.

The play went on as advertised. I only did the act about the 54-inch bed. It was fun, but I was really exhausted when it was over. The Christmas concert came a few days later, and I managed that, too. I was getting stronger with every day, but I still wasn't right. I didn't go down town to eat again.

BACK TO THE USA

Now Ian McDowell was a prodigious drinker. After the trip to Athens, we had become friends. One day that previous summer I went down to the Club with him for Happy Hour. We sat down, and one of the waiters came over and asked what we wanted. Ian stunned him:

> "I'll have an Old Fashioned lunch."
> "What that?"
> "Bring me four Old Fashioneds."
> "Wah! Wahna Allah abu[14]!"
> "Whatever you say. Just bring them now."

The waiter came back, and as he was lining the drinks up in front of him, Ian said,

> "Now, when you come back, bring two more."
> "Wah!"
> "Yeah."

He drank Old Fashioneds two at a time as fast as the waiter brought them. I don't know how many he had in an hour and a half, but it was an enormous amount of liquor. And when we left, he didn't look or act any different than when we had come in. I think he was always at least a little drunk. He always had that sort of sleepy-eyed look that some people get when they drink. His speech was careful, but un-slurred. You would have had a hard time identifying him as an alcoholic.

Now it was December, and we were both due to return to the States. Ian was leaving a few days before me, but we would both be home for Christmas. As I was leaving the barracks to go to the Club for dinner, Ian was coming in.

"Hey, Ian. I'm going down to the Club for dinner. Want to come? It's Happy Hour."
"No. Thanks, John, but I quit."
"Drinking? You quit drinking?"
"Yeah."
"When did you quit drinking?"
"I quit three weeks ago. Haven't had a drink in three weeks."
"That's hard to believe. Cold turkey?"
"Yeah. I just quit."
"How'd you do it, man?"
"Well, I just started thinking about it. I could never afford to drink that much back in the States."
"So, you just quit? That's amazing! Congratulations!"
"Thanks."
"Well, you didn't quit eating, did you? Do you want to come for dinner?"
"I'll wait until later, thanks. I don't want to tempt fate with all that liquor around."

But he did stay off alcohol, at least until he left. And he didn't look or act any different from when he had been drinking all the time. He still looked sleepy-eyed, and spoke carefully.

By then, at long last, my orders had come. I was to leave the week before Christmas, and have three weeks before I had to report to my next duty station. I was astounded at how much irreplaceable...uh...well...junk I had accumulated in a year and a half. I managed to get everything packed into the allotted space. Uncle Sam only paid to ship a certain amount back home, but it was just barely enough.

Wally and a fellow named Charles Nichols and I had decided to rent an apartment together at our next duty station. We were being sent to Fort Belvoir, Virginia, just south of Washington, DC. I didn't know Charles very well, but he had worked with Wally on mids, and Wally thought we would all get along OK. The cost of living was pretty high in the Washington area, so we figured we'd need a three-bedroom apartment.

Wally and Charles left the week before my departure date. I had been counting the days I had remaining in Ethiopia for what seemed like a lifetime. And then, finally, the number was zero. The whole trip back was a blur—from the time I woke up on the morning I left until I got off the jet at O'Hare the next day. But at long last I was home again.

Christmas was wonderful, albeit different. I had a little niece to become acquainted with, and my little brother was now a college graduate. Reading the letters and listening to the tapes from home while I was in Ethiopia had helped me keep current, but I still had a lot of catching up to do. Some of my friends had come home for the holidays, but others had not. And some would never come home again. One of my brother's best friends had been killed in Vietnam—only one of a dreadfully high number of bright, young men. Part of me felt guilty at having managed to escape that experience. I wondered how my friends from language school had made out, but I didn't know any way to get in touch with them again.

I shared my pictures and mementos with my family and friends, and tried to convey to them the other-worldliness of the African country I had spent so much time in. But I never felt I had managed to describe the experience adequately.

ALEXANDRIA

VIRGINIA VILLAGE

Wally and Charles rented a three-bedroom apartment in Alexandria. This third-floor walk-up in the Virginia Village Apartments was to be my home from January, 1970 at least until I got out of the Army on August 25. I had to admit, they had picked a good place. Less than a mile from Interstate 95, we had a short drive against DC rush hour traffic to Fort Belvoir, about 10 miles south. We were to discover, however, that rush hour was just about as bad going toward Fort Belvoir as going toward DC.

There were three other garden apartments sharing the top floor landing. Our rooms overlooked a pleasant courtyard to another building in the development. As the first of us in town, Charles had found the apartment, so he had his choice of rooms. He picked the master bedroom suite, which had its own bathroom. Wally had arrived before me, so he picked the middle bedroom. That left me with the one closest to the living room. Wally and I would share the second bathroom.

An old friend and her husband lived fairly close by. Martin was an artist for the Government Printing Office, and Danielle ran her own dance studio. They had lived there for some time, so they could tell me which stores had the best bargains, and how to get by on a small budget. The first weekend I was there, they drove me to look at a couple of cars people were selling, and I made my first mistake in Washington—I bought a Fiat 124 Sport Coupe. The fellow said he had to move, and had to sell the car. He gave me a great deal on the car. It was a terrific car to drive when it was running well. And that, of course, was the problem. Over the next couple of years, I got to be very friendly with several mechanics in the Alexandria area. The guy who sold me the car either really did get transferred, or he moved, or he got an unlisted number. I never managed to contact him after the sale. At any rate, I had wheels, and for the time being anyway, I loved the car.

A car was just the first thing I needed though. I had no furniture, dishes, or any of the other things you need to furnish an apartment. Danielle and Martin told me not to buy anything until February. In the D.C. area there are phenomenal sales in February called Founders Day sales. Originally these were just between Washington's and Lincoln's birthdays, but now they extend through the whole month. So I slept on a sleeping bag, ate out of paper plates, and saved my money for the big sales.

I started at a Woodward & Lothrop department store looking for kitchen stuff. The first thing I found was a blender. I was looking at one model, when a sales girl came up to me.

> "How much is this blender?"
> "That's just $29.95."
> "I'll give you $5.00 for it."

Then I remembered—I wasn't in Ethiopia any more. The girl was looking at me like I was an idiot. I could feel myself starting to blush. My mouth had slowly dropped open. I stammered,

> "Uh...Uh...No....Uh...I mean...Uh...I'll take it!"

My first purchase for my new apartment. I was so embarrassed. I picked up my package and left post haste. But during the rest of the weekend, I fought my way through hordes of pushy people in a multitude of stores. In the end, I bought pretty much everything I needed, and at very good prices. And I didn't haggle for anything after the blender.

CHERYL ANN GREEN

Two years earlier, when I was traveling to my new duty station at Fort Devens, Massachusetts, I had stopped in Washington and spent the weekend with my Danielle and her husband. She got me a date with a friend of hers. Cheryl had danced with Danielle in several productions and classes. Just out of high school she was almost five feet tall with thick, dark brown hair that fell to the small of her back. I really liked her and she seemed to reciprocate. I had fantasized about her through my stay at Fort Devens and in Ethiopia.

As soon as I had a car, I called and asked her out. We set up a date for the second weekend in February—I figured it would be nice to have furniture first. She offered to drive down to meet me after work that Friday.

She was right on time, and looked more spectacular than I remembered. Over dinner and a show we got better acquainted and found that the mutual attraction was stronger than either of us had thought. Very late that night, we were sitting on my new couch finding that we had more and more in common.

"It's awfully late."
"I wish I didn't have to go home."
"...You know, I'll bet you could spend the night with Danielle. I'm sure she's awake....Or...uh...you could spend the night here."
"...I think I'd sooner stay here."
"That'd be great!"
"Uh...I...brought a little suitcase."
"You did?"
"Well...I was hoping I would want to stay....I mean, I

was hoping I **could** stay."

"Let me go get your bag."

She was phenomenal. I've always been a sucker for good legs, and she had them—plus a lot more. She really only had two drawbacks. First, she was **very** noisy in bed. In fact, I was afraid we would wake the whole building. The next morning when she came into our little dining room in her skimpy nightie and robe, I thought Wally and Charles would croak. She said,

"I hope we didn't keep you up last night. We tried to be quiet."

"Uh...no."

"Not at all."

She was so naive that Wally and Charles basically adopted her—from then on, they treated her like a sister.

Then, again, she wasn't very bright. After that first weekend when most of the talk was about theater and us, there wasn't much more to talk about. I did learn she worked as a Redskinette—one of the Washington Redskin cheerleaders, but that didn't do much to improve our relationship. Actually, the relationship just sort of slowly faded into nonexistence.

The fact that she lived in Burtonsville, Maryland certainly didn't help. It was a 45-minute drive to pick her up or take her home. And in rush hour, it was much longer than that. One Sunday night I took her home late just as Washington was having one of its rare ice storms. It took me six hours to drive home. I got there just in time to wake Wally and Charles so we could all get to work. That wasn't the last nail in the coffin, but by then there weren't many more to seal the lid.

She finally broke up with me one weekend while we were shopping in Georgetown. I thought that was appropriate—I don't like to shop, and I never much liked Georgetown, either.

PARTY NEXT DOOR

Next door lived a single mother and her two daughters. The girls were 17 and 19 years old, and all three were very attractive. Mom guarded the girls like a mother hawk, and was fairly reserved herself. One evening, though, she relaxed just a little. Coming back from the grocery store, I bumped into Mrs. Anderson as she was leaving her apartment.

"Hi, John. It looks like you're cooking tonight."

"Boy, am I cooking! I've been trying to get this friend of mine to part with the recipe for her killer hors d'oeuvre, and tonight's the night."

"Killer hors d'oeuvres?"

"Yeah. They're shrimp, and spices, and all kinds of good things. Hey, why don't you all come over and sample some?"

"Well..."

"How about 8:00?"

"Well...OK. *You all* you said?"

"Unless the girls are allergic to shrimp."

"Well, sure then. We'll be over about 8:00."

Everyone liked the hors d'oeuvres. Everyone liked the beer. Mom even let Terry have a beer or two. Or three. Or....well, who was counting. Cindy was old enough to decide for herself. And when we ran out, Janet (Mrs. Anderson) said,

"Why don't you come over to our place? I have more beer. And bring what's left of those hors d'oeuvres."

So we all toddled next door. Sure enough, there was more beer. Charles left around 11:00—after all, he **was** engaged, and he and Carolyn had to go to church the next morning. Wally and I, however, stayed on. The beer ran out about 1:00 in the morning. By that time, Cindy and Terry were sleeping on sofas in the living room. Wally and Janet and I appeared to be conscious, sitting on the floor talking. As the beer ran out, so did the conversation. There were long pauses between what passed for thoughts.

"Come on, John. We've got to go home...."
"It's a good thing you're not driving, Wall...."
"Yeah...you, too....Are you coming or not?..."
"I'm waiting for you to get up...."
"I don't think I can...."
"You're welcome to sleep on the floor...."
"That wouldn't be proper...."
"Neither would falling down the stairs...."
"That's true...."
"Come on, Wall. Look, **I'm** standing...."
"You're pretty wobbly...."
"Maybe so...but I'll bet I can wobble home...."
"I'm gonna have to crawl...."
"That's all right, Wall....I'll hold the door for you....Why doesn't this lock work like ours?..."
"Are you sure it's locked?..."
"Oh....Now it's not....Come on, Wall....Don't stop....You're getting closer...."

With all the speed of the world's fastest glacier, Wally crawled across the Andersons' living room. I leaned against the door jamb with the door keeping me from falling in the other direction, and watched—or at least my eyes were pointed in the general direction. Janet didn't remain awake to see Wally trying to negotiate the doorway with my help.

"You're blocking the door, John...."

"No, Wall...I'm holding it...."

"Well...hold it open, will you?..."

"Oh...yeah...How's this?..."

"More....That's better....Hey, where're your shoes?..."

"Huh?..."

"Your shoes....Where're your shoes?..."

"I don't know...."

"They're probably back there...somewhere...."

"I don't see them....They'll just have to stay there until tomorrow....Hey...where're **your** shoes?..."

"I don't know....Where are your shoes?..."

"Not my shoes....Where are **your** shoes?..."

"Oh....My shoes?..."

"Yeah...."

"I don't know....Can you see them from up there?..."

"They're probably with mine, somewhere...."

Our shoes spent the night with the lovely Anderson ladies. Eventually, Wally and I made it around the corner to our apartment. It took me quite a while to unlock the door—thanks, Charles. Wally was no help—he couldn't reach the handle. I like to think that I managed to lock their door on my way out.

Janet must have been embarrassed by her (or perhaps, our) behavior. She hardly said a word to us after we retrieved our shoes. She didn't even ask for the recipe.

MUSIC & ARTS

I needed a job. Even as a Spec 5 I wasn't making enough money to make car payments and my share of the lease payments, as well as food, gas, and everything else. What little money I had put away was disappearing fast. I managed to find a part time position with the Kitt Music Company selling sheet music, band instruments, and accessories. We also rented band instruments, primarily for kids in school music programs. It paid just a little more than minimum wage, but the hours fit, and, however remotely, I was working in music.

I had to scramble to get to the store on time after leaving Fort Belvoir. Usually I just had time to stop at home and grab a sandwich, but if traffic was bad, I sometimes had to go straight from one job to the other. I worked week nights from 6:00 until 9:00 and Saturday from 9:00 until 6:00. Of course, I had to help balance the register and close out each night. That added another 10 or 20 minutes.

My immediate boss, head of the band instruments/sheet music shop within Kitt's, was Evelyn Armstrong. She was a sharp, little English woman who had married an American serving in the Air Force in England. She still had a little accent, and was good at her job. She was easy to work for. I often prompted her to talk about her husband just to get her to say his name. Paul, from her, sounded a great deal like *Pool*.

The other full-time employee in our area was Mark Silsby. About six feet four and thin, Mark sported the shoulder-length Prince Valiant hair style that was almost required of pop musicians in the early 70s. Mark only been out of the service for a year or so. He was married and had a baby boy. He had grown up in the Bailey's Cross Roads area, where the store was located, and had been a drummer with the marching band in high school, although he wasn't playing any more. I got along well with Mark. He was so laid back he was nearly horizontal.

The part of the store I worked in was sort of an afterthought for Kitt's, and that spring Music & Arts Centers bought the business from them. After that, we were a store within a store with Evelyn as the store manager.

The real business for Kitt's was piano and organ sales. They specialized in Lowrey organs and Steinway, Everett, and Kawaii pianos. I had never played a Japanese piano before and expected them to be inferior. I found, however, that I liked the touch of the Kawaii better even than that of the Steinway.

A husband and wife team, Lester and Libby Mosley, were the manager and principle salespeople for Kitt's. I think they must have had a pullout bed there. They claimed to have children and a home, but were almost always in the store. I don't think I ever saw their children, except in pictures. Lester had the look of a used-car salesman about him. His hair was always slicked straight back from his forehead in waves. Although he was a good six feet tall, he always stood with his head bowed a bit and never seemed to look directly at you. Instead, he sort of sneaked looks up through his eyebrows at you. Unctuous, almost servile, in manner, he was constantly adjusting his suit jacket and clearing his throat—*harumph*. Libby was somewhat heavyset: she always wore dark, if not black, clothing. She was quiet, always deferential to her husband, and seemed a bit nosey or sneaky. Both of them seemed to regard the rest of us as almost-human.

They also had Willie Thornton working there. His specialty was organ sales. We called him Big Willie. He was about five feet eight and must have weighed 300 pounds or more. He had these pudgy, stubby fingers that you would never have thought would be effective on a keyboard, but he did just fine. He was in some demand to play gospel stuff for revivals and other events. A flamboyant dresser, he had a thick southern preacher's accent and pomaded hair. He wore several gaudy rings, and a flashy watch always dangled from his wrist. He was easier to talk with than the Mosleys, but none of us found him very likable. When he wasn't selling something, and often when he was, he would sit back at one of the organs and play his gospel music—loud. Occasionally, even Lester would get tired of it and ask him to quiet down.

One day Big Willie followed a customer from the organ room right up to the front door of the store. He stopped by our counter, almost in tears.

> "What's the matter, Willie?"
> "Wail, Jahn, Ah've nevah seen anythin' laik thayaht in mah laif."

Well, that's what it sounded like. His jowls all a-quiver, Big Willie had slipped into his finest gospel preacher voice. If you have trouble understanding my transliteration of his speech, I'll translate it in the footnote that follows:

> "What happened?"
> "Wail that mayahn came in a-lookin' fer a orgen. He sayahd he wonted the fahnest orgen he could git fer his home. So Ah took him back to the big Lowrey Theeayter Orgen and sat dayuhwn to show him hahw good it sayounds. *If'n yuh push this key heyur, it'll sayound jest lahk a vahlin*, Ah tolt him. Wail Ah played a beeyuht, and then **he** sayuhd, *Whah, that don't sayound lahk no vahlin*. So Ah tolt him, *If'n yuh push this key, it sayounds jest lahk a bunch uh trumpits*. But when Ah played it, he sayuhd, *Whah, that don't sayound lahk no bunch uh trumpits*. So, real quick lahk, Ah sayahd, *Wail, if'n yuh push this key, it'll sayound jest lahk a banjo quahr*. And Ah played some mower. But he had the audasty to say, *That don't sayound lahk no banjo quahr, neither. Ain't you got a orgen that sayounds lahk a orgen?* Wail, Ah jest din't know whut to say, so he layuft."[15]

We commiserated with him, stifling giggles, but when he went back to his lair in the organ department, Mark and I laughed and laughed and laughed.

Kitts, and later Music & Arts, provided lessons on most instruments. All of the Armed Forces have large bands that remain in the Washington, DC area, except when they are on tour. When you add the members of these service bands to the members of the Washington Symphony Orchestra, the community orchestras and bands, the various college bands and orchestras, and the high school teachers in the area, you have a huge number of very well qualified teachers. Many of them prefer teaching for a music store to teaching at home. The advertising and teaching space is free, and someone else pays withholding taxes, collects money, and does the scheduling.

We had some wonderful instructors at our store. One of the best, and certainly the most eccentric, was Ron Rivers. This man could do incredible things with a guitar. He played with most of the big jazz artists at one time or another as they swung through DC. When I knew him, Ron had just lost a lot of weight—probably 50 or 60 pounds. In everything but his music, he was as cheap a person as you have ever met, so he hadn't bothered to buy new clothes as his weight dropped. As a result, all his clothes hung from him like limp sails on a becalmed yacht. His pants were cinched into multitudinous pleats around his waist, then puffed out everywhere. Shirt collars flopped this way and that around his neck. Ron looked a great deal like Adolph Hitler. He wore the same little mustache, and his hair was dark, generally parted on the right, and usually somewhat mussed. Except when he was playing, he always looked a little wild-eyed—almost surprised. And he had a habit of waving his hands around when he talked. When he got really excited, his suit flowed around him like a cape. He walked with a limp—the result of stepping into a moving car while his mind was working out a counterpoint guitar accompaniment.

Ron collected stringed instruments. He had 14 or 15 at the time. They included such oddities as a harp guitar, a mandola, a couple of mandolins, a lute, and three tenor (4-string) banjos. All had been restored to mint condition by professionals. Ron knew people at most of the famous guitar factories, and had his instruments restored by the companies that originally built them, whenever possible. His collection must have been worth a great deal of money. His cheapest banjo, for example, the one he used for outdoor gigs where there was a chance of rain, retailed for more than $900.00 (in 1970!). Some of the instruments, like the harp guitar, would be difficult to put a price on. Ron didn't have many interests outside of music, but then, he was so good at what he did that I never understood why he bothered teaching for us.

Sandy Young taught bowed instruments. She was a violist for one of the community orchestras and was finishing her Master's Degree at the University of Maryland. Sandy was shy and so quiet that sometimes we didn't even know she had come in and gone back to her teaching studio. Dark hair in tight little waves fell low over her forehead almost like a visor. Well past demure, she was hard to get to know, but over time I found myself liking her a lot. I guess she brought out whatever protective, fatherly feelings I had. Her husband, Ben, taught reed instruments for us, played clarinet for the Army Band, and was working on his Master's Degree at Maryland also.

Sandy had been looking for a new viola. She had traveled all over the East Coast to find one that had just the right timbre, touch, and of course, price. Finally she found the one she wanted in Philadelphia. Although not in the company of a Stradivarius or Amati, it had a good pedigree as well as all the other essentials. After days of haggling, she and Ben drove to Philadelphia on a Sunday to pick it up. She had managed to get the price down to $3,000.00. Well, almost—the bow cost another $600.00. Now $3,600.00 was a **lot** of money in 1970, and Sandy was uneasy at the thought of spending that much for her new viola. The next Monday when she came in to teach she was carrying it like a baby.

"Is that your new viola, Sandy?"
"Yes! Do you want to see it?"

Now, I used an exclamation point where she said "yes," but you have to imagine her voice. She was still so excited that everything she said came out in a sort of husky, breathy tone—quiet and intense. She carefully placed the case on the counter and slowly, deliberately, unzipped the outside, cloth cover. Then, cautiously, she unsnapped the catches and slowly opened the case. Now—oh, so lovingly—she gently lifted the viola and held it toward me.

Just as carefully, I took it and turned it around, looking at it this way and that. It was a beautiful thing. Mark had his turn. Although neither of us would have known why it was worth that kind of money, we both said all the appropriate things. Just as she was nestling it back into its cushions, Ron came walking up from the lesson rooms in the back of the store.

"That your new viola?"
"Oh, yes, Ron. Would you like to see it?"
"Sure."

Again she eased the viola from its sumptuous case and carefully proffered it to Ron. He took it, brusquely flipped it over, knocked on the back a few times with his knuckles, flipped it over again, turned it around, stuck his nose against the strings to get a better view inside through the F holes, plucked the strings a few times, and said,

"Do you mind if I play it?"

Sandy had to close her mouth which had dropped open in terror before she could answer.

"Oh…Well, sure, Ron. Uh…I didn't know you could play.…"

She said as she half turned to get out the bow.

"Well, sure, it's tuned just like a tenor banjo, isn't it?"

Ron flipped the viola around again, snugged the fat end up to his body, and began strumming her precious, new instrument. As he played, lost in his own little world, emotions raced across her face—surprise, horror, blasphemy, hatred, disgust, and more. Finally, he finished with a flourish and returned the viola to her.

"That's nice. It's got a good tone."

And he turned and shuffled back to his teaching room. Sandy stood in shock, watching him walk away. Then she turned, flipped the viola into its case, and briskly sealed it up. In a moment, all of her joy and pride had gone like water down a toilet. Her face a mask, she strode back to her teaching room, went in, and shut the door.

I didn't know whether to laugh or cry. Poor Sandy. That beautiful viola had lost a lot of its luster in that moment. Eventually, however, some of the brilliance must have resurfaced for her. The last I heard from Sandy she was first chair violist with a major orchestra.

CHARLIE LOCKS UP

Now, Charlie was engaged to a nice girl. You do know the difference, don't you, between a good girl and a nice girl? A nice girl goes out, goes home, and goes to bed, while a good girl goes out, goes to bed, and goes home. Chrissy and Charlie were engaged to be married when he got out of the service. They spent a lot of time together, as might have been expected. But despite the fact that he had the master bedroom in the apartment—the one with the attached bathroom—she never spent the night. As far as I knew, she never went into that room. When she came to the apartment, they usually watched television or listened to music.

My relationships were considerably shorter lived, and none of them involved vows of celibacy. Part of me envied Charlie for his engagement with Chrissy, and part of me envied him for the master bedroom suite. My bedroom was one wall away from the living room. This made it difficult to be uninhibited when I had someone sharing my bed. But it was a small price to pay. Charlie and Wally were great roommates, and it was a terrific apartment.

I didn't have that many relationships anyway. Between the hours I spent in the Army and the hours at Music and Arts Center, there weren't many hours left for a love life. On weekdays I usually had to hurry to get home from Fort Belvoir, change clothes, grab something to eat and manage to get to Music and Arts Center by 6:00. At 9:00 when the store closed, I had to help balance the books and clean up. Usually, I didn't get out of there until 9:30. Weekends were somewhat better. I worked Saturdays from 9:30 until 6:00 and after closing up, I was out of there before 6:30. Later, when the blue laws were repealed, I also worked Sundays from 11:30 until 7:00.

Since I did most of the cooking, I also did most of the grocery shopping. That doesn't seem fair, but on the other hand, the other guys did all the cleaning except for my room. One Saturday, after a long day at work and about an hour at the grocery store, I stumbled up the stairs to the third floor with grocery bags, a music case (I was allowed to practice during lunch, if the store wasn't too busy). I didn't want to make extra trips up the stairs, so I had managed, just barely, to carry everything in one shot. I had my key out so I wouldn't have to put everything down to open the door. Not being able to see the lock because of the grocery bags, I groped around with the key, and finally succeeded in getting the thing into the lock. I turned it with a sigh of relief, knowing that soon I could put all that heavy stuff down. The door opened, but only about an inch before it reached the end of the chain. It was dark in the apartment, but I heard scurrying and whispering coming from the living room. Then,

"Just a minute....I'll be right there...."
"Huh?...Well, hurry up! This stuff's heavy!"

Exasperated, I leaned back, allowing the door to close. Finally, I heard the chain slide back and the door opened. The lights were all on and there stood Charlie and Chrissy. Half his shirt buttons were undone, her lipstick was smeared, and she was tucking in her blouse.

"For crying out loud, Charlie!"
"Sorry, John. Uh....Sorry....Uh...that is..."
"Oh, forget it! Just grab some of this stuff!"
"Oh, sure."

Oh, sure indeed. I was less than happy. Chrissy excused herself to go tidy up in the bathroom.

"C'mon, Charlie. What's the idea of chaining the door?"
"Well...we didn't want to be disturbed."

"Why didn't you call me at work? I could have come home later, or something."

"Well...there just didn't seem to be a good time. I mean...well...it just didn't occur to me....Well...you know...."

"Charlie, you have the master bedroom. If you want to do a little kissy face, why don't you go in there and close the door, for crying out loud?"

"Well...we...uh...sort of promised each other...."

"I don't give a shit what you promised each other! Don't lock me out of here again!"

"Yeah...I mean...I'm sorry."

"You said that....Forget it. I'm just a little tired."

Chrissy was considerably embarrassed, although I don't think she heard what Charlie and I had said. They never did that again. But they also never used the bedroom, as far as I know. At any rate, as of 1995 they were still happily married.

RAG TIME

Wally discovered a Shakey's Pizza Parlor in Annandale (the next little town west of us) that featured a live rag time band on Tuesday nights. Soon, a whole bunch of us met there regularly to eat pizza, drink beer, and sing along. There were long, trestle tables with creaky wooden chairs that always seemed on the verge of coming apart and depositing you on the not-too-clean floor. The place was usually packed, especially by the time I got there around 9:30. By then, the other guys would have had a substantial head start on me in beer and pizza consumption. But since the show went on until midnight, I had ample time to catch up.

There were usually a few unattached young women there, and they were the focus of attention for those of our group who were similarly unattached. Wally, in particular, developed a fixation on one of these young ladies.

"Go ahead, Wally. Just walk up and say hi."
"Are you kidding? My appellation would be rebuffed with considerable alacrity."

With a little beer (oh, alright, with a lot of beer), Wally was known to speak with great eloquence. If not with the utmost of sense.

"C'mon, Wally. What have you got to lose?"
"Just my evanescent dream, my fond fantasy of unrequited love."
"Your love can't be quitted. It hasn't even begun."
"What chance have I, a mere mortal, with this

goddess of feminine pulchritudity ...uh...pulchritudinousness...uh...beauty."

"You'll never know unless you try, Wall."

"Then I shall remain secure in my insecurity. She will remain secure in my chaste fantasies. We will remain..."

"Oh, shut up, Wally. Go get another beer."

"A fine idea, that."

A couple of times each night, the band would play a marching song. Stepping off the tiny bandstand, they would begin to march around the room with a hundred or more tipsy patrons following along, as best they could. Sometimes, they would walk right out the front door and march around the parking lot. As mice to the Pied Piper, we, their well-trained followers, would dance along behind, reinvigorated by the fresh night air. Then it was back inside for more beer, more pizza, more stale air, and more general rejoicing.

Now Charlie and Wally each had little sports cars. Wally had a British Racing Green MG roadster, and Charlie had a gray Datsun Fair Lady roadster. I, of course, had my little mustard yellow Fiat 124 Sport Coupe. Not quite a sports car, but sporty enough. We usually arrived at separate times, and therefore, when Shakey's closed for the night, the three of us had to drive home separately. Route 236 (called Duke Street in Alexandria, Little River Turnpike between Alexandria and Fairfax, and Main Street in Fairfax—go figure!) was a four-lane divided highway from Annandale back to our apartment complex.

One night we stood around talking with some of our friends well after Shakey's closed. By the time we got in our cars it was nearly 1:00 in the morning. We pulled out of the little shopping center and drove down Little River Turnpike to the first stoplight on the way home. Charlie and Wally pulled into the two lanes, so I squeezed to the right of Wally, half on the shoulder, half on the highway.

"What the hell are you doing, John?"

"Wanna drag?"

"Are you nuts?"

"I may be nuts, but I'm going to get home before you two in your topless little slot cars."

About then, the light changed and we were all off. Three little four-cylinder engines screamed away as we raced side by side by side to the next light. None of the cars was fast enough to get ahead of the others, so we went abreast from light to light until we arrived at the last red light bumper to bumper to bumper. We paused for a minute. Then, like a group of fighter planes we peeled off to the right into the apartment complex parking lot, laughing like a bunch of maniacs. We didn't try this stunt often, but every once in a while when all of us managed to forget our common sense at the same time, we'd race home again. No one every really won, but that wasn't the point, after all.

PUNNING OUR LIVES AWAY

The work environment at Fort Belvoir was certainly different from any place I'd been in the Army. We worked in a little compound of buildings surrounded by barbed wire with a security guard at the entrance. The buildings were originally barracks like the ones I had lived in Monterey and Fort Devens, but they had been converted into offices. We worked in cubicles on the ground floor. (I don't remember who worked upstairs.) The two squad leader rooms were used by the Warrant Officer and Colonel who were in charge of our little group.

Mr. Hudson was a Chief Warrant Officer (CW4). The Warrant Officer ranked higher than any enlisted rank, but lower than commissioned officers. Many, if not most, were promoted to Warrant Officer after serving in the enlisted ranks. They had to attend a training academy and were generally respected by officers and enlisted men alike—no 90-day wonders here! Mr. Hudson was an affable fellow, reserved and soft-spoken. He was about 50 years old, and had been a career soldier all his working life. He was medium height and build, somewhat nondescript, with an air of weary resignation to the vicissitudes of Army life. A little stand-offish, nevertheless he was always available to anyone who had a question or problem, whether work-related or not.

Major Yousef Sulieman, on the other hand, was a certifiable kook. He was about five feet six and of eastern Mediterranean ethnicity, but he was so intense that he seemed to have just disconnected himself from an electrical socket. His eyes sort of bulged, and he had a wild look about him. Everything he did was hyper.

He didn't walk, he scurried. He didn't talk, he shouted—and with a high-pitched, whiny voice that was just short of being loud enough to shatter glass. He would shout across the narrow corridor that separated his office from Mr. Hudson's.

"Mr. Hudson! Mr. Hudson! Come here! I need you!"

Then, when Mr. Hudson had gone into the Major's office and closed the door, we could all still hear the Major shouting. Poor Mr. Hudson. He must have developed quite a case of tinnitus during his association with the voluble Major Sulieman. I know the rest of us certainly did.

The non-commissioned officer who ranked just below Mr. Hudson was Sergeant Archer. He had a little office cubicle right near the front door and stairwell, so he could keep track of everyone's whereabouts. In addition to being a career soldier, he was a nosy son-of-a-gun. If you even acted like you were going to go outside, he would interrogate you.

"Where you going, troop?!"
"I'm going to the bathroom, Sergeant Archer."
"Oh…I, uh, thought….Never mind!"

We tried to determine what was the minimum body fake needed to get Sergeant Archer to ask us where we were going. After a while, we stopped tormenting him. It was just too easy.

We wore civilian clothes. What a change! After three years of un-relenting uniformity, we all had to re-learn how to select what clothes to wear each day. None of us, surprisingly, had much trouble, although on our incomes, the outfits certainly were not the height of sartorial resplendence. We had to wear security badges on chains around our necks which had to be hidden in our shirt pockets when out of the compound and pulled out to display to the security guard for entry. Then they had to remain in view while we were in the secure compound.

There were three cubicles on each side of the center aisle. Each cubicle held three or four desks and a couple of safes and bookshelves. Our little group was responsible for translating a mountain of documents that had been seized by the Israelis during the Six-Day War. Actually, what we were translating were the dregs from that mountain. The things that really looked important had been translated as soon as possible after the documents had been sorted out by the Israelis. I wouldn't doubt that the most important of the documents captured by the Israelis never even found their way to the United States. More than two years later, what we had left wasn't deemed to be terribly crucial. But there was always the hope that something of note would turn up. During my last eight months in the service, however, I didn't hear of anything worthwhile that came out of our part of the mountain.

The cubicle I worked in was also inhabited by Wally, Gerry Herman (another alumnus of Asmara), and a career soldier, Sergeant Alex O'Neil. Gerry had worked eves with Wally and John Chase, who was also working in our little building in the next cubicle over. Gerry and Chase were both heavy drinkers, intent on solidifying their livers before they reached 30. Gerry and his wife, Arlene, and John and his wife, Sally, often had parties for all of us Asmara alumni at their respective homes. We all drank more than was wise, but all of us somehow survived our youthful stupidity.

Alex O'Neil was about our age, but unlike most of the Army Security Agency soldiers, he had decided to make the Army his home for at least 20 years. Alex wasn't terribly smart, but he made up for it by not having much of a personality. That's not terribly fair. He tried to be one of the guys, but never quite fit in. He didn't flaunt the fact that he was, technically, in charge of our little cubicle, and he tried to participate in what passed for intellectual conversation among us.

Every so often we would spend the day punning. Now, that may sound sort of silly, but it was a whole lot worse than that. One of us would start, intentionally or un-, early in the day with some sort of outrageous pun. Then we would spend the rest of the day making more puns on whatever subject the first one concerned. This might be animals, machines, or some other ordinary thing that, after a while, became more than mundane. (My personal favorite was *parts of the body*.) Sometimes one of us would announce, generally into an unexpecting, silent work environment, the subject of the day. Those who didn't hear the proclamation would be notified while the first examples were forthcoming. People were generally polite, waiting for a split second of silence to take their turn.

When the punning started, everyone on our floor would join in. At first, the puns would come fast and furious, but after a while, the easy ones had all been done. Then, only those of us who were completely nuts would continue to look for more. By the afternoon, finding another pun was a torturous procedure. In order to get to the actual pun, we would have to come up with some outlandish scenario. As the ridiculousness began to coalesce, the punster might announce,

"Uh...Wait a minute, here...I think...Yes...Hold on...Here it is...."

It was sort of like giving birth—on a fundamentally trite level, of course. At the first stuttering, tentative, announcement that the new arrival was imminent, a hush would fall over the office. Everyone would stop typing and talking, and strain to hear the forthcoming silliness. The prologue would begin haltingly, as the punster was still piecing the outrageous tale together. But as he became more sure of himself, the story would come faster and faster, like a snowball rolling downhill. Then would come the awful moment—the pun itself would be triumphantly announced. After a stunned pause would come the punster's reward.

"Oooooooooohhhhhhhh...."
"...That's...disgusting!"
"Ick...."

"Gaaack...."

"Where did you come up with that...with that...with that!"

And much, much more of the same. This particular bit of camaraderie was completely beyond Alex. At first, we found ourselves explaining even the simplest puns. After a while, we didn't bother any more.

One day, Alex invited Wally and me to his house for dinner. We resisted, but he wouldn't take no for an answer. So, one Saturday after I got off work, I picked Wally up, and we drove over to the town house where he and his wife lived. We met his wife, Sally. She was a pleasant woman, but she appeared somewhat flustered, as though she weren't accustomed to entertaining. Alex announced that she was cooking Cornish Hens for the first time. She became even more flustered when Wally and I made all the proper anticipatory comments.

We sat down to get acquainted. After a while, I think we all realized we didn't have much in common. The evening stuttered along, lengthened by the stubborn Cornish Hens, which appeared to be relaxing contentedly in the O'Neil oven—far more serene than the four of us were in the living room. Our conversation had long since degenerated into old Army stories, leaving Sally pretty much bored senseless. She retreated to the kitchen where she pottered around, trying to encourage the hens to brown.

Finally, she announced that they were ready. We sat down at the little dining room table. Dinner was served. Sally was a pretty good cook. Everything looked and tasted just fine—except for the *pièce de resistance*. The unfortunate Cornish Hens needed still more time in their not-so-hot little oven. We ate the parts that appeared to be done, and left a good half of the rest bleeding on the plates.

After-dinner conversation was stilted and, mercifully, brief. We talked in fits and starts for about a half hour, then Wally and I made our excuses and left. We weren't invited back, and we didn't invite them to our bachelor digs.

* * * * *

One day, many weeks later, Alex announced that he wouldn't be in the next day until after lunch. When Gerry, Wally, and I came in the next morning, we sat around talking. After a while, Wally said,

"Well, I guess it's time to get to work...."
"Too bad...."
"Yeah...."
"Maybe not...."
"What do you mean?"
"Well...we don't really have anything to work on, do we?"
"What...?"
"Not until someone opens the safe...."
"Huh...?"
"Well...**I** don't have the combination to the safe. Do you?"
"No. You know Alex opens the safe.
"Well...what if no one opens the safe...?"
"But doesn't Archer have the combination?"
"Maybe...."
"Oh...well...then...I guess...there wouldn't be much to do...."
"But...won't someone notice that we aren't working?"
"Does anyone ever notice if we **are**?"
"No....But the sign...."

Each safe had a little wooden paddle that fit into the handle in the top drawer. One side was painted green with the word *Safe* painted on it. The other side was red with the word *Open* painted on it. That way, you could tell at a glance what the status of the safe was.

"That's a point....I'll just turn it around, like this. Now the safe is officially open."

"Well, then, I guess we're officially working."

Sure enough, no one said a thing. We sat around reading and talking all morning. After lunch, we took up right where we had left off. Alex came in around 1:30. He looked around. Then he looked around again.

"What are you guys doing?"

"We're at work, Alex."

"Well...but...what are you working **on**?"

"Oh. Well, we don't really have anything to work on, Alex."

"What do you mean?"

"Well, we can't get into the safe."

"Huh...? But it's open, see?"

"No. The sign says it's open, but we can't open it."

"What...? The safe **is** locked!"

"That's what we've been trying to tell you."

"Well, why didn't you open it?"

"We don't have the combination, Alex."

"Well, yeah. But Sergeant Archer has the combination."

"He **does**...?"

"You mean you've been sitting around here all day doing nothing?"

"Well, we didn't have anything to work on, Alex...."

"What the hell?! I can't **believe you haven't done A DAMNED THING ALL DAY!**"

"We were just waiting for you to open the safe, Alex."

Alex was none too happy, as you might have guessed. There was one unfortunate consequence to this little escapade. The next time Alex was late coming in, Sergeant Archer checked in on us early and often.

HARD BOILED

Waking Wally was my job. And it wasn't easy, either. This is the same guy I tried to wake up in Ethiopia when I thought I was dying. He didn't sleep any lighter in Alexandria, Virginia. I would generally start by knocking on his door when I got out of the shower.

> "Hey, Wally! It's time to get up."

I'd wait a minute, then open his door. No movement.

> "C'mon, Wally! It's time....I'm going to turn on the light...."

Turning on the light made no difference whatsoever.

> "Get up, Wilkins! We're going to be late...! I'm going to get dressed, then I'll come back in here and throw a bucket of water on you."

No response. After I got dressed, I'd try some more. Eventually, I'd get tired of trying to wake him up, and go have breakfast. After that was cleaned up, I'd try again.

> "Wilkins! If you don't get up, I'm going to leave without you!...C'mon, Wall, get up!"

Well, you can imagine. It was an every-morning hassle. One day, he dragged himself out of bed and got dressed just at the time that we needed to be going.

"C'mon, Wally! You've got your coffee, but there's no time for you to make breakfast. Take a piece of bread to gnaw on, or something."

"I have to have my eggs."

"I'm telling you, there's no time for you to make eggs.... What are you doing?"

"I'll just take them like this."

"You can't eat raw eggs!"

"I'll cook them at work. Just let me get some stuff...."

"How are you going to cook eggs at work?"

"I'll put them in the coffee pot. Then, when they're done, I'll just break them into this bowl, and eat them with this spoon."

"In the coffee pot?"

"Yeah. No one has to know they're in there."

"Whatever! Let's just get going, can we?"

Sure enough, as we walked in, Wally took his two eggs and gently dropped them into the coffee maker. We had one of those 24-cup models at the site.

"Now, how are you going to get them out? They won't float, you know?"

"I brought just the thing for that."

Reaching into his jacket, he pulled a slotted cooking spoon partway out of the inner pocket.

"I didn't see you take that with you."

"There's a lot you don't see. I also have the salt and pepper."

"Your jacket pockets must be filled with the salt and pepper."

"Oh...yeah...Look at that! They sure are."

"You'll have to shake that jacket over the balcony when we get home."

"A small price to pay for breakfast."

But before the eggs had finished cooking, Major Sulieman decided it was time for some coffee. He held his cup under the spout and depressed the spigot.

Nothing happened. He bent down and looked at the water level gauge to make certain there was water in there. Then he put his hand near the side to make sure it was hot. Then he tried again.

Still nothing.

"What the hell is wrong with this coffee maker?!"

He screamed in his typical shrill voice.

"Nothing, Major Sulieman. I filled it this morning."

"Well, just look at this, Sergeant Archer!" See?! There's nothing coming out!"

"Something must be wrong...."

Just then, Wally sauntered up.

"Excuse me, Major."

"What the hell do you want, Wilkins?!"

"My eggs may be blocking the spout. Let me take a look."

"Your eggs?! Your eggs?! What the hell do you mean 'your eggs!?'"

"I put my eggs in there to cook this morning. Just a minute...Let me...Yeah, there they are....See, down there?"

"You've got eggs in my coffee pot!"

"Yeah. Just a minute, let me get my bowl and spoon."

"Are you crazy, Wilkins? You put eggs in my coffee pot!"

"They should be done by now....Let me just...ease them...out. There! Thanks, Major Sulieman. Sorry to inconvenience you."

"What the hell?! Do you think this is a breakfast bar, or something Wilkins?!"

"No, sir. But I just can't work on an empty stomach. Excuse me. I don't want these to get cold."

The shells were a little brown, but the eggs looked pretty good. Wally said he couldn't taste the coffee they had been cooking in.

* * * * *

Wally invited me to come to Cleveland with him for a weekend. I could help him drive, and we could both get out of Virginia for a couple of days. I managed to take a weekend off from my other job, and away we went. By this time, Wally had sold his MG, and replaced it with a gargantuan, old Chrysler 2-door sedan. It suited him about as well as the huge BMW motorcycle he had driven in Ethiopia. On top of everything else, it was sort of a lilac color. Immediately christened the *grapemobile*, it was quite a sight. Wally could see over the dash, but you couldn't see much of him, particularly from the back. It rode well, though, and got us to Cleveland in some kind of style.

Wally's parents lived in Parma, a suburb that long ago had been swallowed by the city of Cleveland. A lovely town for people who translated Arabic, Parma had sets of streets whose spellings were reversed. The street next to Parma was Amrap, the one next to Regal was Lager, and so on and on. Wally's parents house was much like the one I had grown up in. Three little bedrooms, living room, kitchen, dining room, and bathroom on the ground floor with a full basement below. It could have been made from the same plans as the one I had lived in. His parents were easy to get to know, and practically adopted me on the spot, as I did them.

We arrived late Friday night, talked for a while and turned in. I got up early the next morning and wandered out into the kitchen. Mr. Wilkins had already left for work. He drove a truck for a local grocery store chain. Mrs. Wilkins was cleaning up his breakfast dishes.

> "Good morning, John. Would you like some breakfast?"
>
> "Good morning, Mrs. Wilkins. Yes thanks. A bowl of cereal would be fine."
>
> "You can't exist on just a bowl of cereal. Let me make you some bacon and eggs."
>
> "That's too much trouble, Mrs. Wilkins. I'll just have some cereal."
>
> "It's no trouble at all. You do like eggs and bacon, don't you?"
>
> "Well, sure, but...."
>
> "How many eggs would you like?"
>
> "Uh, two, I guess. If you're sure it's not too much trouble?"
>
> "Not at all. Is sunny side up OK?"
>
> "That'd be great. Thanks."

The eggs were good, if a little overcooked. We sat at the little table talking for a while. Then she said,

> "Well, he can't sleep all day. It's time for him to get up."
>
> "Wally? Uh, I mean Mark?"

Although we called Mark Wally, his parents called him Markie or, sometimes, Mark.

> "Yes. I would like to have some time with him before you two have to go back."

"Boy! I hope you know some secret. It takes me forever to wake him up."

"Oh, it's no problem whatsoever. Watch."

And with that, I followed her down the little hall to the door to Wally's bedroom. She opened the door, and called quietly, sort of like a mourning dove,

"Hoo. Hoo. Hoo-ooh."

Wally rolled over in bed and sat up.

"Good morning, Mom."
"See? No problem."

I couldn't reply. In fact, I couldn't close my mouth. With one magic phrase, she had done what normally took me a half hour of cajoling. Wally was out of bed and ready for breakfast in a matter of minutes. I was stunned.

The rest of the weekend was very pleasant. But for once, I couldn't wait for Monday morning. When I got done in the bathroom, I opened the door to Wally's room, and in my best imitation of Mrs. Wilkins said,

"Hoo. Hoo. Hoo-ooh."

Wally rolled over in bed and sat up.

"Good morning, Mom...Uh...Mom?.. Where am I?"
"Oh, I've got you now, Wilkins! You'll never sleep in again!"

And he didn't. That little secret made my mornings much more relaxed for the rest of the time we shared the apartment in Alexandria.

HAND GRENADE

One morning, Gerry Herman came in hung over worse than he usually was. He looked to be in considerable distress when he sat down. He whispered,

> "Please, don't make any loud noises. This is the worst hangover I've ever had."

This was some accomplishment. Gerry had had hangovers that were the stuff of legend. We had seen mornings before when he drank coffee seemingly by the gallon. This day, however, he did, indeed, look worse. We tip-toed around, and whispered. He sat with his head in his hands and his eyes closed, grimacing at each sound.

About ten minutes later, Major Sulieman came storming in the front door, yelling in his high-pitched shriek,

> "Mr. Hudson! Mr. Hudson! Come in my office!"
> "Coming, Sir."
> "Close the door!"

Gerry winced at the sound. We looked at Gerry, then at each other. Things looked bad. Major Sulieman was yelling away in there in top form. It didn't much matter whether the door was open or closed. You could probably hear Major Sulieman driving through Fort Belvoir on Route 1. Gerry's face looked more and more pained. Finally, he exploded. He picked up the metal waste basket sitting next to his desk, and started pounding it on the wall that separated our cubicle form Major Sulieman's office. Oblivious to the pain he must have been causing himself, Gerry screamed,

"Shut the fuck up! Stop screaming in there, you little asshole, or I'll roll a goddamn grenade in there and blow your stupid ass into the fucking Potomac River!"

Gerry collapsed back into his chair holding his head in his hands. He was accompanied by utter silence. We all held our breath, waiting for Sulieman to come out and read Gerry the riot act.

After a couple of stunned minutes, however, we heard Major Sulieman run out of his office and out the back door of the barracks. Wally and I stuck our noses to the window just in time to see him running out of the area. We expected the MPs to come for Gerry, but I think Sulieman was scared to death of him. We didn't see him for the rest of the day.

MIKE'S

If you drive north from Fort Belvoir on Route 1, you will see a little restaurant on the left side of the street about two miles from the fort. It was still there last time I drove by. It used to be called Mike's, but I guess Mike retired. At any rate, it was a favorite lunch place for people who worked at Fort Belvoir. Other folk too, I'd guess. By noon, it was always very busy, but when we went there, we usually beat the rush. Our lunch hour started at 11:30, so we usually got there by 11:40 at the latest.

Mike's was very popular for one primary reason. Draft beer was 25 cents a glass. No matter what comparison you make, in 1970, 25 cents was cheap for a glass of beer. The beer wasn't even too bad. The food was pretty good, also, but most of the guys who went there went for the beer. Some of the fellows I accompanied there could drink an unbelievable amount of beer in the 30 minutes or so that we had to spend. I had begun to like beer in Europe, but could never get enthusiastic about the American brews. So I would normally nurse one, while the other guys inhaled the stuff.

The bar was dark, noisy, and of course, smoky. Smoking ordinances weren't even a fond wish yet for those of us who didn't indulge. The conversation was good, and the camaraderie was first rate. We couldn't afford to go there more than once a week, but when we did, we enjoyed it.

For me, the most interesting aspect of lunch at Mike's was the aftermath. Productivity at the site went straight down the tubes on afternoons when we came back from Mike's. Guys would sit, staring at the wall in front of them. Eyelids would droop, and heads would nod. Fellows who had corner desks might cradle their chins in their hands as though deep in thought and actually go to sleep (perhaps *pass out* would be more accurate). Occasionally, five or six of us would adjourn to John Chase's apartment (a little farther up Route 1), and we'd call in to say we had forgotten to tell Sergeant Archer about some interview we had to go to at the Pentagon, or a job training class, or whatever sounded good. No one seemed to get too sleepy at Chase's place. Of course, we weren't trying to translate Arabic there, either.

It's a pity the Army didn't have computer terminals for us to work on. A productivity analysis program would have had some impressive things to report on those afternoons.

MEDICAL

One morning, Herman, Chase, Wally, and I went up to Sergeant Archer's desk about 9:00.

"Sergeant Archer?"
"Yeah?"
"We have to go to the Pentagon for physicals today. We probably won't be back this afternoon."
"What?!"
"We have to go…"
"I heard what you said! You don't honestly expect me to swallow another cock and bull story like that, do you?!"
"What do you mean, Sergeant Archer?"
"You—all of you bozos—have skipped out of here one time too many! I ain't fallin' for any more of your crap! Get back to work!"
"But Sergeant…"
"You heard me! **Get back to work!**"
"Sergeant Archer, we really do have to take physicals today."
"Bull! I ain't seen no orders! You guys ain't goin' nowhere!"

He had a triumphant gleam in his eyes. He really had us, at last. No one was going to pull the wool over his eyes.

"No fooling, Sergeant. We have to go. Why don't you call to check on us. It's the Pentagon clinic."

"Right! Great bluff, but I ain't buyin' it! Get back to work!"

"It's not a bluff. Call the clinic."

....

He studied us, carefully. We stared back, impassively. Finally, he said,

"All right, assholes! I'm callin' your bluff! You guys are goin' to be in some kinda shit!"

He looked up the number in his directory, picked up the phone, and dialed.

"Yeah. This is Sergeant Archer at Fort Belvoir. I've got some troops here who claim to have physicals scheduled for today....Sure. SP-5 Gerry Herman...with one *n*, SP-5 Mark Wilkins, SP-5 John Chase, and SP-5 John Leeger....Sure, that's L-E-E-G-E-R....Sure, I'll hold...."

He glared at us, triumphantly. We looked back at him, innocently.

"Yeah, this is Sergeant Archer....What?! Are you sure?"

Then, his face began to fall.

"Yeah....Thanks....Uh...all afternoon?...OK."

He hung the phone up carefully. It was very quiet for a minute or so. Then,

"All right. You assholes get outta here. But I'm warning you, I'm checking up on you!"

But the fight had gone out of him. He had picked just about

the only time we actually had something scheduled to check up on us. I don't think he checked again. We didn't skip out too much more any way.

And it didn't take all afternoon. We were back at Chase's house by 2:30.

WILL AND WENDY JONES

Will Jones worked in the cubicle across the aisle from ours. He had about six months longer to go than we did, but other than that, he fit in with the rest of us real well. Will looked like he had an eastern-Mediterranean background, with black hair, a noticeable beard, and a Romanesque nose. The rest of us had met Wendy one night at Shakey's, and she resembled him enough to be his sister. They shared a very dry sense of humor, and loved word games. Will was one of the office's finest contributors to the punning sessions.

At work one day, Will said to Wally and me,

"How'd you guys like to come over Saturday for dinner?"
"Does Wendy know you're asking us?"
"Yeah. She said she pities you poor bachelors—thinks you need some good home cooking for a change."
"What? Wilkins, have you been lying about my cooking?"
"On the contrary...."
"Well, if I were the kind of guy who'd take offense, I might take offense."
"Good thing you're not."
"Yeah."

So we went. They had an apartment in a high-rise on Duke street at Telegraph Road. The dinner was great, and Wendy and Will were a lot of fun. About 11:00, however, Wendy said,

"Well, this has been fun, but I have to get ready for work."

"Work? You work at midnight on a Saturday night?"

"I'm a nurse at the Alexandria Hospital. You don't think we could exist on just what the Army pays Will, do you?"

"I know I'm having to work a second job."

"Well, I'm our family's second job."

"Maybe you're our family's first job. I'd sooner think of the Army as a second job."

"Me, too. One that's going to end, when, Will?"

"174 days. But who's counting?"

Wendy went back to get ready. After a while, she reappeared.

"Wow, Wendy! You look just like a nurse!"

"Yeah....I sure hope Frank died today."

"**What**?! Who...?"

"Oh...I work in the intensive care unit. One of my patients is ready to go. I know this sounds callous, but there's a lot of paper work, and other clean up stuff to do when a patient dies. Frank is 83, after all, so it's not like he's going ahead of his time. I just hope he goes ahead of mine."

"I don't see how you can work there."

"Oh, it's not so bad. In fact I like it—except for the dying stuff. I like Frank Johnston. It's hard to see a patient die, but I guess you do get used to it."

"I don't think I could."

"I didn't think I could, either."

It was a stunning thought, for me. But on the other hand, a lot of guys my age were dying every day over in Vietnam.

GEORGE MALAYTER

George Malayter lived in an apartment complex called Southern Towers. It is right at the intersection of Route 7 and what was then Interstate 95. (Now, it's called Interstate 395, just to keep the tourists confused.) He shared an apartment there with a couple of other guys. The apartment was on the top floor, 16th, I think. It faced sort of north and west, so you couldn't see Washington from his windows. But you could look west toward Bailey's Crossroads. At that time, there was a small airport where the Skyline complex is now. It was just for private planes, mostly one-engine craft like Piper Cubs.

George and his roommates had a party almost every Friday night. The place would be wall-to-wall with people, most of whom were awash with alcohol. I was always nervous when I went to one of these parties. Some of the people were so drunk I was afraid they would jump off the balcony. You see, standing on his balcony, you were right under the flight path for the little airport's runway. When planes were taking off, it looked like they were going to slam right into one side of the balcony. When they were landing, it looked like they might smash into the other side. The darkness intensified the effect, so that even if you were sober, it was pretty intimidating. No one ever jumped off George's balcony (at least during the time I knew him), but I was nervous just the same.

George's parties, like all the parties that we had or went to, were *Bring Your Own Booze*. Usually the kitchen sink held an open bag of ice from the local 7-11 that everyone used for their drinks. The liquor bottles stood on the kitchen table, along with any mixes that might be available. The refrigerator was pretty much reserved for beer.

Now, at that time, I was drinking ultra-dry Martinis. Well,

let's face it, I was drinking straight gin. The Martini recipe I used involved whispering *Vermouth* over the glass that held my gin. And at that, you didn't want to whisper too loud. Obviously, the quality of the drink was determined entirely by the quality of the gin in it (the ice didn't add much), so I only drank Beefeater's. The cheap stuff didn't taste good. The problem I ran into was that when I brought a bottle of Beefeater's to one of these parties, I would get one drink from it. By the time I was ready for another, the bottle would be empty. I think there must have been some kind of secret signal that was passed around the room—*Quality Booze In Kitchen*, or something to that effect.

After a few of these disappointing evenings I hit upon a plan. A couple of days before the next one, I bought a fifth of Beefeater's, took it home, and stuck it in our freezer, still wrapped in its little brown paper bag. When I arrived at the party, I took an ice tea glass, filled it with ice, then covered the ice with Beefeater's. Then, when no one was in the kitchen, I took the bottle in its paper bag, and stuck it in the freezer. Evidently, no one looked up there, so it lasted the whole evening. I had found the answer to my dilemma.

There were two results from this plan. I drank a lot more than I had previously. In fact, on a couple of occasions I drank nearly a whole fifth in one evening. This led to me giving up drinking after a few of these nights. I decided it just wasn't good for me. Probably just as well—if I had continued drinking at that rate, I probably wouldn't be around now.

But the other result was that at about 1:00 a.m. at these parties someone would invariably come up to me and stare at my drink. Then they would say something like this:

> "Boy, I've had too much to drink. That water looks refreshing. Could I have a swallow?"

I could never resist.

"Sure. Have as much as you like."

The poor unsuspecting one would take a big swallow. This was usually followed by a lot of coughing, spraying, hacking, and/or cursing. No one ever took a punch at me, but I think a couple of them considered it.

SUMMER

At last it was summer. The ice storms were behind us, and I, along with thousands of other Washingtonians, was ready for summer. Or so I thought. I had never experienced summer in Washington. After living there for more than a quarter century, I still haven't learned to like it. Washington, DC was built on a swamp, which is one reason that Virginia and Maryland could be persuaded to give the land to the Federal Government in the first place. Summers in Washington are not only hot, they're humid. Sticky. Oppressive. Steamy. Well, you get the picture. It was almost as hot as Masawa in Ethiopia. (Well, **that** might be somewhat of an exaggeration.)

My car wasn't air-conditioned, and it was miserable—especially in stop-and-go traffic! The air-conditioning system in the apartment provided a welcome refuge. In fact, even work at the Music & Arts Center was a better place to be than outside. The building at Fort Belvoir, needless to say, was not a comfortable place to work. Oh, it had a couple of window air-conditioners on each floor, but as fast as they made cool air, the old building leaked it away. The air in the converted barracks was only marginally better than outside. The building did provide a decent sun screen, I guess.

Eventually, Wally and I came up with a routine that made Sundays, at least, enjoyable. We would start by going down to the pool. We'd lie there until we were sweating, then jump in the pool and cool down. After a couple or three cycles like this, we'd be hungry, and/or thirsty. A couple of blocks away was a restaurant called Lum's. The chain has since gone under, but at the time, Lum's provided a welcome respite for us. They had a very American menu, but Wally and I went for three things only: hot dogs with sauerkraut, air conditioning, and schooners of Michelob. The hot dogs were very tasty, and the air conditioning was, of course, wonderful on a hot summer day. But the Michelob....Well, the schooners were about 10 inches high and kept frosty in a cooler. Just looking at that cold, cold glass lowered my temperature some. It was a wonderful thing on a steamy, Washington, summer day.

The schooners provided a new game, as well. The bottom of the base was concave, and when the schooner was placed upside-down and wet in the cooler, some of the moisture would pool there and freeze. After you had a couple of sips, a little nickel-sized piece of ice would detach itself for your pleasure. The thing looked like a little telescope lens. But because the edges where tapered, you could hold it between your thumb and forefinger and squeeze, and it would be launched quite a distance. We tried to keep our little game confined to our table, but if there were more guys than just Wally and me, sometimes the game would get out of hand, and the little frozen flying saucers might end up anywhere. After a while, the hostesses must have begun to recognize us. They seemed to lead us to out-of-the-way booths. And we did go there fairly often. On really hot days, we might make the complete pool/sun/Lum's cycle four or five times—it's hard to remember just what the maximum number might have been.

GET ME TO THE CHURCH ON TIME

Wally's parents arrived one Friday evening to spend a weekend in Washington. They stayed in a little motel down the street. It was nice to see them again when they dropped by to inspect where Wally lived. Wally was their tour guide Saturday. He came back to the apartment about 10:00 p.m.

"John! You've got to help me!"
"What's the problem, Wall?"
"My parents want to go to church with me tomorrow."
"So...?"
"I've been telling them I go to church every Sunday."
"Oh...."
"Well...I don't know where the nearest church is!"
"Oh! Well, why don't we look in the phone book?"
"Great idea!"
"Any particular denomination?
"Catholic, of course!"
"I didn't know you were Catholic."
"Oh, shut up and help me look."

We found a couple that seemed to be nearby, but neither of us was very familiar with the surrounding neighborhoods. We didn't have an area map, of course, so we settled on the next best thing. We would drive in a spiral search pattern until we happened on a Catholic church. By now it was 10:30, so I volunteered to drive while Wally looked.

We drove around in the dark for about an hour and a half, and found nothing. No, that's not quite right. We found Baptist, Methodist, Lutheran, Episcopalian, Presbyterian, Seventh-Day Adventist, and who knows what other kinds of churches. We found a couple of temples and even a mosque. But no Catholic church.

"This is ridiculous, Wally. I thought there were more of you Catholics than this."

"There are....There are....I just don't know where we all meet."

"I don't know how we could have missed them. There must be some closer to home than this. We're almost to Annandale, now."

"I know....I know...."

"I'm going to head back. We must have missed it."

"But where?"

"I don't know....Let's try going down here again."

....

"Stop! Go back! I think I saw a sign."

"From God, I hope."

"Look! Over there!"

"Well, **you** can get out and read it."

....

"What'd it say?"

"It's a Catholic church!"

"Where?"

"The sign said to turn left."

"But that's a residential area."

"Turn left."

"OK...OK."

"It must be....Turn right here!"

"Wall, this is a driveway."

"No! Turn!"

"Alright....Well, I'll be...."

"We found one!"

"Write down the name. Check to see if you can find out what time services are. I'll try to shine the headlamps on the front of the building."

He got the name, but that was all. We weren't even a mile from the apartment. We drove back, laughing at our adventure. When we got back to the apartment, I was ready for bed. It was just about midnight.

"Wait a minute, John. I have to find out what time Mass is."

"Well, call the church. Look up the number in the phone book."

"Oh! I can't do that! I'll wake Father."

"What? The priest? C'mon, Wally. The priest isn't going to answer the office phone at...12:15 in the morning! This is 1970. They'll have an answering machine. Call the number."

"Well...."

"Call the number!"

"OK....It's ringing....Twice....John, I'm afraid...Huh...Oh, excuse me, Father. Well...I...uh...Well...I'm from out of town, and I...uh...just happened to...uh...drive by the church today, and I wondered...well...if I wanted to come to Mass tomorrow...uh...what time would it be?...Yes...Well...Thank you."

"He was awake?"

"Not before the phone rang! And I lied to a priest!"

"You didn't lie to a priest, Wally. You **are** from out of town, and we **did** drive by the church today, right?"

"Yeah....I guess so...."

Well, Wally took his parents to church, and they really enjoyed the service. They remarked about what a lovely, secluded setting the church was in. Wally said later that he kept his head down and tried not to look the priest in the eye when he took Communion.

I slept in.

ETS

Early in June Major Sulieman called me into his office. Well, actually he sort of screamed me into his office.

"Leeger! Come in here!"
"You wanted to see me, Major Sulieman?"
"Close the door....I have a problem with this request you are sending in—the one about your leave time!..."

I had filed a request trying to get the Army to realize that the permissive TDY I had been granted while in Ethiopia shouldn't be counted as leave. If I wasn't successful, I would end up having to pay Uncle Sam for several weeks leave.

"What kind of problem are you talking about, Sir?"
"Right here! You've signed this Spec-5 John W. Leeger! You're not a Spec-5, Leeger!"

Uh oh....All the haggling about length of hair, sideburns, lunches at Mikes, trips to the Pentagon had caught up with me. Well, even one of them could have caught up with me. That stinking Sulieman was going to bust me to Spec-4.

"Uh....I'm not?"
"No....You're a Spec-6! Your orders just came in today! Congratulations!"
"Oh....Thank you, Sir."

I couldn't believe it. I had less than three months to go. Why would they promote me to Spec-6? I sat down at my desk. The Major had followed me out.

"Specialist Wilkins!"
"Yes, Sir?"
"The Army has made a terrible mistake in your behalf!...."
"Oh?...What's that, Sir?"
"They've promoted you to Spec-6!"
"What?"
"You're a Spec-6, Wilkins! Your orders just came in today!"
"Oh....Well...thank you, Sir."
"Colonel Mattingly will be here Monday to present your stripes!"
"Oh....Thank you, Sir."
"Look sharp!"
"Yes, Sir."

Major Sulieman went back into his little office. Wally and I stared at each other.

"Spec-6? Why are they making us Spec-6? We only have a couple more days until ETS[16]."
"75 days, in my case, but who's counting. Who knows why? This **is** the Army, you know."
"I've got it! They're promoting us in the hope that we'll re-up!"
"Not a chance! Why in the hell would they want us for a couple more years? They're having a tough time putting up with us now."
"That's true enough. Well, who knows, indeed?"

Sure enough, Monday morning, Colonel Mattingly arrived accompanied with a photographer. The little ceremony took place in the open area in front of Sergeant Archer's desk. Sergeant Archer didn't look too happy, by the way. I have a copy of the picture the photographer made while the Colonel presented me with my new, never-to-be-worn stripes. Unfortunately, he didn't record the dialogue.

> "Specialist Leeger, I'm proud to present you with these stripes, symbols of your promotion to Specialist Sixth Class."
> "Thank you, Sir."
> "I hope to be able to present you with additional promotions, soon."
> "Don't count on it, Sir."
> "Huh?...Harumph!"

I hadn't said it very loudly, but I guess he heard it well enough. I didn't really mean to offend him, but I didn't plan on being in the Army one day past August 25.

Later that week, some of us who were going to be getting out within the next few months received offers from NSA. We could request immediate transfer to NSA at the equivalent government salary range, and be able to apply our time in the Army toward government retirement. We talked about it among ourselves, but no one was inclined to trade one bureaucracy for another.

In early July, it was time for the yearly Re-Up interview. Poor Mr. Hudson. At least he was enough of a realist not to make things any more uncomfortable for himself than they had to be.

> "Leeger, I guess you know that this is your annual Re-Enlistment Interview."
> "Yes, Sir, and if you'd like to spare us both the hassle, I'd be happy to sign something saying you did your best, but failed."
> "Oh....Well...thank you, Specialist Leeger."
> "No problem, Mr. Hudson."

Most of us were in and out of Mr. Hudson's office about that quickly. And then he came out to get Wally.

"Specialist Wilkins? I'd like you to come into my office for a while."
"Uh....Is this about re-enlistment, Mr. Hudson?"
"Yes, it is, Specialist."
"Well, just let me get my coffee cup, Sir...."

At his own pace, Wally got everything ready, went into Mr. Hudson's office and closed the door. He didn't come out until lunch time.

"Hey, Wall! What were you doing in there so long?"
"Just talking...."
"What do you mean, *just talking*? You're not thinking about re-upping, are you?"
"Oh...I don't know...."
"You don't know? What do you mean, *you don't know*?"
"I don't know, that's all."

He wouldn't say any more about it. After lunch, he re-filled his coffee cup, and went back into Mr. Hudson's office. He was there all afternoon. During the drive back to the apartment, I tried to get him to tell me whether he was thinking of re-enlisting. He just repeated that he *didn't know*. After he spent the next morning in Mr. Hudson's office, we were all over him at lunch— trying to talk him out of re-enlisting. That afternoon, he went back into Mr. Hudson's office for another hour or so. When he came out, he went to his desk and sat down without uttering a word.

"Well...c'mon, Wilkins. What're you doing?"
"Are you going to re-up?"
"I don't think so....No....I guess I'm not."

"Boy! You had us worried for a while there!"

"Yeah! We thought you were going to actually do it!"

"Well...I thought about it for a while....But I guess it's not the right thing."

"What do you mean, *you guess?*"

"You mean you don't **know**?"

"No...I mean it's not the right thing...I guess...."

Nowadays, Wally says he sometimes thinks about that time. If he hadn't let us talk him out of re-enlisting, he could have retired in 1986. I always remind him that he might have gone nuts before then, too.

* * * * *

A couple weeks before I was due to get out, my parents called.

"How'd you like to be our deckhand?"

"Huh?"

"Your mother and I are renting a houseboat for two weeks on the Allegheny River. Why don't you come up and join us. We'll have it from the 22nd until September 5th."

"Well...sure! That sounds great! I'll have to tell people at Music & Arts so they can get someone to fill in, but that should be no problem."

"Why don't we meet you at Hook's on the 26th?"

"Great! I'll be there!"

My Dad had grown up in Kittanning, just north of Pittsburgh. His uncle had a place up-river from there called Hook's Landing. It sounded like the perfect vacation. After four years in Uncle Sam's Army, I'd spend a week and a half in Dad's Navy.

ETS was anti-climactic. After all that had gone on over the last four years, one day I was in the Army, the next day I was out. No ceremony. Here are your papers. Have a nice life. I hadn't been to

Hook's since my Grandfather died in 1956, but I had no trouble finding it. Mom and Dad were there with the houseboat. It was, indeed, a wonderful interlude between the Army and my full-time return to civilian life.

EPILOGUE

The day after I returned from Pennsylvania, Matt Adams called and asked if he could sleep at our apartment for a couple of days while he sounded out the job market in Washington. I answered the door, when he arrived, and he surprised me again when he said,

"مرحباً كيف صحتكم؟"
"Здравствуйтеа Как вы поживáете?[17]"
"Hey! You remembered!"
"So did you!"

We had each learned a tiny bit from the other's language studies at Monterey. It was interesting to compare notes from our field stations. He had spent his time in Saporro, Japan. When I told him about forgetting the German word for bed, he said,

> "That's funny! I had something just like that happen to me! I had some time off, and had decided to spend a few days in Tokyo. I had picked up what I thought was enough Japanese to get around on my own for a couple of days. When I went to the station to get a train ticket, I walked up to the clerk, excited to use what I had learned. What I wanted to say was 'I want a ticket to Tokyo, please, first class.' I started out OK, but then I forgot how to say *first class*. I stood there stammering and muttering to myself. 'How stupid,' I said to myself, 'I've forgotten how to say first class.' Then the clerk said, 'You want a round-trip first-class ticket to Tokyo?' in perfect English. Just like you, I felt like a perfect idiot."

We all laughed. But he had a better story than that.

"I had been in Saporro for a little while when the Russians launched a manned satellite. I was excited to be listening in on these communications. On the third or fourth trip overhead I picked up something I couldn't understand. The astronaut gave the ground controller a letter-number combination, and the ground controller repeated it. I had no reference for anything like this. I talked to my supervisor, and he couldn't relate it to any of their equipment either. The next revolution, the ground controller gave a letter-number combination to the astronaut, who repeated it. Well, everyone started to panic. None of their equipment that we knew about had anything in common with these sequences. Everyone was locked into the building, and we started combing every reference we could find. We were getting pretty frantic when somewhere around the twelfth revolution, the astronaut gave another letter-number combination, and the ground controller responded with, 'Oh, Comrade! You've captured my knight!' Talk about feeling stupid!"

Matt was looking for a government job where he could put his Russian to good use. With his eidetic memory, his command of the language after three and a half years was amazing. One night we had the television on and were half-heartedly watching *Fail Safe*. At one point in the movie, the Premier of Russia calls the President of the United States on the hot line. There is a translator in the President's office, but you can just barely hear the Russian from the speaker phone.

"Wow! Listen to that! That's really Russian!"

Matt ran over to the television, put his ear near the speaker, and started translating in real time. What's more, he even corrected the grammar of the actor in the movie who was supposed to be translating.

That week, Matt went to Voice of America and managed to get an interview with the head of the Russian department there. After he had spoken in Russian with this Russian immigrant for an hour or so, the man told him that he had never heard anyone speak Russian as well as Matt did who hadn't been born and raised there. Nonetheless, they had no openings. In fact, after a week of knocking on the right doors, Matt had to go back to Connecticut.

While he was there, however, we played the weirdest form of Scrabble I'd ever heard of. To make the game more interesting, we allowed words in any language, provided that at least two of us could corroborate whatever was on the board. Between the four of us, we used German, French, Italian, Spanish, and Latin, as well as transliterated Russian, Arabic, and Japanese. Oh, and, of course, English. The game board usually looked like total gibberish, but it was fun!

Before Matt left, we made plans to go to the Formula One race at Watkins Glen in October. But that's a story for another time.

* * * * *

Several of us were contacted by the CIA after we left the Army. I contracted to do some translating by mail. I thought this was pretty weird, considering the documents were supposed to be sensitive, but later decided they must have been testing me to see if I might fit in. I translated a couple of documents, received a couple of checks, and then decided there must be something better. I knew I wouldn't be able to continue with that once I returned to college. I had been accepted at the American University as a transfer student. All those lovely credit hours that the Arabic course at Monterey was supposed to provide would only count if I decided to major in foreign languages. I was determined to finish my music degree, however, so that was one Army benefit that I couldn't make use of. The GI Bill really helped me finish school, however. Especially at American, where costs were higher than I had anticipated.

I thought it felt good to be totally in control of my life again. Despite the fact that I had made some friends that would last a long time, and had seen some places I might never have seen otherwise, I was glad to be out from under the constant discipline of Army life. I had plans for my life, now, and they didn't include wearing a green suit. Within a year, my life was to go skittering off in directions I had never anticipated. But for the time being, the future looked great.

NOTES

1. I can't vouch for the accuracy of my quotation, but matt was right on the money.

2. Killed by his own troops.

3. These open-air markets are a combination supermarket, department store, and flea market.

4. Haile Selassie styled himself as the *Lion of Judah*. From references about King Solomon in the *Bible*, the Ethiopians believed that their's were the first Christian congregations.

5. Many years later mine was stolen when my home was burglarized, but that's a story for another time.

6. One of the duties of the Military Airlift Command was to fly supplies into far-off field stations such as Kagnew. They usually had some seats available on a stand-by basis.

7. This is the high-pitched, warbling sound that Arab and African women and men make as a form of exclamation. It is used, most often, to express excitement or encouragement. Our English word hallelujah is derived from this sound.

8. A single girl was called an ahtee in Asmara.

9. *Ahtah* was Tigrinie for boy.

10. Pidgin Arabic for, "The curse of Allah upon your father.

11. Elapsed Time of Service—the date you were to get out.

12. Situation Normal, All Fouled Up is the Bowdlerized rendition of this acronym.

13. Inspector General

14. Pidgin Arabic for, "The curse of Allah upon your father."

15. Big Willie's speech was sometimes a bit hard to understand, so I'll translate: "Well that man came in looking for an organ. He said he wanted the finest organ he could get for his home. So I took him back to the big Lowrey Theater Organ and sat down to show him how good it sounds. *If you push this key here, it'll sound just like a violin*, I told him. Well I played a bit, and then **HE** said, *Why, that don't sound like no violin* So I told him, *If you push this key, it sounds just like a bunch of trumpets.* But when I played it, he said, *Why, that don't sound like no bunch of trumpets.* So, real quick like, I said, *Well, if you push this key, it'll sound just like a banjo choir.* And I played some more. But he had the audacity to say, *That don't sound like no banjo choir, either. Ain't you got an organ that sounds like an organ?* Well, I just didn't know what to say, so he left."

16. Elapsed Time of Service—the end of your Army career.

17. The Arabic he remembered sounds like, *Marhabban! Kaifa sehahtahkoom?* The Russian I remembered sounds like *Sdrahsvweettsyeh! Kahk vui pozhevaiyetsyeh?* Both phrases mean, *Hello! How are you*

Get Published, Inc!
Thorofare, NJ 08086
12 May, 2010
BA2010132